Microsoft® Money

Microsoft® Money

Microsoft PRESS®

Stephen L. Nelson

PUBLISHED BY
Microsoft Press
A Division of Microsoft Corporation
One Microsoft Way
Redmond, Washington 98052-6399

Library of Congress Cataloging-in-Publication Data
Nelson, Stephen L., 1959–
    Microsoft money / Stephen L. Nelson.
       p. cm.
    Includes index.
    ISBN 1-55615-377-5
    1. Microsoft Money.   2. Small business--Finance--Computer
programs.   3. Finance, Personal--Computer programs.   I. Title.
    HG4027.7.N445   1991
    658.15'92'02855369--dc20   91-37745
                                           CIP

Printed and bound in the United States of America.

1 2 3 4 5 6 7 8 9 MLML 6 5 4 3 2 1

Distributed to the book trade in Canada by Macmillan of Canada,
a division of Canada Publishing Corporation.

Distributed to the book trade outside the United States and Canada
by Penguin Books Ltd.

Penguin Books Ltd., Harmondsworth, Middlesex, England
Penguin Books Australia Ltd., Ringwood, Victoria, Australia
Penguin Books N.Z. Ltd., 182–190 Wairau Road, Auckland 10, New Zealand

British Cataloging-in-Publication Data available.

Quicken™ is a registered trademark of Intuit. Microsoft® is a registered trademark
and Windows™ is a trademark of Microsoft Corporation.

Acquisitions Editor: Marjorie Schlaikjer
Project Editor: Mary Ann Jones

Contents

INTRODUCTION

You may or may not agree with the old saying "Money can't buy happiness," but you would probably go along with the notion that mismanaging money can cause a lot of unhappiness. And stress. And frustration. Helping you avoid these woes by managing your money with Microsoft Money is the purpose of this book.

But before I describe the features of the Microsoft Money program and how to use them, let me quickly tell you about the organization of the book and the conventions it uses.

The Organization of This Book

Altogether, there are ten chapters in this book and one short appendix.

Chapter 1, "Working with Windows," gives you a brief overview of Microsoft Windows, the operating environment that Microsoft Money runs in. If you've worked with other Windows applications, such as Microsoft Excel or Microsoft Word for Windows, and if you feel comfortable choosing commands, starting and stopping applications, working with dialog boxes, and manipulating windows, you can skim this introduction or skip it entirely.

Chapter 2, "Preparing to Use Microsoft Money," describes the initial tasks you need to do before you start using Microsoft Money. These include setting up accounts and defining categories.

Chapter 3, "Keeping Your Checkbook with Microsoft Money," explains how to use Microsoft Money for your day-to-day financial record keeping. In it, you'll find descriptions of how to record checks, deposits, transfers, and other checking account transactions.

Chapter 4, "Supercharging Your Checkbook," explains how to use the Edit, List, and Options menu commands to simplify using your checkbook and transform it into a powerful personal or business financial management tool.

Chapter 5, "Reconciling Your Bank Account," describes how to use Microsoft Money to compare your financial records with the bank's records and track down any discrepancies.

Chapter 6, "Managing Files," discusses maintaining and working with the files in which Microsoft Money stores your financial records. This chapter describes how to back up, restore, and archive Microsoft Money files, how to pass data files between Microsoft Money and the popular checkbook program Quicken, and how to work with multiple sets of files.

Chapter 7, "Printing," explains how to print checks and reports and how to use Microsoft Money's advanced printing features. It describes how to store reports in files on your hard disk so that you can subsequently import them into spreadsheet and word processing applications and how to customize the standard Microsoft Money reports to contain the information you want in the format you prefer.

Chapter 8, "Using Microsoft Money at Home," covers 17 financial management and record-keeping tasks you might perform at home. Even though you probably won't use all the techniques described here, there's a good chance you'll find helpful hints and suggestions in Chapter 8. It might be useful if you're trying to deal with, say, a savings bond on one occasion and a life insurance annuity on another.

Chapter 9, "Using Microsoft Money in a Business," covers roughly two dozen financial management and record-keeping tasks you might perform if you use Microsoft Money in a business. For example, this chapter discusses how to use Microsoft Money for payroll, inventory accounting, accounts receivable, liabilities, fixed assets, and many other tasks as well. If you're using Microsoft Money for more than two or three of the tasks described in this chapter, you're pushing the outer limits of the program's functionality. However, if you're not yet ready to step up to a full-featured small business accounting package, Chapter 9 explains how to use Microsoft Money in all sorts of ways the developers never intended.

Chapter 10, "Making Financial Calculations," describes something that isn't directly related to using Microsoft Money. It explains how to use the Microsoft Windows Calculator to calculate loan payments, loan balances, future investment balances, and even interest rates. Knowing how to make these calculations should make it easier for you to record loan and investment transactions precisely. What's more, knowing how to make these calculations should also make it easier for you to budget—particularly for amounts you want to save and invest.

The appendix, "Installing Microsoft Money," provides step-by-step instructions for installing Microsoft Money on your hard disk.

Conventions Used in This Book

To keep things simple and easy to follow, I've developed a few rules for presenting information.

1. In text discussions, directory names and filenames appear in uppercase letters, as in MONEY.MNY, to make them stand out. However, when you type a pathname or a filename, it appears in lowercase letters, as in "type *money.mny*" because that's the way you type it.

2. If what you type is short, it appears in the text in *italic* type. If it is long or somewhat complex, it appears on a line by itself in type that looks like this:

   ```
   5000 * ( 1 + .10 ) x^y 18
   ```

3. In the text, every word in a menu, command, dialog box, or button name begins with a capital letter, no matter how it appears on the screen. That way, you'll know what I mean when I tell you, for example, "Type *money.mny* in the File Name text box."

4. I call areas in which you enter text in dialog boxes "text boxes," not fields, because the name seems to fit their function. For the same reason, I refer to text boxes that turn into list boxes as "drop-down list boxes." (In the Windows user documentation, these boxes are called "combo boxes" because they combine characteristics of text boxes and list boxes. Sometimes these are also called "auto drop boxes.")

5. I tell you to "choose" commands from menus and dialog boxes and to "select" options from dialog boxes. That way, when I tell you to "choose New," you know to look for a New command on a menu or, if you're in a dialog box, a New command button; and when I tell you to "select New," you know to look for a New option button in the current dialog box.

6. Whenever you follow specific numbered steps, I flag the section with a subhead that always starts with the phrase "Hands-On."

7. Throughout the book, I've scattered notes about using Microsoft Money in a business, pointers about personal finance topics, tips on better use of Microsoft Money, and warnings to caution you about potential problems.

These are marked with icons so that you can't miss them:

 for business notes

 for personal financial tips

 for tips on using the Money program

 for warnings.

With this basic information in hand, you are ready to begin learning about Microsoft Money.

Chapter 1

WORKING WITH WINDOWS

Microsoft Money runs under Microsoft Windows 3.0, a graphical user interface that allows users to select menu options by pointing at icons (pictorial symbols) with a mouse (an electronic pointer) and clicking the mouse button. Before using Microsoft Money, you need to know a thing or two about Windows. For the user of Microsoft Money, there are five important categories of Windows tasks.

1. Choosing commands from menus

2. Starting and stopping applications

3. Working with dialog boxes

4. Working with windows, either through menu commands or with the mouse

5. Using Windows Help

If you are an experienced Microsoft Windows user, you might only need to skim this chapter.

Start Microsoft Windows by typing *win* at the DOS prompt. The Microsoft Windows desktop appears, looking something like the screen in Figure 1-1. You might have a different number of icons at the bottom of the window.

Choosing Commands from Menus

The horizontal strip near the top of the screen is called a menu bar. You can pull down a list of commands either by using the mouse to click on one of the choices on the menu bar or by pressing the Alt key combined with some other key. For example, when you are using the Windows desktop shown in Figure 1-1, the following menus are available: File, Options, Window, and Help. Choosing commands is a three-step process.

1. Activate the menu bar.

2. Select the desired menu.

3. Choose a command.

You can perform the steps one at a time, or you can use shortcuts to perform two or three steps at a time. No matter how you do it, the same three steps are involved.

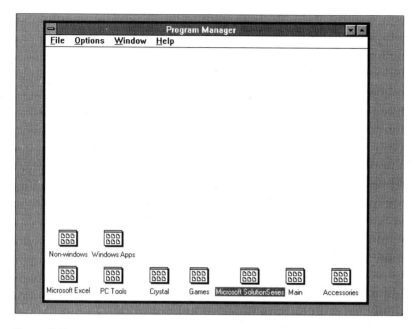

Figure 1-1.
The Microsoft Windows desktop with the Program Manager window displayed.

Activating the Menu Bar and Pulling Down a Menu

You can activate the menu bar in two ways: from the keyboard with the Alt key or with the mouse. When you press the Alt key, Windows activates the menu bar and highlights the first, or leftmost, name on the menu bar. (See Figure 1-2.) From the keyboard, you can then select the menu you want in two ways.

1. By typing the first letter of the menu name

2. By using the Left or Right direction key to move the cursor to the menu name you want and then pressing Enter

If you press the letter *F*, for example, Windows drops down the File menu. (See Figure 1-3.) Don't worry about the commands on these menus. I'll describe the ones that apply to Microsoft Money in later chapters. For now, simply concentrate on how to activate the menu bar and drop-down menus.

Figure 1-2.
When the menu bar has been activated, Windows highlights the first, or leftmost, name on the menu bar.

File	
New...	
Open	Enter
Move...	
Copy...	
Delete	Del
Properties...	
Run...	
Exit Windows...	

Figure 1-3.
The File menu.

If you activate a menu but then realize the command you want is on a different menu, you can use the Right direction key to close the currently displayed menu and pull down the menu to its right. For example, if you press the Right direction key when the File menu is displayed, Windows closes the File menu and drops down the Options menu. (See Figure 1-4.) You can also use the Left direction key to pull down the menu to the left of the currently displayed menu. To close the displayed menu and deactivate the menu bar, press Esc.

If you have a mouse, you can activate the menu bar and pull down a menu simply by pointing to the name of the menu you want and clicking the left button. (In the pages that follow, I call this process "clicking the mouse.") For example, if you click the name of the Window menu, which appears on the menu bar in almost every Windows application, you simultaneously activate the menu bar and pull down the Window menu. (See Figure 1-5.)

Choosing Commands in Windows

After you have activated the menu bar and pulled down a menu, you can choose any active command shown. Active commands on a menu appear in bold type. For example, the Open and New commands shown in Figure 1-3 are active commands. Inactive commands (those not relevant to the context)

Options
Auto Arrange
Minimize on Use

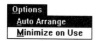

Figure 1-4.
The Options menu.

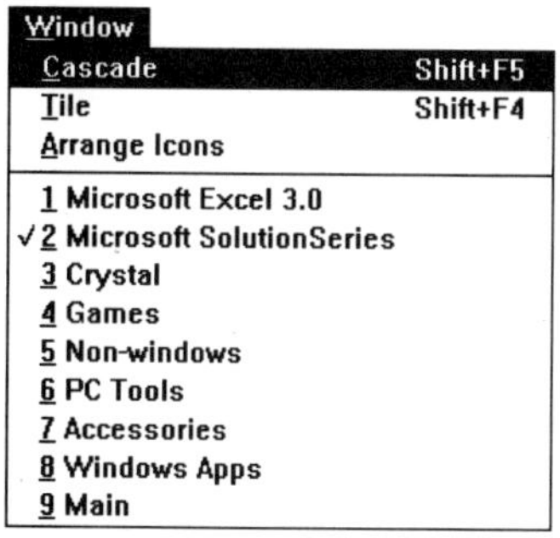
Window
Cascade Shift+F5
Tile Shift+F4
Arrange Icons
1 Microsoft Excel 3.0
✓2 Microsoft SolutionSeries
3 Crystal
4 Games
5 Non-windows
6 PC Tools
7 Accessories
8 Windows Apps
9 Main

Figure 1-5.
The Window menu. You might have different options on your menu.

are shown in gray or lightface letters. The Move and Copy commands shown in Figure 1-3 are inactive commands.

Windows provides four ways to choose active commands.

1. With the character keys
2. With the direction keys and the Enter key
3. With a mouse
4. With shortcut key combinations, such as Shift-F5.

As you work with Windows, you'll develop your own preferences for choosing particular commands.

Using the Character Keys

To choose commands using the character keys, press the one-character abbreviation, which Windows identifies by underlining it on the menu. For example, suppose you have activated the menu bar and pulled down the File menu. (Refer to Figure 1-3.) You can see that the letter *N* is the abbreviation for the New command because it is underlined; similarly, *O* is the abbreviation

for Open. You can choose any command from the File menu simply by pressing the letter that is underlined in the command name. A command abbreviation is not necessarily the first letter. The abbreviation for the Exit command, for example, is the letter *X*.

Using the Direction Keys and the Enter Key

A second technique for choosing commands (after you have activated the menu bar and pulled down a menu) is to use the Up or Down direction key to highlight the command you want and then to press Enter. For example, to choose the New command, you first activate the menu bar and pull down the File menu. (Refer to Figure 1-3.) Because *New* is highlighted, pressing Enter chooses the New command. To choose Open, press the Down direction key once to highlight the Open command, and then press Enter.

If you press the Up direction key when you're already at the top of a menu, Windows moves you to the bottom of the menu. Similarly, if you press the Down direction key when you're already at the bottom of a menu, Windows moves you to the top. This shortcut provides a quick way to go from the top to the bottom or from the bottom to the top of long menus.

Using a Mouse

A third technique for choosing commands is to use a mouse. After activating the menu bar and pulling down a menu, simply use the mouse to point to the command you want, and click the mouse button.

Using the Shortcut Keys and Key Combinations

The final method for choosing commands is to use the shortcut keys, which simultaneously activate the menu bar, pull down a menu, and choose the command. For example, to choose the File Open command (see Figure 1-3), you could simply press Enter. To choose the Window Cascade command (see Figure 1-5), you could press the Shift and F5 keys simultaneously. As you can see from Figures 1-3 and 1-5, the shortcut key or key combination that executes a command appears to the right of the command name on the menu. (The function keys are labeled F1, F2, F3, and so on, and appear either along the top of your keyboard or in two columns on the left side.)

Starting and Stopping Programs in Windows

Once you know how to work with Windows menus, you're ready to learn how to start and stop Windows applications such as Microsoft Money. In Windows, related programs are installed as groups, which are displayed near the bottom of the Program Manager window. Starting a program is a two-step process. First you display the program group window that includes the program you want to run. Because Microsoft Money creates its own program group, Solution Series, when you install it, you first need to display the Solution Series program group window by choosing the Solution Series command from the Window menu. (See Figure 1-5.) When you do, Windows displays the Solution Series program group window shown in Figure 1-6.

When you've displayed the correct application program group window, you will see an icon, or picture, representing each program in the group. In the case of Microsoft Money, the icon is a picture of an open checkbook. When it appears, you can open the program with the mouse or with the File Open command.

To start a program such as Microsoft Money with the mouse, simply point to the icon that identifies the application program and double-click the mouse. When Microsoft Money loads, you will see its first screen, the Account Book, shown in Figure 1-7. (If you've just installed Microsoft Money, a prompt directs you to set up an account. Instructions for setting up accounts are covered in Chapter 2, so click on the Cancel button to skip the account setup for now.)

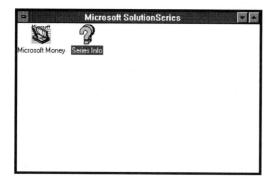

Figure 1-6.
The Microsoft SolutionSeries program group window.

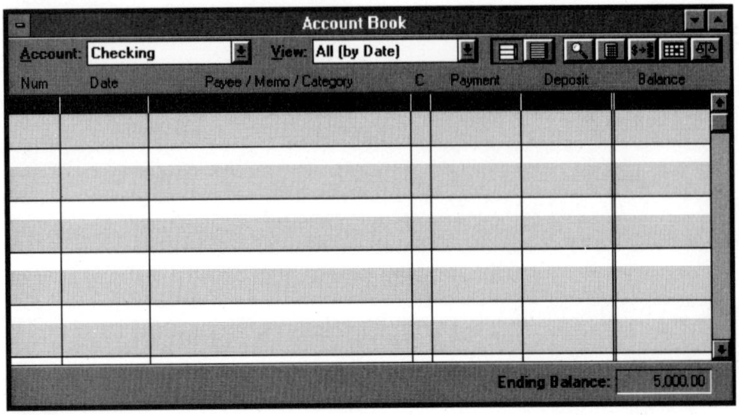

Figure 1-7.
The first Microsoft Money screen.

A second way to start a program is with the File Open command. You first identify the program you want to start by pressing Tab until the icon representing the application program is highlighted. You then either select the File Open command or use the shortcut key for File Open and press Enter.

When you've finished working with an application program, you need to quit the program before turning off your computer. To end a Windows program such as Microsoft Money, you simply choose the Exit command from the applications File menu. To exit from Windows as well, you choose the Exit Windows option from the File menu on one of the Windows desktops.

Working with Dialog Boxes

Dialog boxes provide a way for you to communicate with the software efficiently. They appear as squares or rectangles on the screen and contain text boxes you fill in, buttons you highlight to choose commands or select options, and items you check. (If you've worked with other graphical user interface software, you are already familiar with dialog boxes and can probably simply skim this section.)

First start Microsoft Money by using either the mouse or the File Open command, as described in the previous section. Then display the Options menu (see Figure 1-8) and choose the Settings command. When you do, Microsoft

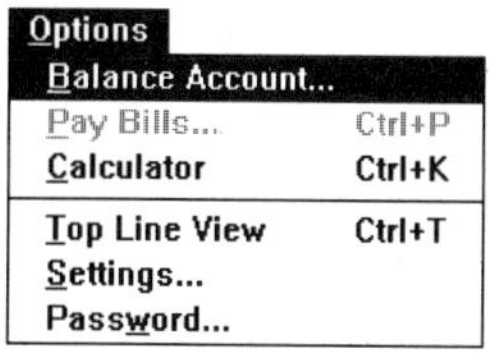

```
┌─────────────────────────────┐
│ Options                     │
├─────────────────────────────┤
│ Balance Account...          │
│ Pay Bills...        Ctrl+P  │
│ Calculator          Ctrl+K  │
├─────────────────────────────┤
│ Top Line View       Ctrl+T  │
│ Settings...                 │
│ Password...                 │
└─────────────────────────────┘
```

Figure 1-8.
The Microsoft Money Options menu.

Money displays the Settings dialog box shown in Figure 1-9 on page 10. When you choose any command followed by three periods (an ellipsis), a dialog box pops up. Not surprisingly, different commands display different dialog boxes, but you work with all of them in similar ways.

(The Settings command and dialog box shown in Figure 1-9 are described in detail in Chapter 4. For now, simply concentrate on the general techniques of using dialog boxes.)

Dialog boxes contain four basic elements.

1. Text boxes

2. Scrollable and drop-down list boxes

3. Command buttons

4. Option buttons

The Settings dialog box provides at least one example of each element.

Text Boxes

Text boxes are simply input fields; blank spaces in which you enter data. In the Settings dialog box, for example, you use the Days In Advance To Remind text box. (See Figure 1-9.) Enter the number of days in advance that you want Microsoft Money to remind you of scheduled transactions. If the text box is already highlighted, you can simply type in a number. If it isn't highlighted, you can either use the Tab and Shift-Tab keys to highlight it or click the text box with the mouse.

List Boxes

List boxes display possible entries you could make in a text box. Some list boxes are displayed when you first see the dialog box; others require you

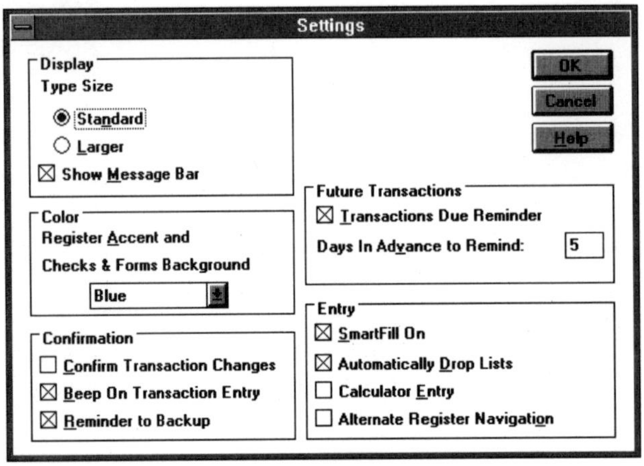

Figure 1-9.
Microsoft Money's Settings dialog box.

to ask for the list of possible entries to be displayed. The latter are called drop-down list boxes. In the Settings dialog box, Color is a drop-down list box; the down arrow that appears to the right of the input field identifies it as such. To use a list box, you press the Tab or Shift-Tab keys to highlight the first item in the list box. To activate a drop-down list box, you either click on the down arrow or simultaneously press the Alt and Pg Dn keys. To highlight different items in the list, you either use the Up and Down direction keys or type the first letter of the item. For example, if you type the letter *M*, Windows highlights the first item in the list that starts with that letter. Figure 1-10 shows the Color drop-down list box.

Sometimes the list of possible selections is too long to be displayed in the list box at one time. In these cases, repeatedly pressing the Down direction key scrolls the list down; repeatedly pressing the Up direction key scrolls the list up. You can also use the Home and End keys to go directly to the top

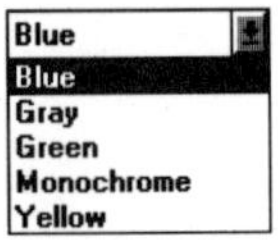

Figure 1-10.
The Color drop-down list box.

or bottom of the list and the Pg Up and Pg Dn keys to scroll up and down several items at a time. When the item you want is highlighted, press Enter to insert it in the text box.

You can also use the mouse to select an item from a list box and to scroll up and down in a list box. To select an item from a list box with the mouse, click on the item; to scroll up or down one item in the list, click on the scroll arrow that appears at the top or bottom of the scroll bar—the thin, vertical bar that runs along the right side of the list box. Not all list boxes have scroll bars. Windows adds them only when the list of possible entries is too long to fit in a single list box.

You can also click on the scroll bar in the general area of the scrollable list you want to see. If you click at the top of the scroll bar, Windows displays the beginning of the list. If you click in the middle of the scroll bar, Windows displays the middle of the list. And if you click at the bottom of the scroll bar, Windows displays the end of the list.

The square box on the scroll bar, called the scroll box, shows where you are in the scrollable list. You can use this box to scroll up and down the list. Simply hold down the left mouse button, and drag the box in the direction in which you want to scroll. Release the mouse button when the cursor's location on the scroll bar approximately corresponds to where you want to be in the list.

Command Buttons

Command buttons represent specific commands you can choose from within a dialog box. The Settings dialog box (refer to Figure 1-9) has three command buttons—OK, Cancel, and Help. There are four ways to choose a particular command button.

1. If the command button is the default selection, indicated by a bold border around the button, press Enter to choose that command.

2. Use the Tab or Shift-Tab keys to highlight the command button you want and then press Enter.

3. Use the mouse to click on the command button you want.

4. If the button has an underlined character in its name, choose it by pressing the Alt key and then pressing the underlined character key.

The Cancel command button appears in almost every dialog box; like Esc, it lets you close the dialog box and return to the menu or dialog box previously displayed.

Option Buttons

Option buttons let you give Windows more information about how to carry out a command. For example, the Settings dialog box shown in Figure 1-9 includes two types of option buttons: a square check box for options such as Show Message Bar (shown near the top left-hand corner of the dialog box) and two round buttons representing mutually exclusive options, such as the Type Size option buttons that give you a choice between a standard type size and a larger type size.

To use check boxes such as the Show Message Bar box in Figure 1-9, you press the Tab or Shift-Tab keys to highlight the correct option and then press the Spacebar to select or deselect the option. Selected options display X in the check box.

You can also use the mouse to turn a check box on and off by clicking on the check box. Clicking on a check box displaying X turns it off, while clicking on a check box that is blank turns it on.

To use the round option buttons, such as the Type Size buttons in Figure 1-9, pick one of the mutually exclusive options by inserting a bullet, or dot, in the circle. To do so, use the Tab or Shift-Tab keys to highlight the currently selected option button (the one with the bullet), and then press the Up or Down direction key to highlight the option you want. Note that the bullet moves to the highlighted option, indicating which option is selected.

You can also use the mouse to click on the option button that you want to select. Windows then moves the bullet to the option you clicked, indicating that it has been selected.

Working with Windows

Microsoft Windows gets its name from the fact that it displays different activities in different enclosed areas of the screen, called windows. Because these are a basic feature of any Windows-based application, including Microsoft Money, it is important to have a good grasp of the mechanics of working with windows in the following three areas.

1. The Control menu commands

2. The Window commands

3. Controlling windows with the mouse

The Control Menu Commands

The Control menu icon is the square with a dash that appears in the top left-hand corner of every window. When you select the Control menu icon by clicking the mouse or pressing Alt-Spacebar, Windows displays a menu of commands for use with the window that is currently displayed on the screen. (See Figure 1-11.)

The commands on the Control menu let you control the appearance and location of the various windows. The menu lists up to seven commands: Restore, Move, Size, Minimize, Maximize, Close, and Switch To. Not all seven appear on every window's Control menu—some list only two or three of the commands.

Maximizing, Minimizing, and Restoring Windows

The Maximize, Minimize, and Restore commands let you change the size of the active window. The Maximize command simply expands the size of a window to a full screen. (When Windows first displays a window, it is slightly smaller than the full screen.) The Minimize command shrinks the window, leaving only a small icon in the lower left-hand corner of the screen. (In Figure 1-7, for example, the Future Transactions and Checks & Forms icons in the lower left-hand corner of the Microsoft Money screen are actually minimized windows.) To change a window back to its original size, choose the Restore command. (Because a minimized window icon is too small to

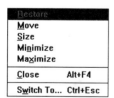

Figure 1-11.
The Control menu.

display the Control menu icon, you display its Control menu by selecting the minimized window itself.)

Moving and Resizing Windows

Initially, Windows displays the active window roughly in the middle of your screen. Often, particularly when you work with more than one open window, you will want to reposition the window. When you choose the Move command from the control menu, Windows changes the border around the active displayed window from a solid dark line to a dashed gray line. You can then move the window up, down, left, or right on the desktop by using the direction keys. You can even move a window off the desktop!

The Size command works in a similar fashion. When you choose this command, Windows changes the border around the active displayed window from a solid, dark line to a dashed gray one. You can then change the height of the window by moving the top window border up or down using the Up and Down direction keys, or you can change the width of the window by moving the right window border left or right with the Left and Right direction keys.

Closing and Switching the Active Window

The last two options on the Control menu (shown in Figure 1-11), Close and Switch To, don't appear on every window's Control menu because they relate to the specific application you are working with. For example, the Close command permanently removes the application window from the desktop. It is equivalent to choosing the File Exit command to stop an application.

The Switch To command lets you flip between the Windows Program Manager and any other application programs you've started and are running under Windows. When you choose Switch To, Windows displays a list that includes the Program Manager and any other running applications. Describing the Switch To command in more detail would require a lengthy discussion of the Windows operating environment. If you have questions about this command, you can refer to the Windows user documentation.

The Window Commands

Every menu bar in Windows lists a Window menu. (Refer to Figure 1-5.) Most of the commands shown in Figure 1-5 do not apply directly to Microsoft

Money; some pertain to the arrangement of the windows on the desktop. For example, Cascade and Tile arrange the windows. (Refer to the Windows user documentation if you have questions about these Window menu commands.)

The Window menu also lets you flip between the various windows available in a particular application by selecting the command corresponding to the window you want to display. Figure 1-12 shows the Microsoft Money Window menu, which lists as commands the three windows you can use in Microsoft Money: Account Book, Checks & Forms, and Future Transactions. A check mark appears next to the name of the active, or displayed, window. To display a different window, you select the corresponding command. Figure 1-13, for example, shows the Checks & Forms window that appears when you choose the Checks & Forms command from the Window menu.

Controlling Windows with the Mouse

If you have a mouse, you can carry out many commands simply by clicking on or dragging various parts of the window. (Moving an object by keeping

Figure 1-12.
Microsoft Money's Window menu.

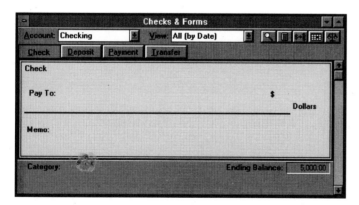

Figure 1-13.
The Checks & Forms window appears when you choose the Checks & Forms command.

the mouse button depressed as you move the mouse is called dragging.) Figure 1-14 shows the Microsoft Money Account Book window.

Activating and Moving Windows with a Mouse

You can activate and move windows directly with the mouse. To activate a window, simply click anywhere on it, and Windows brings it to the top of the stack of open windows.

Obviously, to click on a window to activate it, you must be able to see it. If you need to move another window out of the way, point to its name in the title bar ("Account Book" in Figure 1-14), and, while holding down the mouse button, drag the window to the location you want it to occupy.

Resizing with a Mouse

You can resize a window by using the mouse to point to one of its four borders or one of its four corners. Point to the border or corner that you want to move, and, while holding down the mouse button, move the mouse to make the window shorter or taller or wider or narrower. To make the window shorter or taller, you can drag either the top border or the bottom border up or down. If you want to make the window narrower or wider, drag the left or

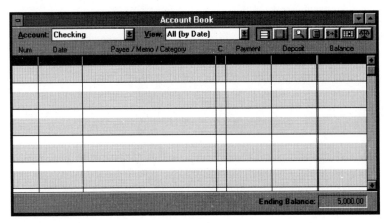

Figure 1-14.
The Microsoft Money Account Book window.

right border to the left or right. Dragging one of the four corners makes the window shorter and narrower or taller and wider at the same time.

Sizing Windows with Buttons

In the top right-hand corner of the screen are two size buttons, each containing an arrowhead. Clicking on the left-hand size button, which points down, is equivalent to choosing the Control menu's Minimize command. The right-hand size button, which shows either an arrowhead pointing up or a double-headed arrow that points up and down, is equivalent to the Control menu's Maximize and Restore commands. If the window hasn't already been maximized, only the arrowhead pointing up is displayed, and clicking on it maximizes the window. If the window has been maximized, the double-headed arrow appears, and clicking on its box restores the window.

Scrolling with a Mouse

Many windows, including the Account Book window, have a scroll bar along their right border; some also have a scroll bar along the bottom border. The right-hand scroll bar is a thin, vertical bar with scroll arrows at its top and bottom. The bottom scroll bar is a thin, horizontal bar with scroll arrows at its left and right ends. You use these scroll bars to browse through the contents of the window or locate a particular entry. For example, suppose you have an Account Book that is several pages long. Even if you zoom the window to full size, the window cannot display all of it; with the scroll bars, you can scroll through all the Account Book pages.

To scroll down one line, click the scroll arrow at the bottom of the right scroll bar. To scroll down continuously, one line at a time, point to the scroll arrow and hold down the mouse button until you find what you are looking for. To scroll up, use the scroll arrow at the top of the right scroll bar in the same way.

The bottom scroll bar, when it appears on a window, works the same way but lets you scroll from side to side. To scroll one column to the right, click the scroll arrow at the right end of the bottom scroll bar; to scroll left, click the scroll arrow at the left end. You can also scroll continuously by pointing to the scroll arrow and holding down the mouse button.

You can also click on the scroll bar to indicate which part of the window you want to see. If you click at the top, middle, or bottom of the right-hand scroll bar, Windows moves the scroll box—the square box on the scroll bar—to the place you indicated and displays the corresponding portion of the window. The bottom scroll bar operates approximately the same way, letting you click on the left, middle, or right of the scroll bar to display the left-hand column, the middle column, or the right-hand column of a report.

The scroll box indicates approximately where you are within the information displayed in the window. You can use it to move through the data by holding down the mouse button while dragging the scroll box in the direction you want to go.

Using Windows Help

The Help files for a Windows application amount to a reference book stored in the computer's memory. You open this reference book either by activating the Help menu or by choosing the Help command button that appears in many dialog boxes.

The best way to learn about Help is simply to use it. If you have a question about a menu option or about how to perform a task such as setting up an account, you can click on Help for assistance. A few hints will make it easier to use. If you follow this discussion at your computer terminal, you'll be able to explore some of the techniques for working with Windows.

Reviewing the Help Menu

The Help menu is the extreme right-hand item on the menu bar in every Windows application. Figure 1-15 shows Microsoft Money's Help menu, which

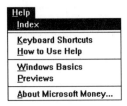

Figure 1-15.
The Microsoft Money Help menu.

lists six commands: Index, Keyboard Shortcuts, How To Use Help, Windows Basics, Previews, and About Microsoft Money.

Index

The Index command displays a list of Help topics such as Working with Accounts, Future Transactions, and Investments. (See Figure 1-16.) These categories are underlined and displayed in green on a color monitor.

When you find a topic you want to learn more about, move the mouse until the mouse pointer changes to a pointing hand, and then click the mouse button. Microsoft Money displays a list of Help subtopics like that shown in Figure 1-17 on the next page.

When you select a Help subtopic, the Help program displays the first screen of what is usually a multiple-screen discussion of the topic. Figure 1-18 shows

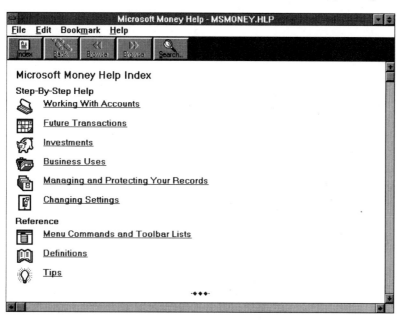

Figure 1-16.
The Help Index window.

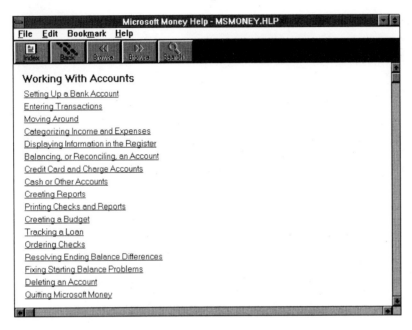

Figure 1-17.
The Help subtopics list for Working With Accounts.

the first screen for the Help subtopic Setting Up A Bank Account. (Notice that this screen has both vertical and horizontal scroll bars.) To leave Help, choose Exit from the File menu.

Keyboard Shortcuts

The Keyboard Shortcuts command, as its name indicates, lists Help subtopics explaining the keyboard shortcuts for Microsoft Money. Figure 1-19 on page 22 shows the subtopics list of Keyboard Shortcuts. When you select the first Help subtopic, Moving Around The Register, Windows displays the first screen of that subtopic, as shown in Figure 1-20 on page 23.

How To Use Help

The How To Use Help command lists Help topics having to do with Help's own commands, screens, and dialog boxes. After reading through this brief description of its features, you might want to use this command to learn more about Help.

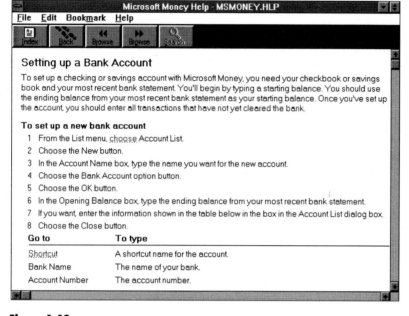

Figure 1-18.
The first screen for the Help subtopic Setting Up A Bank Account.

Previews

The Previews option lets you review briefly some of the different ways you can organize your personal or business finances using Microsoft Money. At this point, you might like to get a feel for what you can do with Microsoft Money. If so, you can stop here for a demonstration or two before reading on.

About Microsoft Money

The final Help option, About Microsoft Money, displays a dialog box containing the product name and version number, the name of the person the software is licensed to, and a copyright notice. To close the About Microsoft Money dialog box, click on the OK command button.

Working with Help

For the most part, working with Help uses skills you've acquired in the preceding pages of this chapter or through your previous experiences with

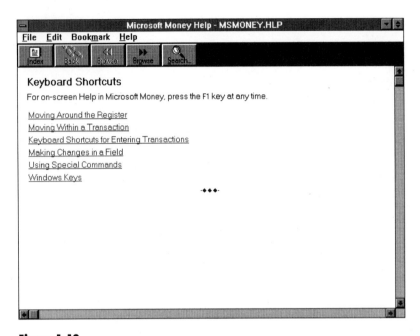

Figure 1-19.
The list of Keyboard Shortcuts Help subtopics.

Windows. The section below will familiarize you with the particular features of the Help windows' menus and command icons.

Using the Help Windows'
File, Edit, and Bookmark Menus

Four menus appear at the top of each Help window: File, Edit, Bookmark, and Help. (Refer to Figures 1-16 through 1-20.) The rightmost Help menu lists the options discussed in the preceding pages of this section.

The File menu lists options for printing information shown in the Help window, changing the printer setup, and exiting from the Help program. (If you need help or have questions about the Printer Setup command, refer to Chapter 7, "Printing.")

The Edit menu lists two options: Copy and Annotate. The Copy command copies the text displayed in the Help window to a temporary storage area in

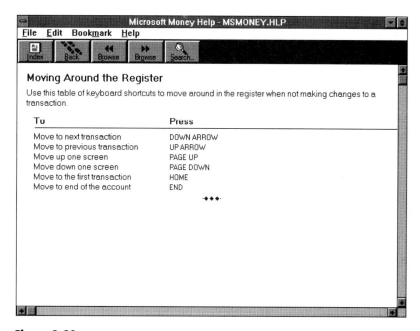

Figure 1-20.

The first screen of the Help subtopic Moving Around The Register.

memory called the Clipboard. Although you probably won't use it frequently, you might at some point want to use this option to paste text from a Help window into another application.

The Annotate command allows you to add a note to a Help window. You do so by typing the note in the dialog box that appears when you choose this command. To remind you that you have created the note, Help puts a picture of a paper clip on the Help window. To read or edit the note later, you click on the paper clip.

You use the Bookmark command to create a list of "pages" you want to turn to quickly, just as you would use bookmarks in a book. Initially, the Bookmark menu lists only one command, Bookmark. When you select this command, however, the title of the currently displayed Help window is added to the Bookmark menu. In the future, therefore, when you want to return to that particular Help window, you simply select its title from the Bookmark menu.

Using the Help Command Icons

As Figure 1-16 indicates, the Help window also displays five command icons
just below the menu bar: Index, Back, Browse (back), Browse (forward), and
Search. You choose each command by clicking on its icon. Index, for example,
displays the Help Index window shown in Figure 1-16. Back displays the
previous Help window; Browse (back) and Browse (forward) display the
preceding and next pages of a multiple-page discussion. And, finally, the
Search icon displays a dialog box into which you enter the Help topic you
want to search for.

Conclusion

This chapter has covered a lot of ground regarding the basic operating procedures of Windows programs like Microsoft Money. At this point, if you are
new to Windows, you might feel a bit intimidated by the richness and diver-
sity of the system. Don't be discouraged. Even though there seem to be half
a dozen ways to carry out each action, you'll soon figure out which one or
two ways work best for you. Then you'll be ready to move on to Chapter 2,
"Preparing to Use Microsoft Money."

PREPARING TO USE MICROSOFT MONEY

Successfully using a tool like Microsoft Money requires you to follow a sequence of steps. This chapter describes what you need to do from the very beginning. It describes what accounts are, how to know which ones you want, and how to set up the accounts. It explains what categories are, describes how you use them, and gives you tips on picking them.

Setting Up Accounts

The first steps in using Microsoft Money involve learning what Microsoft Money considers an account, which accounts make sense for you in your specific situation, and what information you need to gather before you can set up an account.

What Is an Account?

An account, as far as Microsoft Money is concerned, is simply a list of the events or transactions that affect an asset or liability. Microsoft Money uses accounts to keep track of personal or business assets and liabilities. Assets are resources you own, such as cash, bank accounts, cars, and real estate. Liabilities are debts you owe, such as credit card balances, car loans, and mortgages.

The basic rule in Microsoft Money is to set up one account for each asset or liability you want to track. Suppose, for example, you want to track a checking account, a savings account, your residence's value, and a mortgage. In that case, you would set up four accounts, one for each item.

Choosing Which Accounts

Should you set up an account for every item you own and every dollar you owe? Probably not. When you track an account, you keep records of two

BUSINESS NOTE: A business generally needs many more accounts than an individual because it owns more and owes more. Common business assets, for example, include cash, inventory, accounts receivable (the amounts customers owe the business), furniture, equipment, and real estate. Common business liabilities include accounts payable (the amounts the business owes vendors), taxes payable, credit lines, and bank loans.

aspects: value, or the balance of the asset or liability, such as the cash in a checking or savings account, the value of your home, or the outstanding principal on a mortgage, and the reasons why the balance has changed. Realistically, you will probably have no reason to keep track of changes in every asset and liability.

You can apply two tests to determine whether you need to set up an account for a particular asset or liability. The first test is, do you need to track the asset or liability balance? If the answer is yes, then you should probably set up the account. For example, because you want to know how much money is in your checking account—you don't want to bounce checks—you'll want to keep track of your checking account balance.

A second test is, do you need to know the reasons for changes in an account balance? For example, a checking account balance changes because you write checks and make deposits. You might also need to track certain types of withdrawals and deposits for income tax purposes. Charitable contributions, for instance, are tax deductions, so tracking checks written to charities lets you track your charitable deductions.

Each asset and liability that you decide to track will have a Microsoft Money account of its own.

Table 2-1 shows some common personal and business assets and liabilities and the reasons you might want to track them. Start by setting up the one or two accounts you'll benefit most from tracking. You can add others later as you become more comfortable with the mechanics of Microsoft Money.

Description	*Reasons for tracking*
Personal assets	
Cash in pocket	Track spending
Checking accounts	Track account balances for cash available, income deposited, and expenses withdrawn
Savings accounts	Track account balances for cash available and interest earned

Table 2-1.   (continued)
Common types of personal and business accounts.

Table 2-1. *continued*

Description	Reasons for tracking
Investments	Track investment values, interest and dividend income, and capital gains and losses on sales of investments
Residence	Track fair market value and cost of home and improvements to calculate taxable gains on sale
Personal liabilities	
Credit cards	Track balances, available credit, and card spending
Car loans	Track principal owed
Mortgages	Track principal owed and interest paid, for tax purposes
Business assets	
Petty cash	Track spending
Bank accounts	Track account balances for cash available, income deposited, and expenses withdrawn
Accounts receivable	Track amounts customers owe and when payments are due, to encourage timely collections
Inventory	Track dollars of inventory held and cost of goods sold
Equipment and real estate	Track book values, depreciation, and gains and losses on sales of assets
Business liabilities	
Credit lines	Track balances and available credit
Bank loans	Track principal owed and interest and principal paid
Taxes payable	Track federal income taxes and payroll taxes owed

Gathering Account Information

After you identify the assets and liabilities you want to track, you need to gather accurate, up-to-date information on account balances or amounts owed. For example, to set up a bank account record, you need the account balance, and to track a credit line, you need to know what you actually owe on the date you begin tracking it. All this sounds, and is, pretty simple. However, the tips in the following discussion might make it even easier. (In addition, the last two chapters of the book—Chapter 8, "Using Microsoft Money at Home," and Chapter 9, "Using Microsoft Money in a Business"—describe in detail the steps for using Microsoft Money in several dozen common personal and business applications.)

Bank Accounts

For a bank account, enter the account balance as of the last time you reconciled the account. From that point forward, you'll simply use Microsoft Money to record transactions. Don't use the bank's statement balance unless it agrees with your record of the balance; the bank's balance often doesn't include recent deposits and withdrawals you've made since the last statement.

Residence

How you will use the account information for your residence determines what you should enter as the starting balance. If you are tracking the fair market value of your home—perhaps to monitor your own net worth—you can simply enter the fair market value on the date you set up the account. Most people guess about the fair market value, but you could, I suppose, hire an appraiser and get a very accurate estimate.

Credit Cards, Credit Lines, Bank Loans, and Mortgages

To set up a Microsoft Money liability account, including accounts for credit cards, credit lines, bank loans, and mortgages, start with the principal balance owed as of the date of the last payment. (If you don't have your last payment statement, call or write the lender.) Record changes in the liability balance from that date forward. In the case of credit cards and credit lines, you also have to record charges or withdrawals.

PERSONAL FINANCIAL TIP: If you're tracking the adjusted cost basis of your home for income tax purposes, you need to do a bit more work. Begin by entering as the starting balance the initial purchase price plus all the other costs of acquiring the home, including escrow and title insurance. Next enter as changes in the balance all the things you've done up to the present time to improve the property, for example, landscaping, additions, renovations, and so on. From that point forward, you'll simply record the cost of additional improvements as you make them.

Step-by-Step Instructions for Setting Up Accounts

After you've decided which accounts you need and have gathered all the pertinent information, you are ready to begin working with Microsoft Money. Setting up each account should take only a few seconds.

Hands-On: Setting Up an Account

To set up an account in Microsoft Money, follow these steps.

1. Start Microsoft Money. You'll briefly see the hourglass as your computer loads the program. Then the Account Book window appears, as shown in Figure 2-1. The account you created as part of the installation will be displayed in the Account Book window, although it will not yet contain any transactions.

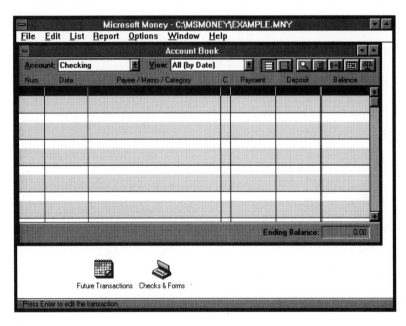

Figure 2-1.
The Account Book window.

2. Click on the down arrow next to the Account field to display the Account drop-down list box. When you do, Microsoft Money displays the list box shown in Figure 2-2. The account you created as part of the installation is listed, as well as three additional items: All Accounts, Multiple Accounts, and New Account.

3. Click on the New Account item in the drop-down list box. When you do, Microsoft Money displays the Create New Account dialog box, shown in Figure 2-3.

4. In the text box, type the name you want to use for the account, such as *checking*, *residence*, or *mortgage*.

Figure 2-2.
The Account drop-down list box.

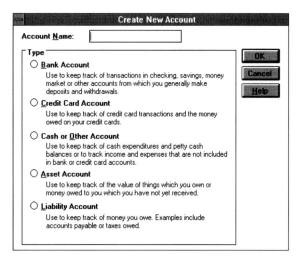

Figure 2-3.
The Create New Account dialog box.

5. Select the option button that describes the type of account you're setting up: Bank Account, Credit Card Account, Cash Or Other Account, Asset Account, or Liability Account. Then choose the OK command button.

6. When prompted for the account opening balance in the Opening Balance dialog box shown in Figure 2-4, enter the opening balance and choose OK.

That's all there is to it. You need to repeat steps 2 through 6 for each account you want to set up. Then you'll be ready to define a few categories.

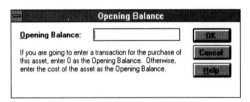

Figure 2-4.
The Opening Balance dialog box for an asset account.

Defining Categories

Besides setting up your accounts, you'll also find it helpful to identify and define the categories you need from the very start.

What Are Categories?

Categories classify your income and expenses and give Microsoft Money its power. Microsoft Money provides three types of categories: income categories, expense categories, and subcategories. Here's how they work: Whenever you record a transaction, or change, for an account, you can assign the transaction to a category. For example, an individual might have categories that track such income items as wages and bank account interest and others that track expenses such as groceries, rent, and gasoline. Similarly, a business might have categories to track such income items as product and service sales and such expenses as advertising and employee benefits. At the end of the month or year, Microsoft Money summarizes transactions by category so that you can see how much has been received in any income category or spent in any expense category.

A subcategory is simply a category within a category. Suppose, for example, you are married and both you and your spouse work. You might have an income category called Wages and two subcategories: My Wages and My Spouse's Wages. You can also have expense categories; for example, under the general category Utilities, you can have the subcategories Electricity, Water, Natural Gas, Sewer, and Garbage.

Choosing Categories

Microsoft Money comes with two sets of categories already defined: one for home use and one for business use. However, you might want to modify these to suit your own situation. The categories you need depend on two things: the types of income and expense items you want to track for budgeting purposes and the types of income and expense you must report on your income tax return.

When you want to keep track of something simple, such as how much you spend to maintain your car, you create a simple expense category such as Car Expenses. Other simple categories might record how much money you make working overtime or how much you spend on take-out food.

With regard to income tax reporting, however, you need to do a little more work. You'll want to categorize your income and expenses in ways that let you easily fill in the blanks on your tax forms. Unfortunately, the tax forms change almost every year, so it's impossible to know exactly which categories you'll need for, say, 1992, until almost the end of it. (Usually, the final forms come out in November or December.) Nonetheless, if you create income and expense categories to coincide with every line on last year's forms, you should have no difficulty modifying the categories to reflect the current year's tax changes.

To help you identify the categories you need, Table 2-2 shows the most common individual income and deduction categories, and Table 2-3 shows common business income and expense categories. Although this information is based on 1990 tax forms, which will be out of date by the time you read this, it can provide a good starting point.

The tables are based on Form 1040 and Schedules A, B, and C. Taxpayers use Form 1040 to report income and adjustments to income, Schedule A to report itemized deductions, Schedule B to report interest and dividend income, and Schedule C to report profits and losses from a business or profession. If you are a real estate investor or a farmer who needs to file Schedule E or Schedule F, you can look at last year's copies of these forms to help you set up the necessary income and expense categories.

Income

Wages, salaries, tips	Total IRA distributions
Taxable interest income	Total pensions and annuities
Tax-exempt interest income	Unemployment compensation
Dividend income	Social security benefits
Taxable refunds of state and local income taxes	Other income
Alimony received	

Adjustments

IRA deductions	SEP and Keogh deductions
Self-employment tax deduction	Penalty on early withdrawal of savings
Self-employed health insurance deduction	Alimony paid

Itemized deductions

Medical and dental expenses	Real estate taxes
State and local income taxes	Other taxes
Home mortgage interest	Unreimbursed employee expenses
Deductible investment interest	Other miscellaneous expenses
Charitable contributions	

Table 2-2.
Common individual income and deduction categories from Form 1040 and Schedules A and B.

Income

Gross receipts or sales	Other income
Sales returns or allowances	Cost of goods sold

Expenses

Advertising	Pension and profit-sharing plans
Bad debts from sales or services	Rent or lease on vehicles, machinery, and equipment
Car and truck expenses	
Commissions and fees	Rent or lease on other property
Depreciation	Repairs and maintenance
Employee benefit programs	Supplies
Insurance	Taxes and licenses
Interest on a mortgage	Travel
Interest, other	Meals and entertainment
Legal and professional services	Utlities
Office expense	Wages
	Other expenses

Table 2-3.
Common business income and expense categories from Schedule C.

Step-by-Step Instructions for Defining Categories

After you decide which categories you want, you can create new ones that don't appear on Microsoft Money's category list.

Hands-On: Adding a Category

To add a category, follow these steps.

1. With the Account Book window displayed, choose the Category List command from the List menu. (See Figure 2-5.) When you do, Microsoft Money displays the Category List dialog box shown in Figure 2-6.

2. Choose the New command button in the Category List box. When you do, Microsoft Money displays another dialog box, Create New Category, as shown in Figure 2-7.

3. With the cursor in the Name text box, type a brief descriptive name for the category, such as *wages* or *real estate taxes*.

Figure 2-5.
The List menu.

Category List		Category List

Figure 2-6.
The Category List dialog box.

4. Select the Income Category option button if the category summarizes income or the Expense Category option button if the category summarizes expenses.

5. (Optional) Microsoft Money lets you print special reports that include only those income and expense categories you mark Include On Tax Reports. If you want to use this report feature—which I describe in detail in Chapter 7, "Printing"—select the Include On Tax Reports check box.

6. Choose OK. Microsoft Money adds the new income or expense category and updates the Category List box to show it.

7. You can create a shortcut or abbreviation to use in place of the full category name. To do this, move the cursor to the Shortcut text box (see Figure 2-6), and enter the abbreviation, using no more than six characters.

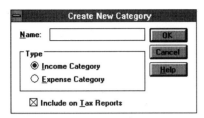

Figure 2-7.
The Create New Category dialog box.

8. If you want to describe the category further, perhaps for your own documentation purposes, move the cursor to the Comment text box, and type the description. To use more than one line, press Ctrl-Enter at the end of each line.

9. You can also set up a budget account for a category by using one of three approaches: (1) Select the Monthly Budget option button, and enter the monthly amount you expect for the income or expense category in the Amount text box; (2) select the Yearly Budget option button, and enter the annual amount you expect for the income or expense category in the Amount text box; or (3) select the Custom Budget option button, and when Microsoft Money displays the Custom Budget dialog box (shown in Figure 2-8), enter the monthly amounts you expect for the income or expense category in the monthly amount text boxes. As Figure 2-8 shows, the Custom Budget dialog box has two unique command buttons: Fill Down and Total Subcategories. Total Subcategories appears only when a category actually has subcategories. If you choose Fill Down, Microsoft Money enters the amount in the currently selected month's budget amount text box into each of the subsequent months. If you choose Total Subcategories, Microsoft Money calculates the budget amount for the currently selected month as the total of all the subcategory budget amounts for that month.

You can think of expense categories as the ways in which you spend your income. Simply by receiving the income, you incur expenses that are easy to overlook. To begin with, earned income up to $53,400 (for 1991) is subject to social security tax of 7.65 percent or self-employment tax of 15.30 percent. Then there's a 1.45 percent medicare tax in effect for those whose income is between $53,400 and $125,000, as well as state and federal income taxes.

Figure 2-8.
The Custom Budget dialog box.

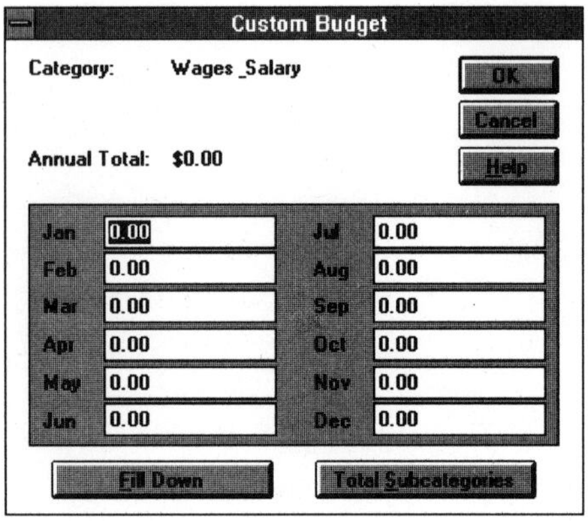

For precision, try to include estimates of income, social security, and other taxes in your budget. It's also a good idea to know exactly what percentage of your income the total of these expenses represents. A raise or bonus of, say, $1,000 does not mean you have $1,000 to spend. A large chunk might go to federal and state income taxes and, probably, to social security or self-employment taxes. Still other expenses might be incurred in earning the extra $1,000. It's painful but not unusual to find that 40 to 50 cents of each dollar of income is consumed by these kinds of expenses.

In budgeting your personal expenses, you can borrow several tricks from the business world: zero-based budgeting, contingency allowances, expense (or spending) breakdowns, and variance analysis.

> **PERSONAL FINANCIAL TIP:** Budgeting begins with identifying your probable sources of income and their amounts. Income sources include wages or salary from a job, retirement or pension benefits, and investment income. Because both timing and amounts are important, you need to estimate not only how much income you receive but also when you receive it.

Zero-based budgeting refers to the practice of always starting the budgeted amount for an expense category at zero. The idea is that no expense category is so sacred that it's not reviewed every time you create a budget. Zero-based budgeting doesn't mean that you cannot include a trip to Disneyland in the budget again this year; in fact, you might choose to make such an expense one of your top priorities every year. Nonetheless, zero-based budgeting does help you think carefully about your spending priorities. It usually saves you money because the current year's priorities—not last year's or 1968's—determine how you spend your money.

Contingency allowances are simply financial cushions. Nobody can forecast income and expenses with certainty. Cars break down. Children get sick. People lose jobs. A contingency allowance gives you room to maneuver financially if unforeseen circumstances arise.

The term *expense breakdown* (sometimes called *spending breakdown*) refers to classifying expenses into various categories, which is exactly what you do with Microsoft Money's expense categories. If you always run out of money a few days before your next payday, you can easily conclude that you're spending too much. But that's not a very helpful insight. You need to pinpoint the area in which you're spending too much. For example, you might be overspending by eating out too often or by purchasing too many new clothes. If you know what expense items are driving you over the financial edge, you can at least consider curbing them.

The term *variance analysis* refers to comparing planned spending with actual spending. If you choose to use this tool—which Microsoft Money's Budget Report makes simple—you're on your way to sophisticated personal financial management. If you are spending too much in a particular category, you can look for ways to get back on track—perhaps simply by fixing more meals at home or postponing buying a new pair of jeans or a new coat. Or you might decide that your original budget for a category was too low and that you need to cut back elsewhere. Although it might be more personal financial management than you're currently looking for, variance analysis gives you a way to keep your finger on the pulse of your finances.

Hands-On: Adding a Subcategory

To add a subcategory to an expense or income category, follow these steps.

1. Display the Category List dialog box by choosing the Category List command from the List menu.

2. Select from the list the income or expense category under which the new subcategory should be added. When you do, Microsoft Money displays any subcategories that already exist for the category in the Subcategory List box.

3. Choose the New command button. When you do, Microsoft Money displays the Create New Subcategory dialog box (see Figure 2-9), which closely resembles the Create New Category dialog box in Figure 2-7.

4. With the cursor in the Name text box, type a brief but descriptive name for the subcategory.

5. Verify that the Subcategory For drop-down list box shows the correct income or expense category for this subcategory. If it doesn't, activate the Subcategory For drop-down list box, and then select the appropriate category from the list.

6. If you want the subcategory to appear on Microsoft Money Tax Reports, select the Include On Tax Reports check box.

7. Choose OK. Microsoft Money adds the new subcategory and updates the Subcategory List box to show it.

You can also create shortcuts for a subcategory, further describe the subcategory using comments, and even budget for the subcategory—just as you can for regular categories. The steps for doing so are essentially the same as those outlined in the discussion on adding a category.

If you make mistakes and find that you added categories or subcategories you don't want or that you incorrectly named categories or subcategories, you can also use the Category List dialog box to correct these errors.

Hands-On: Deleting a Category or Subcategory

To remove a category or a subcategory from your list, follow these steps.

1. With the Account Book window displayed, choose the Category List command from the List menu. When you do, Microsoft Money displays the Category List dialog box shown in Figure 2-6.

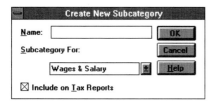

Figure 2-9.
The Create New Subcategory dialog box.

2. Highlight the category or subcategory you want to remove.

3. Choose the Delete command button.

4. If you have previously used the category or if it's a category that has a subcategory, Microsoft Money displays a message box asking you to confirm
   the deletion. If the category is used in other transactions, Microsoft Money
   also prompts you to provide a replacement category and, optionally, a replacement subcategory.

Hands-On: Changing
a Category or Subcategory Name

To change a category or subcategory name, follow a similar sequence of steps.

1. With the Account Book window displayed, choose the Category List command from the List menu.

2. When Microsoft Money displays the Category List dialog box, highlight the
   category or subcategory you want to rename.

3. Choose the Rename command button. When you do, Microsoft Money displays the Rename Category dialog box shown in Figure 2-10.

4. Type the correct category or subcategory name, and choose OK.

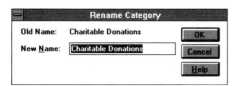

Figure 2-10.
The Rename Category dialog box.

If you spend a few minutes thinking about the categories you need, the process of creating the perfect category list will be quick and easy. All you need to do is use the New, Delete, and Rename command buttons in the Category List dialog box. When you finish, you can print out your category list by choosing the Report command.

 MICROSOFT MONEY TIP: *An important issue to consider when you buy a new accounting package is timing: when to begin using the program to track your account balances, income, and expenses. Fortunately, with a checkbook program such as Microsoft Money, timing isn't all that critical. Still, the easiest time to begin using Microsoft Money for accounting is at the start of the year. If you can't start at the beginning of the year, the next best time is at the beginning of a month, preferably right after you've reconciled the bank accounts you plan to track with Microsoft Money.*

The main thing, no matter when you begin, is to have a clean cut-off point. You want to know that your financial records through June, say, are all in a shoe box and that from July forward they are in Microsoft Money data files. Without a clear-cut beginning, you could have difficulty determining whether you missed recording some transactions or whether you recorded others twice.

Conclusion

By following the steps in this chapter, you've built a sturdy foundation of accounts and categories—the basic building blocks of Microsoft Money. At this point, you're ready to begin using the program.

Chapter 3

KEEPING YOUR CHECKBOOK WITH MICROSOFT MONEY

Assuming that you've already learned the rudiments of working with Microsoft Windows, set up your accounts, and defined the categories you use, you're ready to use Microsoft Money. Although you can use Microsoft Money for almost any type of financial record keeping, the easiest task is automating your checkbook. This chapter covers everything you need to know to keep your checkbook using Microsoft Money.

Recording Checks

Microsoft Money provides two ways to record checks. You can use either the Checks & Forms window or the Account Book window, depending on your personal preference. To find out which you like better, simply read through the next two sections.

The Checks & Forms Window

To record checks in the Checks & Forms window, you first display the window and then fill in the text boxes.

Hands-On: Entering a Check
Using the Checks & Forms Window

The step-by-step instructions are as follows.

1. Display the Checks & Forms window, either by clicking on the Checks & Forms icon at the bottom of the window or by choosing the Checks & Forms command from the Window menu. Figure 3-1 shows the screen with the Account Book window displayed and the Window menu activated. The Checks & Forms icon and the Future Transactions icon appear in the lower left-hand corner of the screen. Figure 3-2 shows the Checks & Forms window.

2. Verify that the name of the checking account on which you want to write a check appears in the Account drop-down list box at the top of the Checks & Forms window. If it doesn't, click the down arrow to the right of the Account drop-down list box to display the Account list box shown in Figure 3-3. Then select the correct account.

3. If necessary, select the Check option button so that the Check version of the Checks & Forms window is displayed. The word *Check* will appear in the upper left-hand corner of the Check form.

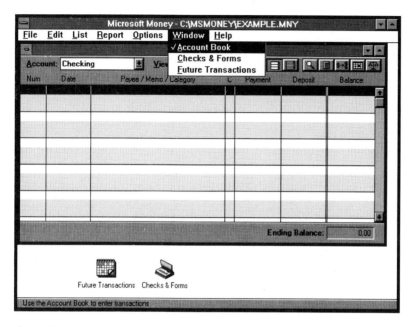

Figure 3-1.
The Account Book window displayed with the Window menu activated.

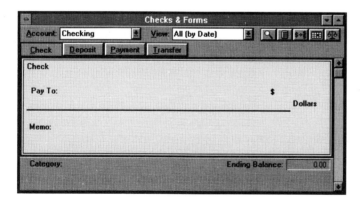

Figure 3-2.
The Checks & Forms window.

Figure 3-3.
The Account drop-down list box.

4. Press Enter or click on the window to open the text boxes for input. Figure 3-4 shows the Checks & Forms window with its input fields opened.

5. If necessary, select the check number text box (#). If you want to print this check, type the word *print*; if you don't want to print it, type the actual check number. (When you're ready to print a group of checks, Microsoft Money prompts you to enter the next check number on your preprinted check forms. If you have a rear-feed-tractor or laser printer, enter the number on the first form; if you have a top-feed-tractor printer, enter the number on the second form. Microsoft Money then adds this information to the Num field in the Account Book. The process of printing checks is described fully in Chapter 7, "Printing.")

6. Press Tab or use the mouse to move the cursor to the Date text box. Microsoft Money automatically fills the Date text box with the system date; you can change it by typing over it or moving the date ahead by one day with the plus (+) key or back by one day with the minus (–) key.

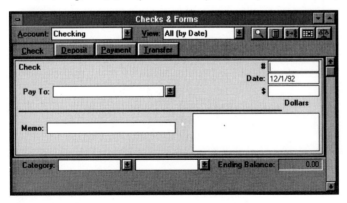

Figure 3-4.
The Checks & Forms window with its input fields opened.

7. Move the cursor to the Pay To text box. Type in the name of the person or business to whom you're writing the check. Or, because Microsoft Money automatically records whatever you enter into the Pay To text box, you can click the down arrow to the right of the Pay To text box and select a payee from the drop-down list box.

8. Move the cursor to the amount ($) text box. Type the amount of the check, using a period to indicate dollars and cents. You don't need to type commas because Microsoft Money adds them for you.

9. (Optional) Move the cursor to the Memo text box. Enter a brief description of the check. For example, when paying the electric bill, you might want to note which month the bill covers.

10. (Optional) Move the cursor to the four-line address text box. If you're using envelopes with address windows, type the payee's name and address in the address-block input area. Or you can copy the payee's name by following these steps: Highlight the payee name you entered in step 7, choose the Copy command on the Edit menu (see Figure 3-5), move the cursor to the first line of the address-block input area, and then choose the Paste command on the Edit menu. (If you included the payee's address on the Payee list, both the name and address will appear automatically in the address-block input area as soon as you fill in the Pay To text box.)

11. Move the cursor to the Category drop-down list box. Type the category name or shortcut, or click the Category down arrow or press Alt-Down direction key to display the Category drop-down list box, and select a

Figure 3-5.
The Edit menu.

category from the list. For example, if you configured Microsoft Money during installation to use the defined list of home categories, you can select the Utilities category to record a check to the electric company.

12. Move the cursor to the subcategory drop-down list box. Type the sub-category name or shortcut, or click the subcategory down arrow or press Alt-Down direction key to display the subcategory drop-down list box; then select a subcategory from the list. (Figure 3-6 shows an example check written to Washington Electric Company and categorized as a utilities expense.)

13. Review the text boxes for errors, and then press Enter to record the check. Microsoft Money records the check in the Account Book, updates the ending balance, and clears the text boxes so that you can enter another check.

That's all there is to it! If you want to record another check, repeat the process. If you don't, either close the Checks & Forms window or reactivate the Account Book window.

The Account Book Window

You can also record checks in the Account Book window. The procedure is similar to that for using the Checks & Forms window and uses many, although not all, of the same text boxes in a slightly different arrangement.

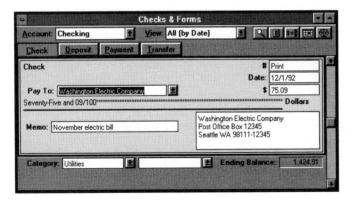

Figure 3-6.
A check recorded in the Checks & Forms window.

Hands-On: Entering a Check
Using the Account Book Window

To record a check in the Account Book window, follow these steps.

1. Display and activate the Account Book window either by clicking on the window or choosing the Account Book command from the Window menu. Figure 3-7 shows the Account Book window. Any checks or deposits you've previously entered will show in the Account Book.

2. Verify that the name of the checking account on which you want to write a check appears in the Account drop-down list box at the top of the window. If it doesn't, click the down arrow to the right of the Account field so that Microsoft Money displays the Account drop-down list box; then select the correct account. Refer to Figure 3-3, which shows the Account drop-down list box.

3. Press Enter or click on the window to open the text boxes. Figure 3-8 shows the Account Book window with its input fields opened.

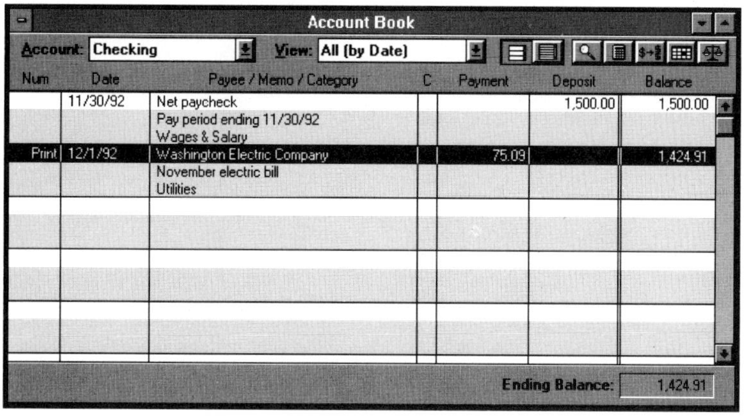

Figure 3-7.
The Account Book window.

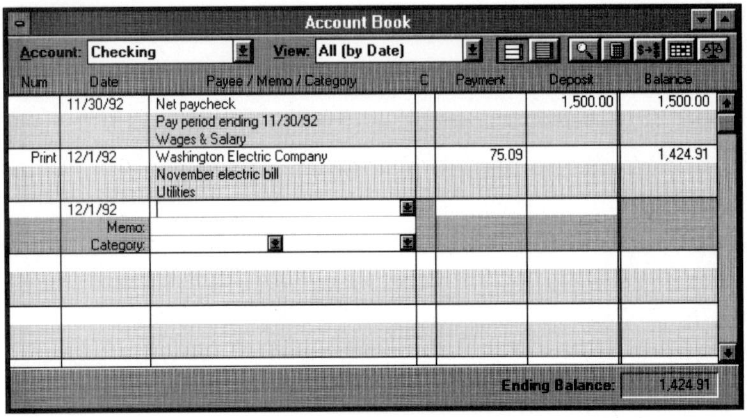

Figure showing the Account Book window:

Num	Date	Payee / Memo / Category	C	Payment	Deposit	Balance
	11/30/92	Net paycheck Pay period ending 11/30/92 Wages & Salary			1,500.00	1,500.00
Print	12/1/92	Washington Electric Company November electric bill Utilities		75.09		1,424.91
	12/1/92	Memo: Category:				

Ending Balance: 1,424.91

Figure 3-8.
The Account Book window with its text boxes opened for input.

4. If necessary, move the cursor to the Num text box. Then type *print* to identify this check as one you want to print. If you don't want to print the check, type the actual check number.

5. Press Tab or use the mouse to move the cursor to the Date text box. Microsoft Money fills the Date text box with the system date. You can, however, change this date by simply typing over it or by moving the date ahead one day with the plus key or back one day with the minus key.

6. Press Tab or use the mouse to move the cursor to the Payee text box. Type in the name of the payee, or use the drop-down list box and select a payee.

7. Press Tab or use the mouse to move the cursor to the Payment text box. Type the amount of the check, using a period to indicate dollars and cents. You can type a dollar sign and commas if you like, but Microsoft Money will add commas for you and will always remove the dollar sign.

8. (Optional) Move the cursor to the Memo text box, which is on the line below the Payee text box. Enter a brief description of the check. When paying your credit card bill, you might, for example, want to note which month the bill covers.

9. Move the cursor to the Category drop-down list box. Type the category name or shortcut, or click on the Category down arrow or press Alt-Down

direction key to display the Category drop-down list box, and then select a category.

10. Move the cursor to the subcategory text box. Type the subcategory name or shortcut, or click on the subcategory down arrow or press Alt-Down direction key to display the subcategory drop-down list box, and select a category.

11. Review the text boxes for errors, and then press Enter to record the check. Microsoft Money records the check in the Account Book, updates the ending balance, and opens the text boxes on the next line of the Account Book so that you can enter another transaction.

If you want to record another transaction, simply repeat the process. If you don't, you can either close the window, activate another window, or exit from Microsoft Money.

Recording Other Transactions

Once you know how to record checks, entering other transactions—deposits, automated-teller-machine withdrawals, interest, service charges—is a snap. Because of the similarities, I won't repeat the sequence a third time. I will, however, briefly highlight some minor differences in the procedures for recording other types of transactions.

Deposits

Deposits, like checks, can be recorded in one of two ways: by using either the Checks & Forms window or the Account Book window. Not surprisingly, the steps for recording a deposit parallel those for recording a check. Figure 3-9 shows the Deposit version of the Checks & Forms window, which you can display by selecting the Deposit option button in the Checks & Forms window. The fields are arranged slightly differently from those in the check version of the window, but the Deposit form uses similar text boxes for input: a deposit number instead of a check number, a deposit date instead of a check date, a Received From instead of a Pay To field, and Memo, Category, and subcategory. When you fill in the last text box and press Enter, Microsoft Money adds the deposit amount to the ending balance.

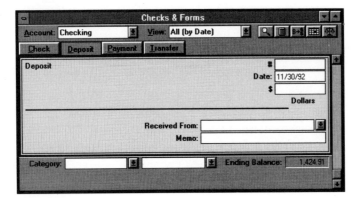

Figure 3-9.
The Deposit version of the Checks & Forms window.

Of course, you also have the option of recording deposits directly into the Account Book window. (Refer to Figures 3-7 and 3-8.) In this case, however, the deposit amount is entered in the Deposit column.

Other Withdrawals

Besides checks, you frequently need to record other withdrawals from a checking account. Every time you use a cash machine to take money out of an account, you withdraw money, and when the bank charges you a service fee, it withdraws money from your account.

You can record these withdrawals either in the Payment version of the Checks & Forms window (see Figure 3-10) or in the Account Book, which records the transactions in the Payment column. The process of recording these kinds of payments or withdrawals is the same as that for recording checks.

Transfers Between Accounts

You need to know how to record one final type of transaction: transfers—using the Transfer version of the Checks & Forms window. Transfers occur when you move money from one account to another—for example, from your savings account to your checking account.

Transfers sometimes get a little tricky, especially if you've set up asset accounts other than bank accounts or liabilities such as credit card balances or a home mortgage. Transactions will occur in which it seems as if you're

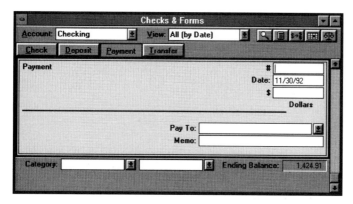

Figure 3-10.
The Payment version of the Checks & Forms window.

recording income or expenses when you are actually only moving money from one account to another.

One such transaction occurs when you transfer money from a checking account to an investment account. If you write a check for deposit in, say, a broker's money market fund, it's clear that you've simply moved money. However, you're also moving money when you use money in one account to buy another asset—stocks, bonds, real estate, or equipment. For example, if you write a check to buy $1,000 worth of stock, you decrease your checking account balance by $1,000; and, if you've set up an account for stock investments, you increase your stock investments account balance by $1,000. One asset account decreases by the amount you move, and the other asset account increases by the same amount.

A second type of transfer occurs when you move money from an asset account to a liability account. Suppose you want to pay an extra $500 on your car loan. When you write the $500 check, you decrease your checking account balance by $500. At the same time, because you are decreasing your car loan liability by $500, you need to decrease that balance by $500. In this situation, you're simply moving money from an asset account to a liability account. The balances in both accounts decrease by the same amount.

Clearly, in these sorts of transfer transactions, you earn no income and incur no expense—you only move money around. You don't, therefore, specify a category when you record the transaction but simply specify the account you want to move the money into. The difference between the Transfer version of the Checks & Forms window and the other versions of the window is that there is no text box in which to record the category. You simply record the date, the amount, the name of the account you're transferring from, the name of the account you're transferring to, a receipt number (optional), a Pay To description, and a memo. Figure 3-11 shows the Transfer version of the Checks & Forms window.

Hands-On: Recording a Transfer with the Checks & Forms Window

The specific steps you follow to record a transfer from one account to another are as follows.

1. Display the Checks & Forms window by either clicking on the Checks & Forms icon or choosing Checks & Forms from the Window menu.

2. Verify that the account from which you want to move money appears in the Account box at the top left of the window. If it doesn't, click the down arrow to the right of the Account field so that Microsoft Money displays the Account drop-down list box. Then select the correct account. The account you select will appear simultaneously in the From text box on the Transfer form.

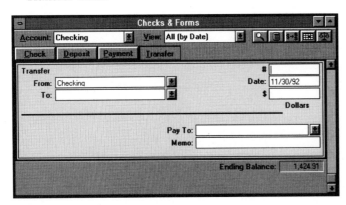

Figure 3-11.
The Transfer version of the Checks & Forms window.

3. Select the Transfer option button to display the Transfer version of the Checks & Forms window. The word *Transfer* will appear in the upper left-hand corner of the Transfer form.

4. (Optional) Enter a receipt number for the transfer transaction.

5. Press Tab twice or use the mouse to move the cursor to the Date text box. Microsoft Money fills the Date text box with the system date, but you can change this simply by typing over it or using the plus or minus key.

6. Move the cursor to the To text box. Then type the account name or short-cut, or select an account from the drop-down list box that displays available accounts when the cursor is on the To text box.

7. Move the cursor to the amount ($) text box and type the amount of the transfer.

8. (Optional) Move the cursor to the Pay To text box. You can enter a de-scription of who or what you're paying in the Pay To text box. Most of the time, you won't have a Pay To entry. Suppose, however, that you are transferring funds from a savings account at one bank to a checking ac-count at a different bank. In this case, you would type the name of the latter bank in the Pay To text box.

9. (Optional) Move the cursor to the Memo text box. If you want to, type a brief description of the transfer.

10. Review the text boxes for errors, and then press Enter to record the transfer.

Microsoft Money records the transaction in both accounts, updates the ending balances for both accounts, and clears the text boxes for another transfer trans-action. Figure 3-12 shows a completed Checks & Forms window recording a transfer of $500 from a checking account to a savings account.

Hands-On: Recording a Transfer with the Account Book window

As you might have guessed, you can also record transfers using the Account Book by following these steps.

1. Display and activate the Account Book window. Verify that the account from which you want to move money is displayed. If it isn't, click the down arrow to the right of the Account drop-down list box so that

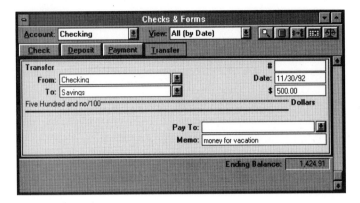

Figure 3-12.
An example of a completed Checks & Forms window recording a $500 transfer.

Microsoft Money displays the Account drop-down list box; then select the correct account.

2. Press Enter or click on the window to open the text boxes of the next empty space in the Account Book. (Refer to Figure 3-8, which shows the Account Book window with its text boxes opened for input.)

3. If necessary, move the cursor to the Num text box, and type the identifying number of the transaction, if it has one.

4. Press Tab or use the mouse to move the cursor to the Date text box. If needed, change the default transaction date supplied by Microsoft Money.

5. Move the cursor to the Payee text box. Type in the payee name if one is needed, or select a payee from the drop-down list box.

6. Move the cursor to the Payment text box. Type the amount of the transfer, using a period to separate dollars from cents.

7. (Optional) Move the cursor to the Memo text box, which is on the line below the Payee text box. Enter a brief description of the transfer.

8. Move the cursor to the Category drop-down list box. Either type the word *transfer*, or click on the Category down arrow or press the Alt-Down direction key to display the Category list box, and then select Transfer, the first item in the list.

9. Move the cursor to the subcategory drop-down list box. Type the account name or shortcut, or click on the subcategory down arrow or press Alt-Down direction key to display the subcategory list box. Because you indicated that the transaction is a transfer, Microsoft Money lists all your accounts instead of subcategories. You then select the correct account for the transfer.

10. Review the text boxes for errors, and then press Enter to record the transfer. (Figure 3-13 shows the Account Book window with a transfer transaction as the third item.)

Microsoft Money records the transaction in both accounts, updates both accounts' ending balances, and opens the input fields on the next space in the Account Book so that you can enter another transaction.

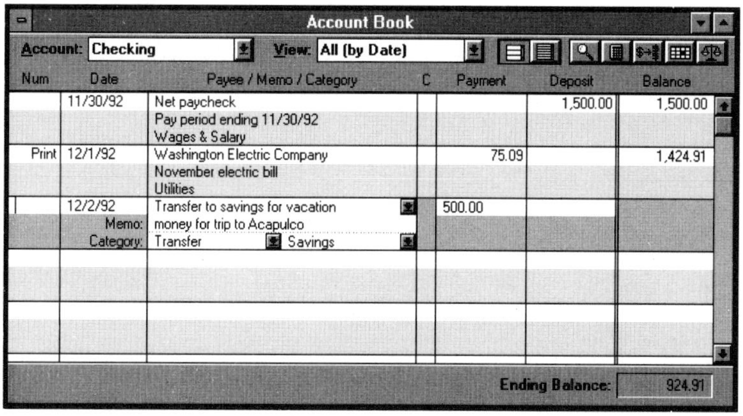

Figure 3-13.
An example of a completed Account Book window recording a $500 transfer.

Making Things Easier

You're already well on your way to using Microsoft Money as a personal or business accounting tool. There are, however, a few additional topics you should know about as soon as possible; they include split transactions, payee lists, SmartFill, automatic transaction copying, date changing with a keystroke, automatic check numbering, and view options. These features make working with Microsoft Money much, much easier.

Split Transactions

So far, the descriptions of recording a transaction have assumed you only
need one category or, in the special case of a transfer, one account. In practice, however, many transactions require more than one category or account
and sometimes even a combination of categories and accounts. To deal with
these situations, Microsoft Money provides for split transactions.

Split transactions are simply transactions that use more than a single category
or account. Suppose, for example, you go to a large grocery store and spend
$50 on groceries and $25 on motor oil for your car. Further suppose that you
want to keep track separately of the amounts you spend on groceries and
your car. This is where Microsoft Money's Split Transaction feature comes in.
It allows you to assign more than one category to a transaction.

Hands-On: Splitting a Transaction

To split a transaction, follow these steps.

1. Enter the program as you normally do, but when you get to the step at
   which you would usually enter a single category or account, choose Split
   Transaction from the Edit menu or click on the Split command button at
   the top of the window—it's the fifth icon from the left and shows a big
   dollar sign pointing to two smaller dollar signs. When you do, Microsoft
   Money displays the Split Transaction dialog box, along with the Category
   drop-down list box you'll need to assign the first category. (See Figure 3-14.)

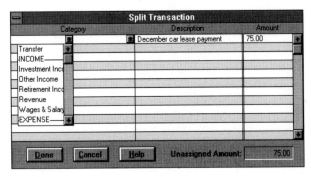

Figure 3-14.
The Split Transaction dialog box.

2. If the first part of the transaction is an income or expense transaction, enter the category in the first Category list box and, optionally, the subcategory in the second Category list box. If the first part of the transaction is a transfer, type the word *transfer* in the first Category list box and the name of the account in the second Category list box.

3. (Optional) Move the cursor to the Description text box. If you want, enter a description of the portion of the transaction assigned to that category.

> **MICROSOFT MONEY TIP:** *If you have questions about how to enter category names, refer to the earlier sections in this chapter on recording transactions. If you have questions about how to enter transfer accounts, refer to the earlier section on transfers between accounts.*

4. Move the cursor to the Amount text box, and type in the amount you want to assign to the category.

5. Move to the next line of the Split Transaction dialog box. With the next line's text boxes open for input, repeat steps 2 through 4 for each category or account you want to use in splitting the transaction. Figure 3-15, for example, shows a $75 check split into $50 for groceries and $25 for car supplies.

6. When the assigned total equals the transaction total, choose the Done command button. Microsoft Money closes the Split Transaction dialog box and

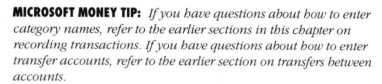

Figure 3-15.
An example of a completed Split Transaction dialog box.

returns you to the window in which you were recording the transaction. To identify split transactions, Microsoft Money puts the word *Split* in the Category drop-down list box. (See Figure 3-16.)

Payee Lists

Payee lists are another handy feature. Every time you record a transaction, Microsoft Money adds the payee name to a list. Then, instead of re-entering the payee name, you can retrieve it from the Payee list.

Hands-On: Using the Payee List

To use the Payee list, follow this two-step procedure.

1. With the cursor in the Payee text box, click on the Payee down arrow or press Alt-Down direction key to open the Payee list box. Figure 3-17 shows the Payee list box.

2. From the list, select the payee name you want to re-use.

SmartFill

SmartFill is Microsoft Money's ability to guess what you want placed in a particular field. Here's how it works: After you enter the first three characters in a text box, Microsoft Money compares them to the lists of possible entries

Account Book						
Account: Checking		View: All (by Date)				
Num	Date	Payee / Memo / Category	C	Payment	Deposit	Balance
	12/1/92	Madison Street State Bank		500.00		1,000.00
		money for trip to Acapulco				
		Transfer To : Savings				
	12/1/92	Barton's Drug Store		13.95		986.05
		presciption from Dr. Dewclaw				
		Healthcare				
	12/1/92	Carter's Car Repair		65.72		920.33
		tune for convertible				
		Automobile				
	12/1/92	Del Fonda Mexican Restaurant			0.00	920.33
		lunch with Peter and Tom				
		Leisure				
	12/1/92	Erwin's Truck Stop		75.00		
	Memo:					
	Category:	Split				
				Ending Balance:		270.24

Figure 3-16.
To identify split transactions, Microsoft Money places the word Split *in the Category drop-down list box.*

Figure 3-17.
The Payee list box.

maintained for the relevant field. If it can find a matching entry, it fills the text box with it.

Suppose, for example, that you type the three characters *Wal* in the Payee text box. Microsoft Money looks for a name on the Payee list that starts with those letters and finds that you've previously recorded a check to Walter's Pawn Shop. It fills in the rest of the Payee text box so that the payee name reads Walter's Pawn Shop. If Microsoft Money guesses correctly, you press Enter or Tab to accept the entry. If you want to enter some other payee, such as Wallingford Insurance, you simply keep typing. Microsoft Money deletes the characters it has added and replaces them with what you type.

SmartFill works on any field for which you maintain a list of possible entries. You should find this a handy feature when you're entering payees, assigning categories and subcategories, and making account transfers.

SmartFill can be turned off in the Settings dialog box. (Choose Settings on the Options menu.)

Automatic Transaction Copying

Another time-saving feature, automatic transaction copying, works in a fashion similar to SmartFill. If you enter a payee name that's the same as the name on a previously recorded transaction, Microsoft Money fills all the text boxes in the window with data from the previous transaction.

At first glance, this might seem like a mistake, but it's not. Two transactions to the same payee probably also have other things in common. The monthly rent check to your landlord, for example, might always be the same amount, and the monthly check to the power company will probably always be assigned to the Utilities expense category.

Changing the Date with a Keystroke

As mentioned earlier, Microsoft Money automatically fills in any date field with the system date. Sometimes, of course, the system date isn't appropriate to the transaction, and you'll need to type over it. In addition, you can change a date with the plus (+) and minus (−) keys—moving it ahead by one day using plus and back by one day using minus.

Automatic Check Numbering

Another time-saving feature is Microsoft Money's automatic transaction numbering. When you set the previous transaction number as print, you indicate that you're printing a check; consequently, Microsoft Money enters the current transaction's number as print, assuming that the current transaction will also be a check.

If the previous transaction's number wasn't set as print, Microsoft Money fills in the current transaction's number for you by adding one to the previous transaction number. So, for example, if the last check you recorded was number 1123, Microsoft Money fills in the current transaction's number as 1124.

Using Different Views

At the top center of each window, you probably noticed the View drop-down list box. (Refer to Figure 3-7.) As Figure 3-7 indicates, the usual way to view an account is to see all transactions for the account arranged by date [All (By Date)]. However, Microsoft Money identifies several other possibilities when you open the View drop-down list box. (See Figure 3-18.) Each View option represents a way you can arrange the data in an Account Book. You don't actually change or remove transactions; you only change the way the information is displayed.

Why would you want to change the view? There are a lot of reasons, some of which I illustrate in subsequent chapters. For example, when you're searching for a particular transaction—such as the last time you had your car engine tuned—you might want to view transactions by payee or category. When you're reconciling a bank account, you might need to find a transaction that was incorrectly recorded and to mark transactions that have cleared the bank. In this case, you might want to view unreconciled transactions by date or by number. There are many other ways to use these different views, too. But let's

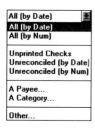

Figure 3-18.
The View drop-down list box.

postpone those discussions and consider only the mechanics of the View menu options here.

To change the view, you simply select the option that describes the view, or arrangement, you want. In its standard, or default, organization, Microsoft Money displays all transactions in the order of their transaction dates. This view is represented by the All (By Date) option, and it gives you a chronological history of the changes to an account.

All (By Num)

The All (By Num) view arranges transactions in numerical order. Because checks and deposits have different numbering schemes, this view tends to group similar kinds of transactions together. For example, all checks and all deposits will probably be grouped in separate lists.

Unprinted Checks

The Unprinted Checks view displays checks to be printed—those with the check number set as print—in the order you entered them. This view is useful for reviewing the checks you've written before you actually print them.

Unreconciled (By Date)

This view, which arranges uncleared transactions in the order they were originally entered, is sometimes useful when reconciling an account. I'll talk more about it in Chapter 5, "Reconciling Your Bank Account."

Unreconciled (By Num)

The Unreconciled (By Num) view arranges uncleared transactions by their transaction numbers—the usual view for reconciling an account.

A Payee

The A Payee view lets you display all the transactions for one payee, which can be useful for reviewing business with a particular company or individual. When you select this option, Microsoft Money displays the Select Payee dialog box (see Figure 3-19), which simply displays the Payee list. You select the payee you want and then choose OK. Microsoft Money redisplays the Account Book showing only the transactions for that payee.

A Category

The A Category view lets you display all transactions assigned to a particular category. It's useful when you want to review the transactions that have affected some type of income or expense, such as your payroll deposits or your utility bills. When you select this option, Microsoft Money displays the Select Category dialog box (see Figure 3-20), which lists the categories you've defined. You select the pertinent category and then choose OK. Microsoft Money redisplays the Account Book, showing only the transactions assigned to that category.

Other

The Other view option lets you organize transactions any way you want. You choose which payees, which categories, and which transaction types are displayed. Despite the power of this view, it's not at all difficult to use. When you select this option, Microsoft Money displays the Other View dialog box shown in Figure 3-21.

As Figure 3-21 shows, you can arrange transactions based on several factors: date, type of transaction, payee, transactions marked cleared, category, a

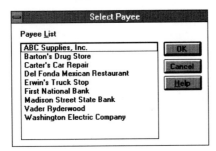

Figure 3-19.
The Select Payee dialog box.

range of dates, a range of transaction numbers, and a range of amounts. You can use all these factors, some combination of them, or only a single one. If you don't use a particular factor, Microsoft Money ignores it as long as you leave its text box or list box empty. The fields for the Other View dialog box work very much like those you already know about.

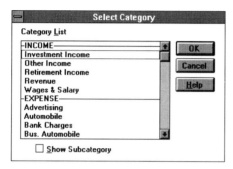

Figure 3-20.
The Select Category dialog box.

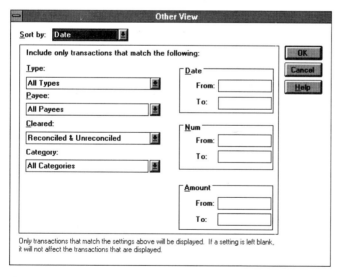

Figure 3-21.
The Other View dialog box.

The Sort By drop-down list box, which appears at the top of the dialog box, lets you specify the order of the transactions. The default order is by transaction date, but if you select the Sort By field, the Sort By list box displays some other sorting options: by number, by accounts (if you've chosen to display all the transactions in all accounts), alphabetically by payee, and alphabetically by category.

To specify that only certain types of transactions should be displayed, you use the Type drop-down list box. When you open the Type drop-down list box, you'll see a list that includes the four types of transactions —payments, deposits, unprinted checks, and transfers — and accounts with no amount. Or you can choose to view all four types of transactions.

Sorting by the Payee field lets you specify that you want to see only the transactions pertaining to a specific business or individual. When you select this option, Microsoft Money displays the Payee list. You identify the payee you want and then choose OK.

The Cleared drop-down list box is useful when you're reconciling or balancing a bank account: It lets you display only cleared transactions, only uncleared transactions, or both types. (I'll talk more about this option in Chapter 5, "Reconciling Your Bank Account.")

To display only the transactions assigned to a specific category, you can open the Category drop-down list box, which displays a list of the categories you've defined. You identify the category and then choose OK.

The Date From and To text boxes let you limit the transactions displayed to those with dates falling within a certain period. You enter the starting date in the From text box and the ending date in the To text box.

Similarly, the Num From and To text boxes let you limit the transactions displayed to those with transaction numbers falling within a certain range. You enter the starting transaction number in the From text box and the ending transaction number in the To text box.

The last two text boxes on the Other View dialog box let you limit the transactions displayed in the Account Book to those with amounts falling within a certain range. You enter the lower amount in the Amount From text box and the higher amount in the To text box.

Conclusion

You're now ready to use Microsoft Money productively as a personal or business accounting tool. You'll want to explore some additional topics, however. For example, the next chapter, Chapter 4, describes how to supercharge your checkbook by using the rest of the Microsoft Money menu commands. Chapter 5 explains how to reconcile bank accounts with Microsoft Money. Chapter 6 provides tips on file management, and Chapter 7 walks you through the steps for printing checks and producing the many reports Microsoft Money can provide.

Chapter 4

SUPERCHARGING YOUR CHECKBOOK

If you've been reading this book from the beginning, you know quite a bit about working with Microsoft Money—how to work with Microsoft Windows, how to set up accounts and define categories in Microsoft Money, and how to keep your checkbook. You've probably noticed the Edit, List, and Option menus that appear at the top of Microsoft Money windows. I've already discussed a few of the commands in these menus in earlier chapters. In this chapter, I describe how to use the rest of them to supercharge your checkbook.

Using the Edit Menu Commands

In Chapter 3, you learned how to use the Edit menu's Split Transaction command. In this section, I describe each of the other Edit menu commands (see Figure 4-1): Undo, Cut, Copy, Paste, Delete Transaction, Void Transaction, Schedule In Future, Mark As Cleared (or Mark As Reconciled), and Find.

Using the Undo Command

The Undo command reverses the effect of your most recent changes to an input field. For example, suppose you change the payee name for a transaction from Bill Richards to William Richards but then decide you really want to use Bill Richards. To do so, you can simply choose the Edit Undo command; you can even change your mind again by choosing Edit Undo a second time.

There's only one catch to using Undo. You can't undo your changes after you move to the next text box. So, for example, you can't use Undo to switch the name Bill Richards back to William Richards after you move to, say, the Memo text box.

Edit	
Undo	Ctrl+Z
Cut	Ctrl+X
Copy	Ctrl+C
Paste	Ctrl+V
Delete Transaction	
Void Transaction	
Split Transaction...	Ctrl+S
Schedule in Future...	Ctrl+E
Mark as Cleared	Ctrl+M
Find...	Ctrl+F

Figure 4-1.
The Edit menu.

Using the Cut, Copy, and Paste Commands

The Cut, Copy, and Paste commands work together to let you duplicate or move text or numbers (data) between text boxes. The Cut and Copy commands allow you to store data on the Clipboard, a temporary storage area in memory. After you use the Cut or Copy command to move data to the Clipboard, you employ the Paste command to retrieve it and place it at the new location you select.

Cut and Copy

The Cut command removes the marked data from its original location and places it on the Clipboard. The Copy command makes a copy of the selected data and places it on the Clipboard, while leaving it in its original place.

You need to know a couple of things about the Clipboard to use it efficiently. First, you can store only a single piece of data on the Clipboard at a time. The data stored by the previous cut or copy operation is replaced when you cut or copy new data. Second, Microsoft Money stores the contents of the Clipboard only as long as Windows is running. If you quit Windows or turn off your computer, the Clipboard contents are discarded.

Before you can cut or copy any data, you need to mark it so that Microsoft Money knows what you want to store on the Clipboard. There are two ways to mark data: using the keyboard and using the mouse.

To mark data using the keyboard, you use Shift and the direction keys. The process is simple. First move the cursor to the first or last character or digit of the data you want to mark. To store more than one character or digit on the Clipboard, hold the Shift key down and use the direction keys, Home, or End to highlight all the data to be cut or copied.

To mark data with the mouse, simply move the mouse pointer to the first or last character or digit you want to cut or copy; then, while holding down the mouse button, drag the mouse pointer to highlight the rest of the data.

After you mark the data you want to cut or copy, choose the appropriate command from the Edit menu—Cut to move the data and Copy to duplicate it. If you make a mistake and highlight text or numbers you don't want to cut or copy, press Esc to remove the highlight.

Paste

To retrieve the cut or copied data, first position the cursor where you want to insert the data. When you choose the Paste command from the Edit menu, Microsoft Money inserts the data stored on the Clipboard at the cursor location.

You don't have to paste data into the same text box it was cut or copied from, or even into the same window. You can cut or copy a block of text from the active window, activate another window, and paste the Clipboard contents into the newly active window. Chapter 1, "Working with Windows," describes how to switch the active window.

Deleting and Voiding Transactions

Whereas the Cut, Copy, and Paste commands work on individual input fields, the fifth and sixth commands on the Edit menu affect entire transactions. Delete Transaction removes the selected transaction from the Account Book entirely. Void Transaction retains the selected transaction but marks it void and does not include it in the account balance or category total. In Figure 4-2, for example, the check to James D. Hughes, Attorney, has been voided. To use either command, you select the transaction you want to delete or void and then choose the command.

How do you know whether you want to use Delete Transaction or Void Transaction? The basic rule is that you should void a transaction if you want to

Account Book

Account: Checking		View: All (by Date)						
Num	Date	Payee / Memo / Category	C	Payment	Deposit	Balance		
1127	12/4/92	James D. Hughes, Attorney	R	1,000.00		**VOID**		
		retainer for legal services						
		Bus. Services						
1124	12/29/92	Washington Electric Company	R	75.09		640.24		
		November electric bill						
		Utilities						
1125	12/30/92	Madison Street State Bank	R	500.00		140.24		
		money for trip to Acapulco						
		Transfer To : Savings						
1126	12/31/92	ABC Supplies, Inc.	R	34.63		105.61		
		hardware to fix garage door						
		Housing						
	1/1/93	Service Charge	R	5.00		100.61		
		Bank Charges						
					Ending Balance:	101.61		

Figure 4-2.
A voided transaction in the Account Book.

keep a record of the transaction's existence. For example, checks you void by writing the word *void* across the check face should probably also be recorded as void in your Account Book; checks on which you stop payment should be voided, as well as deposits made with a check that turns out to be bad—perhaps because of insufficient funds in the check writer's account.

If you don't want or need a record of the transaction's existence, however, you can simply delete the transaction. This usually happens when you incorrectly enter a transaction or make an error part way through entering it and want to start over again.

Scheduling Future Transactions

Microsoft Money's Future Transactions feature permits you to maintain a list of transactions for re-use. For instance, instead of re-entering the same information when you pay the rent each month, you can store all the transaction information on the Future Transactions list. When you want to pay the monthly rent, you simply tell Microsoft Money to copy the necessary information from the Future Transactions list.

There are two steps to using Future Transactions: recording a transaction in the Future Transactions list and entering that transaction in the Account Book. The Edit menu's Schedule In Future command accomplishes the first step, and the Enter From Schedule command, which appears on the Edit menu when the Future Transactions window is displayed, accomplishes the second step.

Hands-On: Adding a Future Transaction

To add a transaction to the Future Transactions list, follow these steps.

1. Highlight the transaction you want to add, either by using the cursor keys or by clicking the mouse.

2. Choose the Schedule In Future command from the Edit menu or click on the Schedule In Future command button at the top of the window. (It's the second button from the right—the icon that resembles a calendar.) Microsoft Money next displays the Schedule Future Transaction dialog box shown in Figure 4-3.

3. Specify the frequency of the future transactions. To do so, click on the down arrow to the right of the Frequency drop-down list box. Microsoft Money lists 11 frequency choices: Daily, Weekly, BiWeekly, SemiMonthly,

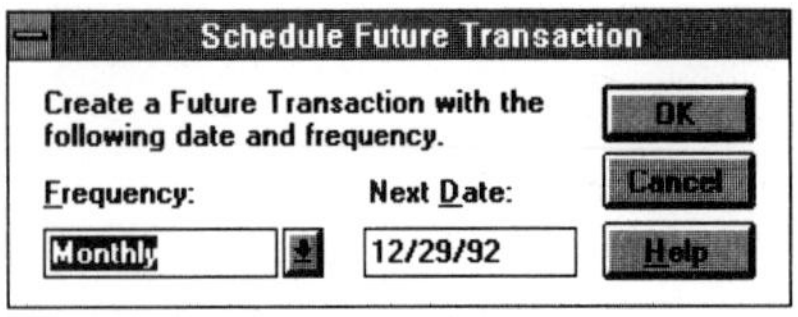

Figure 4-3.
The Schedule Future Transaction dialog box.

Monthly, BiMonthly, Quarterly, SemiAnnually, Annually, BiAnnually, and Only Once. Select the appropriate frequency from the list.

4. After you specify the frequency, Microsoft Money guesses the date on which you want to enter the next transaction into the Account Book. For example, if the current system date is December 1, 1992, and you specify a monthly frequency, Microsoft Money assumes that the next transaction date is January 1, 1993. If the date Microsoft Money guesses is correct, choose OK. If not, move the cursor to the Date text box and type the correct date.

5. When the Schedule Future Transaction dialog box is complete, choose OK.

6. To verify that the transaction you specified was correctly added to the Future Transactions list, you'll want to view the Future Transactions window. You can do so either by double-clicking on the Future Transactions icon in the bottom left-hand corner of the screen or by choosing Future Transactions from the Window menu. Figure 4-4 shows the Future Transactions window with a newly added transaction.

From this point on, Microsoft Money keeps track of this information.

As Figure 4-4 shows, the Future Transactions window resembles the Account Book window and displays several pieces of information for each transaction: the next transaction date, transaction frequency and account, transaction number, payee, memo, category, and payment or deposit amount. To see more detailed transaction information, choose the Entire Transaction View command from the Options menu.

Recording Future Transactions

You can use the Future Transactions feature simply as a tickler to remind you of a transaction a specified number of days before the expected transaction date. You can also use it to automate scheduled transactions when it's time to

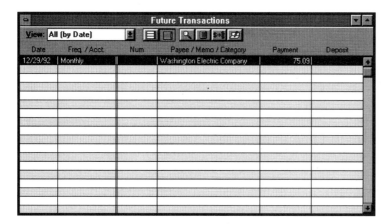

Figure 4-4.
The Future Transactions window.

execute them. When the Future Transactions window shown in Figure 4-4 is displayed, Microsoft Money replaces the Schedule In Future command (see Figure 4-5) with the Enter From Schedule command. This command simply enters the selected future transaction into the Account Book.

Hands-On: Entering a Future Transaction

To use the Enter From Schedule command, follow these steps.

1. Select the future transaction you want to enter into the Account Book by using the cursor keys, clicking the mouse, or clicking on the Future Transactions icon at the top of the screen—the icon on the far right that resembles a pen writing in a checkbook. Microsoft Money displays the Enter Scheduled Transactions dialog box shown in Figure 4-6.

2. Verify that the Enter In drop-down list box names the correct account. If it doesn't, click the down arrow to the right of the Enter In list box. After Microsoft Money displays a list of accounts, select the one you want to use.

3. Verify that the Num text box shows the correct transaction number. If it doesn't, select the Num text box and type the correct number over the incorrect one or leave it blank.

```
┌─────────────────────────────────┐
│ Edit                            │
├─────────────────────────────────┤
│ Undo                     Ctrl+Z │
│ Cut                      Ctrl+X │
│ Copy                     Ctrl+C │
│ Paste                    Ctrl+V │
├─────────────────────────────────┤
│ Delete Transaction              │
│ Void Transaction                │
├─────────────────────────────────┤
│ Split Transaction...     Ctrl+S │
│ Schedule in Future...    Ctrl+E │
│ Mark as Cleared          Ctrl+M │
├─────────────────────────────────┤
│ Find...                  Ctrl+F │
└─────────────────────────────────┘
```

Figure 4-5.
The Future Transactions window's Edit Menu.

```
┌──────────────────────────────────────────────────────────────────┐
│                    Enter Scheduled Transactions                   │
├──────────────────────────────────────────────────────────────────┤
│  Enter In:  [Checking    ▼]  Remaining Balance:   101.61          │
│                                                        [ Enter ]   │
│   Num    Date      Payee/Memo/Category  Spend     Receive         │
│  ┌────┐ ┌────────┐ Washington Electric Compa┌──────┐ ┌──────┐     │
│  │    │ │12/29/92│                     │75.09 │ │      │          │
│  └────┘ └────────┘ November electric bill └──────┘ └──────┘       │
│                    Utilities                                      │
│                                                        [ Cancel ]  │
│  [ Split... ]                                          [ Help ]    │
└──────────────────────────────────────────────────────────────────┘
```

Figure 4-6.
The Enter Scheduled Transactions dialog box.

4. Verify that the Date text box shows the correct transaction date. If the date isn't correct, select the Date text box and type the correct date over the incorrect entry.

5. Verify that the amount shown is correct. If the transaction is a withdrawal, the correct amount should appear in the Spend text box. If it is a deposit, the correct amount should appear in the Receive text box. If the amount is wrong, select the appropriate text box and type in the correct amount.

6. (Optional) If the transaction is split, you can choose the Split command button to review or change the amounts assigned to the categories. Microsoft Money then displays the Split Transaction dialog box. (Chapter 3, "Keeping Your Checkbook with Microsoft Money," describes the Split Transaction command.)

7. When all the text boxes in the Enter Scheduled Transactions dialog box are correct, choose the Enter command button. Microsoft Money then enters the transaction in the Account Book.

Marking as Cleared or Uncleared

The Mark As Cleared and Mark As Uncleared commands let you designate transactions as having cleared the bank—something you do as part of reconciling, or balancing, your bank accounts. (Chapter 5, "Reconciling Your Bank Account," discusses this process in more detail.)

When you receive your bank statement, you mark all the transactions that have cleared the bank and use only the cleared transactions to calculate the ending balance, which you compare to the balance shown on the bank statement. If the balances match, your account is reconciled.

To mark transactions as cleared or uncleared, use the Mark As Cleared or Mark As Uncleared commands. If the selected transaction was not previously marked cleared, the command Mark As Cleared appears on the Edit menu. When you choose that command, Microsoft Money places the letter *C,* for cleared, in the C-column of the Account Book.

If the selected transaction has been previously marked cleared—that is, if the transaction already has a *C* in the C-column of the Account Book—the Mark As Uncleared command appears on the Edit menu.

When you choose this command, Microsoft Money removes the letter *C* from the C-column.

Finding Transactions

The last command on the Edit menu, Find, lets you search through the transactions listed in the current view of the Account Book. Suppose, for example, you are looking for the last check you wrote for your car insurance. You could use Find to look for a transaction that contained the words *car, insurance,* or *car insurance.*

Hands-On: Finding Transactions

To use the Find command, follow these steps.

1. Choose the Find command from the Edit menu. When you do, Microsoft Money displays the Find dialog box shown in Figure 4-7.

Figure 4-7.
The Find dialog box.

2. Type the word, phrase, or part of a word or phrase you want to search for in the Find What text box.

3. Use the Look In drop-down list box (see Figure 4-8) to indicate which text boxes you want to search. The default Look In setting is All Fields, but when you open the drop-down list, Microsoft Money displays the list of input fields: Number, Payee, Amount, Memo, Category, and Subcategory. If you have defined a classification, the first classification will also appear on the list. (I discuss classifications in more detail later in this chapter.) Simply select the fields you want to search.

4. Use the Direction option buttons to specify whether you want to search transactions listed above or below the selected transaction.

5. When you're ready to begin searching, choose the Find Next command button, and Microsoft Money begins the search. If it finds a transaction matching the criteria you specified in the Find What and Look In text boxes, it displays that transaction. If it doesn't, it shows an information message.

Using the Edit Menu
Commands on the Other Windows

In the preceding paragraphs, I've described the use of the Edit menu commands in the context of the Account Book window. You can also use all

Figure 4-8.
The Look In drop-down list box.

these commands when working in the Future Transactions and the Checks & Forms windows. For example, you might find the Undo, Cut, Copy, and Paste commands handy for editing text boxes in both these windows, or you might need to delete and void transactions, mark transactions as cleared or un-cleared, and search using the Find command.

Exploring the List Menu Commands

The List menu, shown in Figure 4-9, contains commands for maintaining Microsoft Money's lists. As you've already used three of the four lists—the Account, Payee, and Category lists—the sections on using the Account List and Payee List commands will seem familiar. (Refer to Chapter 2 for a full description of the Category List command.) I describe the fourth list, Other Classification, in greater detail at the end of this section.

Using the Account List Command

The Account List command lets you add, rename, and delete accounts. The simplest way to set up accounts, as described in Chapter 2, uses the New Account command on the Account drop-down list box. The Account List command on the List menu, however, lets you describe accounts more fully.

When you choose the Account List command, Microsoft Money displays the Account List dialog box. (See Figure 4-10.) As the command buttons indicate, you can use the dialog box to add, delete, or rename accounts. Several additional text boxes—not available when you set up accounts using the New Account command—allow you to use a longer account name, create a shortcut abbreviation for the account, specify the account number if applicable, and use a Comments field to describe the account.

Figure 4-9.
The List menu.

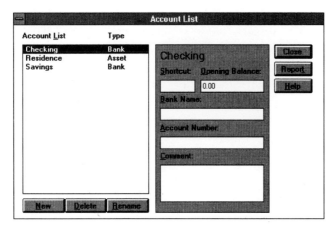

Figure 4-10.
The Account List dialog box.

Hands-On: Describing an Account in More Detail

To use the Account List dialog box to describe an existing account more fully, follow these steps.

1. Select the account you want to describe more fully.

2. Move the cursor to the Shortcut text box, and enter an account abbreviation of six characters or less. (You'll be able to use this shortcut in place of the account name when entering the account name in a text box.)

3. Move the cursor to the Bank Name text box and enter a second, longer name for the account. An account with the First National Bank called Checking, for example, might have the longer second name *First National Checking.*

4. If the account has an account number—as is the case with bank accounts, credit cards, and mortgages, for example—move the cursor to the Account Number field, and enter the account number.

5. (Optional) To describe an account further, use the Comment block. For example, if you had set up an account for a piece of real estate, you might use the Comment block to record its address. To move from one line of the Comment block to the next line, press Ctrl-Enter.

6. To close the Account List dialog box and save your changes, choose the Close command button.

Hands-On: Setting Up an Account from Scratch

You can use the Account List dialog box to set up accounts from scratch by following these steps.

1. Choose the New command in the Account List dialog box. When you do, Microsoft Money displays the Create New Account dialog box, with which you are already familiar because you used it to set up your accounts initially. (Refer to Figure 2-3 in Chapter 2.)

2. Type in the name you want to use for the account, such as *checking*, *savings*, or *credit card*.

3. Click on the option button describing the appropriate type of account: Bank Account, Credit Card Account, Cash Or Other Account, Asset Account, or Liability Account. Then press Enter or click on the OK command button.

4. When Microsoft Money displays the Opening Balance dialog box, enter the starting balance, and press Enter or click on OK. (Refer to Figure 2-4.)

5. With the cursor on the Shortcut text box, enter an account abbreviation of up to six characters.

6. Move the cursor to the Bank Name text box and enter a second, longer name for the account.

7. If the account has an account number, as is the case with bank accounts, credit cards, and mortgages, for example, move the cursor to the Account Number text box, and enter the account number.

8. (Optional) You can use the Comment block to describe the account further. To move from one line to the next, press Ctrl-Enter.

9. To close the Account List dialog box and save your changes, choose the Close command button.

Deleting and Renaming Accounts

With the Delete and Rename commands, you can also use the Account List dialog box to remove accounts you've set up previously or to change their names. If you're careful and thoughtful in setting up your accounts initially, you won't often need these command buttons. However, you might want to delete a fictitious account you created while learning the mechanics of Microsoft Money. Or your bank might change its name.

Hands-On: removing an account. To remove an account you previously set up, follow these steps.

1. With the Account List dialog box displayed, select the account you want to delete from the list box.

2. Choose the Delete command button to remove the account.

3. If the account you select has transactions in its Account Book, Microsoft Money alerts you to the existing transactions and asks you to confirm that you want to delete the account.

4. Choose the Close command button to close the dialog box.

Hands-On: renaming an account. To rename an account you previously set up, follow these steps.

1. With the Account List dialog box displayed, select the account you want to rename from the list box.

2. Choose the Rename command button. When you do, Microsoft Money displays the Rename Account dialog box (see Figure 4-11), which simply identifies the old account name and provides an input field for entering the new name.

3. Enter the new account name in the New Name text box.

4. Choose the OK command button to return to the Account List dialog box.

5. Choose the Close command button to close the dialog box.

Rename Account		
Old Name: Residence		OK
New Name: Residence		Cancel
		Help

Figure 4-11.
The Rename Account dialog box.

Printing Account Lists

The Report command button in the Account List dialog box displays a list of your accounts, along with the information stored about each one, in a window called the Account List Report window. (See Figure 4-12.) To print this list after you've displayed it, simply choose the Print command button. (For more information on printing reports, refer to Chapter 7.)

Using the Payee List Command

As described in Chapter 3, "Keeping Your Checkbook with Microsoft Money," the program maintains a list of all your payees. After you've entered a payee, you can retrieve the individual's or business's name from the list rather than retyping it.

The Payee List command lets you add new payees to the list, delete payees, and even change the payee name stored on the list. In addition, you can define shortcut abbreviations, record the payees' telephone numbers and addresses, and include comments.

Particularly for businesses using Microsoft Money, the ability to store information about the people or firms you do business with should prove invaluable. But the Payee list—in conjunction with Microsoft Money's SmartFill feature,

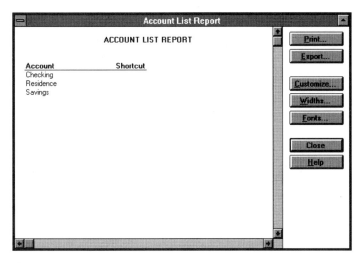

Figure 4-12.
The Account List Report window.

which utilizes the lists of accounts, payees, and categories—also benefits home users. (SmartFill is described in Chapter 3, "Keeping Your Checkbook with Microsoft Money.")

Hands-On: Adding a Payee

To add a payee to the list using the Payee List command, follow these steps.

1. Choose the Payee List command from the List menu. When you do, Microsoft Money displays the Payee List dialog box, shown in Figure 4-13.

2. Choose the New command button. When you do, Microsoft Money displays the Create New Payee dialog box (see Figure 4-14), which simply provides a text box in which to enter the payee name.

3. Enter the payee name and choose OK. Microsoft Money closes the Create New Payee dialog box, leaving the Payee List dialog box displayed.

4. With the cursor on the Shortcut text box, enter an abbreviation for the payee of up to six characters.

5. Move the cursor to the Phone text box, and enter the telephone number for the individual or business.

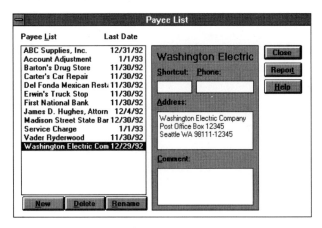

Figure 4-13.
The Payee List dialog box.

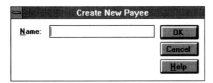

Figure 4-14.
The Create New Payee dialog box.

6. Move the cursor to the Address text box and enter up to a four-line address. To move from one line of the Address block to the next, press Ctrl-Enter.

7. (Optional) If you want to describe a payee further, use the Comment block. To move from one line of the Comment block to the next, press Ctrl-Enter.

8. To close the Payee List dialog box and save your changes, choose the Close command button.

Removing and Renaming Payees

As noted earlier, you can also use the Payee List command to remove entries from the Payee list and to rename payees. Typically, however, you won't use these command buttons unless you incorrectly enter a payee name when recording a transaction.

Hands-On: removing a payee. To remove a payee from the Payee list, follow these steps.

1. With the Payee List dialog box displayed, select the payee you want to delete from the list box.

2. Choose the Delete command to remove the payee.

3. Microsoft Money then displays a confirmation message alerting you to existing transactions and asking you to confirm the deletion. Choose OK.

4. Choose the Close command button to close the dialog box.

Hands-On: renaming a payee. To rename a payee, follow these steps.

1. With the Payee List dialog box displayed, select the payee you want to rename from the list box.

2. Choose the Rename command button. Microsoft Money then displays the Rename Payee dialog box (see Figure 4-15), which simply identifies the old payee name and provides a text box in which to enter the new name.

3. Enter the new payee name in the text box.

4. Choose the OK command button to return to the Payee List dialog box.

5. Choose the Close command button to close the dialog box.

Printing Payee Lists

The Report command button in the Payee List dialog box will not be particularly useful if you're only using the Payee list indirectly—for example, with Microsoft Money's SmartFill feature. If, however, you decide to store information about the individuals and firms you do business with on the Payee list, you can use this button to print a list of your payees and all the information you have about them. To create such a list, simply choose the Report command button; Microsoft Money then displays the Payee List Report window shown in Figure 4-16. To print the Payee List Report, choose the Print command button. (Refer to Chapter 7 if you have questions about printing.)

Using the Other Classification List

In Chapter 2, I described how to summarize income and expenses by category. Microsoft Money provides a second way to summarize financial data by classification. Classifications can be whatever you want them to be. For example, a general contractor who builds single-family homes might want

Rename Payee	
Old Name:	Erwin's Truck Stop
New Name:	Erwin's Truck Stop

OK
Cancel
Help

Figure 4-15.
The Rename Payee dialog box.

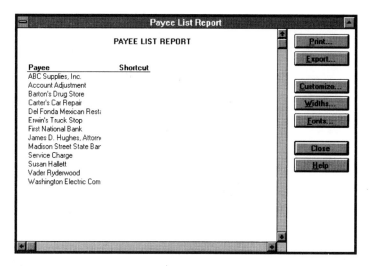

Figure 4-16.

The Payee List Report window.

to summarize income and expenses not only by category but also by each single-family home. Using this classification, the contractor would know not only how much he or she spent on expense items such as two-by-fours, nails, sheetrock, and shingles, but also what each of these items cost for each house built. Similarly, an accounting or law firm might want to classify expenses by client, and a real estate investor to tally income and expenses by property.

Other classifications might be appropriate to your personal or business situation. Microsoft Money lets you identify and use two classes and create subclasses as well. Classes are powerful tools for summarizing the financial information you collect in the way that is most meaningful to you. Table 4-1 lists how and why individuals or businesses of various sorts might choose to use Microsoft Money's classifications feature.

Individual/firm	Classification	Why used
Real estate investor	Property	Track income and expenses by property to determine the profitability of specific properties
General contractor	Job	Track income and expenses by job to determine revenues, costs, and profits of a job
Retailer	Customer	Track sales and expenses by type of customer—retail, wholesale, and so on—to determine profitability of different segments of business
Manufacturer	Region	Track sales and expenses by region—county, state, country, and so on—to determine profits by region
Any business	Salesperson	Track sales or sales and expenses by salesperson to determine each salesperson's contributions and perhaps to calculate sales commissions

Table 4-1.
Examples of other classifications.

Creating Other Classifications

To create your own classifications, use the Other Classification command on the List menu. The process has two steps. First you name the classification, using the Other Classification command; then you identify the items in the class. The general contractor who builds single-family homes, for example, would name the classification Homes. After that, he or she would identify the individual homes to which income and expense items pertain, such as 512 Wetmore Street and 5461 Sandpoint Way. Microsoft Money would then add a new text box, Homes, to the Account Book, Checks & Forms, and Future Transactions windows for entering information about relevant transactions.

Hands-On: naming classifications. To name the classification you want, follow these steps.

1. Choose the Other Classification command from the List menu. When you do, Microsoft Money displays the Other Classification dialog box, as shown in Figure 4-17.

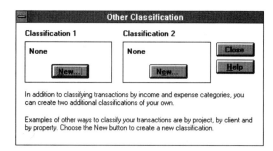

Figure 4-17.
The Other Classification dialog box.

2. To add the first classification, choose the New command button in the Classification 1 box. When you do, Microsoft Money displays the New Classification dialog box shown in Figure 4-18. It displays a list of predefined class names: Client, Department, Job, Project, Property, and Work Order.

3. Select the option button that corresponds to the class name you want to use, or create your own name by selecting the last option button and entering a class name in the text box.

4. If you want the class you name to be broken down into subclasses, mark the Allow Sub-items check box. Although not every class lends itself to

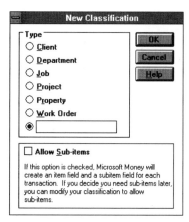

Figure 4-18.
The New Classification dialog box.

sub-items, this option can be useful in certain cases. For example, if you define a class called Clients, you could create sub-items for multiple projects that you do for the same client.

5. Choose OK to display the Classification List dialog box shown in Figure 4-22. (In this figure, the dialog box is titled Property List because the classification description selected in the New Classification dialog box was Property.) Choose the Close command.

To add a second classification, follow the same sequence of steps with one minor difference: choose the New command button in the Classification 2 box.

Renaming and Deleting Classifications

You can also use the Other Classification command on the List menu if you decide later to delete or rename a class.

Hands-On: renaming a classification. To rename a class, follow these steps.

1. Choose the Other Classification command from the List menu. When you do, Microsoft Money displays the Other Classification dialog box shown in Figure 4-19. Note that after you define a class, Microsoft Money replaces the New command button shown in Figure 4-17 with the Modify and Delete command buttons shown in Figure 4-19.

2. Choose the Modify command button in the appropriate classification box. When you do, Microsoft Money displays the Modify Classification Scheme dialog box shown in Figure 4-20.

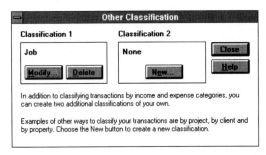

Figure 4-19.
The Other Classification dialog box displays the Modify and Delete command buttons after you define a class.

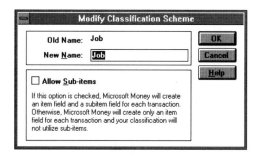

Figure 4-20.
The Modify Classification Scheme dialog box.

3. Type the new name you want to use for the class in the New Name text box.

4. If the renamed class has subclasses, verify that the Allow Sub-items check box is checked. If it isn't, check it.

5. Choose OK to return to the Other Classification dialog box.

6. Choose the Close command button in the Other Classification box to return to the window.

Hands-On: deleting a classification. To delete a classification, follow these steps.

1. Choose the Other Classification command from the List menu.

2. Choose the Delete command button in the appropriate classification box. When you do, Microsoft Money displays a confirmation message asking you to confirm that you want to delete the classification.

3. Choose OK.

4. Choose the Close command button on the Other Classification box.

Identifying the Items in a Class

Once you name the classification scheme, you're ready to identify the specific items within the classification. For example, if the classification scheme uses property as a class, you identify individual properties—the property on Maple-wood Drive, the property on Broadway, and so on—as items. There are two ways to do this.

If you want to identify all items at once, you can use the List menu again. After identifying a classification scheme, you can choose a new command from the List menu that lets you identify the items. (See Figure 4-21. To refresh your memory of the usual version of the List menu, refer to Figure 4-9.)

Hands-On: identifying items. To use the List menu to identify items, follow these steps.

1. Choose the List menu command that corresponds to the class—it will be either the fifth or sixth option. (In Figure 4-21, the sixth option reads *2. Property List* because Property was identified as the second classification scheme.) Microsoft Money then displays the Property List dialog box. (See Figure 4-22.)

    Microsoft Money always uses the name of the class you've identified in its dialog box titles and text box and check box names. Because this example

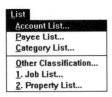

Figure 4-21.
After you name a class, the List menu includes options for identifying items.

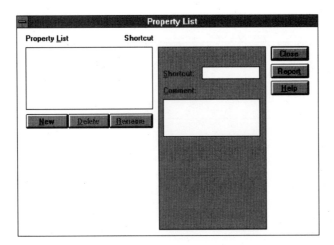

Figure 4-22.
The Property List dialog box.

used Property as the classification scheme, Microsoft Money uses the word Property. If you use some other classification, such as Client, Job, or Department, Microsoft Money uses that class description in its dialog box titles and text box and check box names.

2. Choose the New command button. When you do, Microsoft Money displays another dialog box, the Create New Property dialog box. (See Figure 4-23.)

3. With the cursor in the Name text box, type a brief description of the property.

4. If you marked the Allow Sub-items check box when defining the class, you can now choose the main Property New button to enter a full-fledged item and then the Sub-Property New button to enter a sub-item. Then use the drop-down list box on the Create New Sub-Property dialog box to identify the main Property the sub-item corresponds to. (These buttons don't appear in Figure 4-23 because Property wasn't set to allow sub-items.)

5. Choose OK. Microsoft Money adds the new item. If you've added a sub-item, Microsoft Money displays it in a second list box in the Sub-Property List dialog box.

6. To create a shortcut, or abbreviation, for the item or sub-item, highlight the item in the list box, move the cursor to the Shortcut text box, and enter the abbreviation of up to six characters.

7. To describe the item further for your own records, highlight the item in the list box, move the cursor to the Comment text box, and type the description. To use more than one line, press Ctrl-Enter at the end of each line.

After you identify a classification, Microsoft Money adds a new text box for the classification to each window. (If you've defined a subclassification, Microsoft Money adds a new text box for that, too.) Figure 4-24 shows the Account Book with a line for the classification in each transaction. As usual,

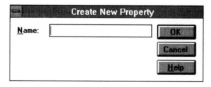

Figure 4-23.
The Create New Property dialog box.

(Figure 4-24 window)

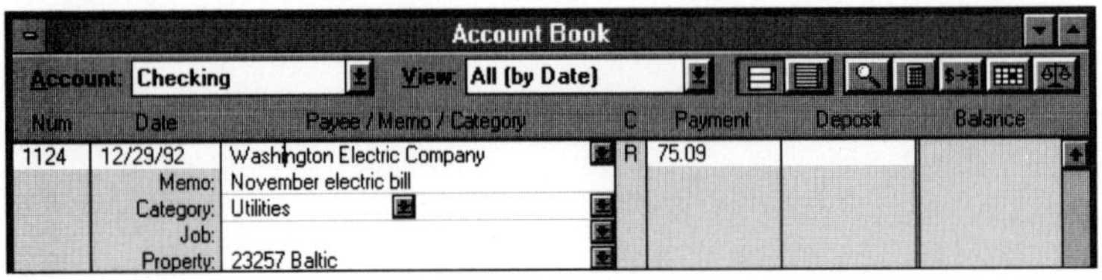

Figure 4-24.
The input fields for a transaction when you've defined Property as a class.

the down arrow to the right of the list box indicates that you can display a scrollable list of all the items named by clicking on the down arrow with the mouse or by pressing Alt-Down direction key with the cursor on the drop-down list box.

You can also add items and sub-items while entering transactions. Simply type a new item or sub-item name in the input field. When you do, Microsoft Money displays the Create New dialog box for the item, which you complete as described in steps 3 and 4 of the preceding section.

Removing and Renaming Items

If you make mistakes or add items or sub-items you don't want, you can use the List dialog box for the classification to correct the errors.

Hands-On: removing an item. To remove an item or sub-item you no longer want on your classification list, follow these steps.

1. Choose the List menu command that corresponds to the class. When you do, Microsoft Money displays the appropriate List dialog box, such as the Property List dialog box shown in Figure 4-22.

2. Highlight the item or sub-item you want to remove.

3. Choose the Delete command button.

4. (Optional) If you've previously used an item or sub-item, Microsoft Money won't let you remove it without first specifying a replacement for all the transactions that use it. In this case, Microsoft Money displays the Delete Property dialog box shown in Figure 4-25 for you to specify the replacement item. Enter the replacement item in the left-hand input field, and the sub-item, if appropriate, in the right-hand input field. Then choose OK.

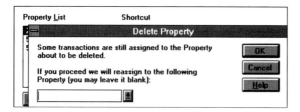

Figure 4-25.
The Delete Property dialog box.

Hands-On: renaming an item. To change the name of an item or sub-item, follow a similar sequence of steps.

1. Choose the List menu command that corresponds to the class. When you do, Microsoft Money displays the List dialog box for the class, such as the Property List dialog box shown in Figure 4-22.

2. Highlight the item or sub-item you want to rename.

3. Choose the Rename command button; Microsoft Money displays a Rename dialog box for the item, such as the one shown in Figure 4-26.

4. Type the new item or sub-item name and choose OK.

If you've spent at least a few minutes thinking about the items you need, you'll find the process of creating the perfect classification list quick and easy. All you'll do is repeatedly choose the New, Delete, and Rename command buttons in the List dialog box for the class.

When you're done, you can generate a list of the items in a class by choosing the Report command button. Microsoft Money displays a List Report window, such as the one shown in Figure 4-27. To print the report, simply choose Print. (Refer to Chapter 7 if you have questions about printing.)

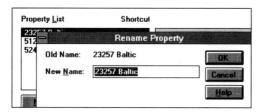

Figure 4-26.
The Rename Property dialog box.

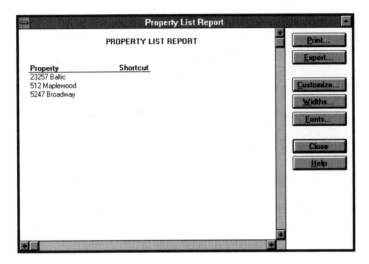

Figure 4-27.
The Property List Report window.

Setting Microsoft Money's Options

The Options menu lists a half dozen commands of different types. The first three commands are useful tools for record keeping. Balance Account helps you reconcile bank accounts, Pay Bills lets you enter transactions on the Future Transactions list into the Account Book, and the Calculator command accesses the Windows calculator, which you can use to make calculations while you work with your financial records. I describe the Pay Bills and Calculator commands in the following paragraphs and the Balance Account command in Chapter 5, "Reconciling Your Bank Account."

The last three commands on the Options menu affect the mechanics of working with Microsoft Money. The fourth command, Top Line View/Entire Transaction View, controls the appearance of the Account Book. Settings controls miscellaneous processing options, such as whether Microsoft Money beeps when you record a transaction. Password, the final command, lets you define a password to use subsequently to gain access to your financial records.

Using the Pay Bills Command

The Pay Bills command enters into the Account Book all future transactions that have expected transaction dates falling on or before a specified date. When you choose the Pay Bills command, Microsoft Money displays the Record Due Transactions dialog box. (See Figure 4-28.) To indicate the future transactions you want recorded, you enter a date; future transactions with dates falling on or before that date are recorded in the Account Book. If the date is correct, choose the OK command button. It's that simple.

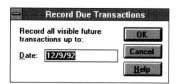

Figure 4-28.
The Record Due Transactions dialog box.

Using the Windows Calculator

The Calculator command accesses the Windows Calculator. (See Figure 4-29.) If you've worked with a handheld calculator, you know how to use the Windows Calculator. In case you haven't, I'll review the basics.

Figure 4-29.
The Windows Calculator.

To add, subtract, multiply, or divide, use the mouse to select the calculator buttons for the arithmetic operation you want to perform. For example, to add 2 to 4, you enter *2 + 4 =*. To multiply, use the asterisk (*) symbol; to divide, use the slash (/).

The Windows Calculator also allows you to calculate more powerful arithmetic functions, including square roots, percentages, and inverse numbers. To find the square root of a number, first enter the number, then select the sqrt button. For example, to calculate the square root of 100, enter the number *100* and then select the sqrt button.

The percent key lets you add, subtract, multiply, and divide a number by a percentage of itself. For example, to add 35 percent of 200 to 200, enter *200 + 35 %*. To multiply 200 by 35 percent—which is the same thing as 35 percent of 200—you enter *200 * 35 %*. Interestingly, you can't calculate what number 200 is 35 percent of by entering *200 / 35 %*; that expression also calculates 35 percent of 200.

The 1/x key calculates the inverse of a number. For example, the inverse of 5 is 1/5. So if you enter *5 1/x*, the calculator divides the number 1 by 5.

The C, CE, and Back buttons let you clear the calculator display of any numbers entered. The C button clears the current calculation, the CE button clears the number displayed on the calculator, and the Back button erases the far right digit of the number displayed.

The memory buttons are MC, MR, MS, and M+. MC sets the calculator's memory to zero. M+ adds the number currently displayed to the number in memory. If you previously cleared memory by using the MC button, M+ has the effect of memorizing the displayed number. MR displays the number stored in memory, and MS subtracts the displayed number from the number in memory.

The Calculator has its own Edit menu, which contains Copy and Paste commands. These commands work exactly like the Copy and Paste commands on Microsoft Money's Edit menu described earlier in the chapter; you can use them to transfer calculations into your Microsoft Money files. Suppose, for example, that you need to pay three invoices to the same vendor: one for $45.61, one for $17.03, and one for $68.89. The check amount should be the total of these three amounts. You can add these three numbers using the Calculator, use the Copy command to copy the total—$131.53—to the Clipboard, and close the Calculator to return to the Account Book window. You can then move the cursor to the Payment text box and choose Edit Paste to paste the number, still stored on the Clipboard, into the Withdrawal field.

To learn more about the Calculator, refer to the *Microsoft Windows Users Guide* or to Chapter 10, "Making Financial Calculations." Chapter 10 describes how to use a special version of the Windows Calculator to compute loan payments and estimate future investment balances.

Switching Between Top Line and Entire Transaction Views

The illustrations showing the Account Book have all used the Entire Transaction view. Microsoft Money also lets you use a single-line or Top Line view. In fact, this Top Line view is used by default for the Future Transactions window. Figure 4-30 shows a Top Line view of the Account Book. To switch from the Top Line view of the Account Book or Future Transactions windows to the Entire Transaction view, choose the Entire Transaction View command from the Options menu. If the window shows the entire transaction and you want to switch to a Top Line view, choose the Top Line View command.

You can also change the view using the Top Line View and Entire Transaction View icons at the top of the Account Book and Future Transactions windows. To see the entire transaction, click on the leftmost icon—which looks like a miniature account book set to display an entire transaction. To see only a

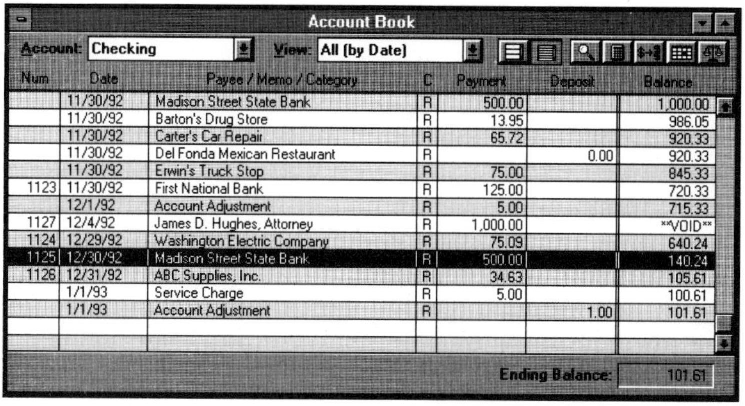

Num	Date	Payee / Memo / Category	C	Payment	Deposit	Balance
	11/30/92	Madison Street State Bank	R	500.00		1,000.00
	11/30/92	Barton's Drug Store	R	13.95		986.05
	11/30/92	Carter's Car Repair	R	65.72		920.33
	11/30/92	Del Fonda Mexican Restaurant	R		0.00	920.33
	11/30/92	Erwin's Truck Stop	R	75.00		845.33
1123	11/30/92	First National Bank	R	125.00		720.33
	12/1/92	Account Adjustment	R	5.00		715.33
1127	12/4/92	James D. Hughes, Attorney	R	1,000.00		**VOID**
1124	12/29/92	Washington Electric Company	R	75.09		640.24
1125	12/30/92	Madison Street State Bank	R	500.00		140.24
1126	12/31/92	ABC Supplies, Inc.	R	34.63		105.61
	1/1/93	Service Charge	R	5.00		100.61
	1/1/93	Account Adjustment	R		1.00	101.61

Figure 4-30.
The Top Line view of the Account Book window.

single line, click on the second-to-the-left icon, which looks like a miniature account book set to display a single line.

Setting Your Preferences

The Settings command lets you control how Microsoft Money works. When you choose this command, Microsoft Money displays the Settings dialog box shown in Figure 4-31, which contains a series of option buttons.

The Type Size option buttons let you specify the point size you want Microsoft Money to use for text it displays: either Standard (10 point) or Larger (12 point). The Show Message Bar check box turns off or on the message bar at the bottom of the screen. The Color drop-down list box lets you specify the accent color and check background color shown on the screen.

The Confirm Transaction Changes check box determines whether confirmation messages appear when you edit transactions. The Beep On Transaction Entry check box lets you specify whether Microsoft Money beeps when you record a transaction. The Reminder To Backup check box lets you turn on and off the message that asks if you want to back up your data files whenever you exit from Microsoft Money.

The Transactions Due Reminder check box lets you turn on and off a reminder alerting you to future transactions that will soon require action.

```
┌─────────────────────── Settings ───────────────────────┐
│ ┌─Display────────────┐          ┌──────┐                │
│ │ Type Size          │          │  OK  │                │
│ │                    │          └──────┘                │
│ │  ● Standard        │          ┌──────┐                │
│ │  ○ Larger          │          │Cancel│                │
│ │ ⊠ Show Message Bar │          └──────┘                │
│ └────────────────────┘          ┌──────┐                │
│                                 │ Help │                │
│ ┌─Color──────────────┐          └──────┘                │
│ │ Register Accent and│  ┌─Future Transactions─────────┐ │
│ │ Checks & Forms Back-│  │ ⊠ Transactions Due Reminder │ │
│ │ ground             │  │ Days In Advance to Remind: 5 │ │
│ │  [ Blue        ▼]  │  └─────────────────────────────┘ │
│ └────────────────────┘                                  │
│ ┌─Confirmation───────┐  ┌─Entry───────────────────────┐ │
│ │ ☐ Confirm Trans-   │  │ ⊠ SmartFill On              │ │
│ │   action Changes   │  │ ⊠ Automatically Drop Lists   │ │
│ │ ⊠ Beep On Trans-   │  │ ☐ Calculator Entry          │ │
│ │   action Entry     │  │ ☐ Alternate Register        │ │
│ │ ⊠ Reminder to Backup│  │   Navigation                │ │
│ └────────────────────┘  └─────────────────────────────┘ │
└─────────────────────────────────────────────────────────┘
```

Figure 4-31.
The Settings dialog box.

You specify how far in advance you want to be warned, using the Days In Advance To Remind text box.

The SmartFill On check box lets you turn Microsoft Money's SmartFill feature on and off. (Chapter 3, "Keeping Your Checkbook with Microsoft Money," describes SmartFill.) The Automatically Drop Lists check box controls whether Microsoft Money opens drop-down list boxes for payee names and categories when you enter transactions. Marking the Calculator Entry check box causes Microsoft Money to assume that the last two digits in any number are decimals and to add a decimal point whenever you type an entry. (For example, 3456 would be displayed as 34.56.) The Alternate Register Navigation check box, if marked, lets you move from text box to text box by pressing the Enter key instead of Tab.

Using Passwords

If you're concerned about the confidentiality of your financial records, you can assign a password that Microsoft Money will require before giving you or anyone else access to your records. To assign a new password, choose the Password command from the Options menu. When you do, Microsoft Money displays the New Password dialog box. (See Figure 4-32.) To assign a password, enter any combination of letters and numbers that you want to use in the dialog box's text box. Microsoft Money will not display your password; to confirm that you have entered it as you intended, the program will ask you to enter it a second time.

If later you want to change your password, you use the Password command again. When you already have a password and you choose the Password command, Microsoft Money displays the Change Password dialog box,

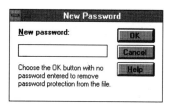

Figure 4-32.
The New Password dialog box.

which prompts you for the current password. After you type in that password, it displays the New Password dialog box, into which you can type your new password.

Don't forget or lose your password! Doing so is equivalent to shredding your financial records. If you do forget or lose your password, you'll need to follow the same procedures for recovering your data that would be necessary if the data files on your disk became corrupted. (Refer to Chapter 6, "Managing Files," for further information about this problem.)

Microsoft Money allows you to segregate your financial records by using different files; each password applies only to a single file. (Chapter 6 describes how you create and work with multiple files.)

Conclusion

This chapter has covered a lot of ground. If you've read it from start to finish, you're now well versed in the mechanics of the Edit, List, and Options menu commands that will make Microsoft Money easier to use and your financial management more powerful.

Chapter 5

RECONCILING YOUR BANK ACCOUNT

Let's face it. One of the most tedious tasks in keeping a checking account is reconciling, or balancing, the account. Yet it's extremely important to do. Verifying your records against the bank's often catches errors you've made in recording transactions and usually catches the bank's errors. There are even problems, such as forgery and embezzlement, that you can only protect yourself against by regularly reconciling an account.

Fortunately, reconciling an account using Microsoft Money is a snap. This chapter explains the steps for using the reconciliation tools built into Microsoft Money. Before stepping through the process, however, I'll review the logic behind reconciling bank accounts.

The Reconciliation Process

On any given day, a comparison between what your records show as the balance in your bank account and what the bank's records show will yield a discrepancy. Reconciling a bank account explains the difference between your records and the bank's records. It's that simple.

Three general circumstances create differences between the two sets of records. Discrepancies can be caused by

1. Transactions you've forgotten to record that have cleared, or been recorded by, the bank.

2. Transactions you don't know about until you see them on the bank statement.

3. Transactions you've recorded but that haven't yet cleared the bank.

The process of reconciling an account involves looking carefully at each of these three kinds of circumstances. To do so, follow six steps.

1. On your monthly bank statement, look for any transactions you forgot to record. Electronic teller or cash machine transactions often seem to fall into this category.

2. Look for any transactions that appear on your statement that you wouldn't have known to record because the bank, not you, initiated them. For example, if your checking account pays interest, you won't know the monthly interest added to your account until you see the bank statement. Or if your

monthly service charges are based on a combination of factors, such as the number of checks you write and the average daily balance, you might not be able to record these transactions until you get the bank statement.

3. Record any transactions you identified in steps 1 and 2.

4. Identify all the transactions you've recorded but that haven't yet been cleared by the bank. For example, checks you write on the last day of January probably won't appear in the January statement because the bank won't receive the checks until sometime in February. A deposit mailed to the bank near the end of the month might also be outstanding for the same reason.

5. Add up all the transactions you've recorded but that haven't been cleared by the bank. Include withdrawal transactions, such as checks, as positive amounts and deposit transactions as negative amounts.

6. Compare the total calculated in step 5 to the difference between your recorded balance and the bank's balance. The difference between them should equal the total of uncleared transactions. If it doesn't, you've made an error on one of the six steps and must simply repeat each of them until you find your mistake.

How to Reconcile Bank Accounts in Microsoft Money

If you understand the basic logic of the process outlined above, you'll find using Microsoft Money to reconcile your bank accounts to be simple and straightforward. You follow the same reconciliation steps, but Microsoft Money does most of the work for you.

Hands-On: Reconciling a Bank Account

To use Microsoft Money to reconcile a bank account, follow these steps.

1. With the Account Book window displayed, choose the Balance Account command from the Options menu dialog box. (See Figure 5-1.) If you previously selected All Accounts, the Select Account dialog box appears, and you must select a single account to balance. When you do, Microsoft Money displays the Balance dialog box for the account you selected. (Figure 5-2 shows the dialog box for a checking account.) Normally, you

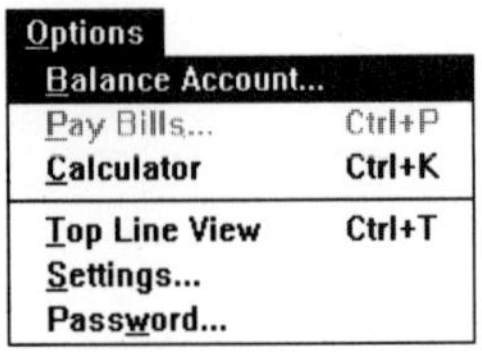

Options	
Balance Account...	
Pay Bills...	Ctrl+P
Calculator	Ctrl+K
Top Line View	Ctrl+T
Settings...	
Password...	

Figure 5-1.
The Balance Account command appears on the Options menu.

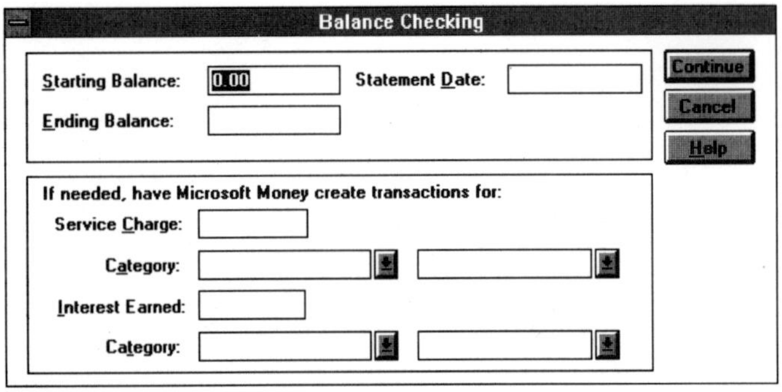

Balance Checking

Starting Balance: `0.00` Statement Date: `_____` Continue
Ending Balance: `_____` Cancel Help

If needed, have Microsoft Money create transactions for:
Service Charge: `_____`
Category: `_____` `_____`
Interest Earned: `_____`
Category: `_____` `_____`

Figure 5-2.
The Balance Checking dialog box.

reconcile only the accounts for which you receive a statement, such as checking accounts, savings accounts, and your credit card account.

2. Move the cursor to the Starting Balance text box, and enter the opening, or beginning, balance from the bank statement. If you're reconciling two or more months of transactions and balances, enter the opening balance from the earliest bank statement. (If you reconciled the account the month before, the Starting Balance text box shows your previously entered Ending Balance; this should be the same as the current statement's beginning balance.)

3. Move the cursor to the Ending Balance text box, and enter the closing, or ending, balance printed on the bank statement. If you're using two or more months' bank statements, enter the closing balance from the most recent statement.

4. Move the cursor to the Statement Date text box, and enter the last date covered by the bank statement.

5. If you haven't recorded the service charge on an account, move the cursor to the Service Charge text box, and type the service charge amount.

6. Move the cursor to the Service Charge Category and subcategory text boxes, and type in the appropriate categories.

7. If you haven't recorded the interest income earned on an account, move the cursor to the Interest Earned text box, and type the amount of interest earned.

8. Move the cursor to the Interest Earned Category and subcategory text boxes, and type in the appropriate categories.

   Microsoft Money records transactions in the Account Book for the service charges and interest earned that you specified in steps 5 and 7.

9. When the Starting Balance, Ending Balance, Statement Date, Service Charge, and Interest Earned text boxes are correctly filled in, choose the Continue command button. (Figure 5-3 shows a completed Balance Checking dialog box.) When you do, Microsoft Money displays a single-line view of the Account Book that includes only uncleared, or unreconciled, transactions, as shown in Figure 5-4.

10. Select those transactions that appear as cleared on the bank statement, and then press the Spacebar to mark these transactions as cleared. Cleared transactions display a *C* in the C-column of the Account Book. (If you

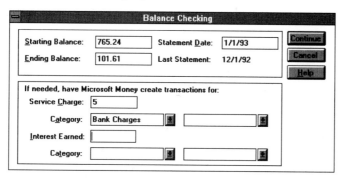

Figure 5-3.
The Balance Checking dialog box.

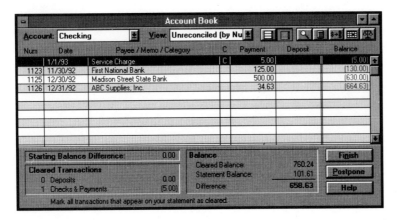

Figure 5-4.
The Account Book window view used to reconcile an account.

inadvertently mark an uncleared transaction as cleared, you can click the mouse or use the Spacebar to change cleared transactions to uncleared.)

The Mark As Cleared and Mark As Uncleared commands, which appear on the Edit menu (see Figure 5-5), provide another way to mark transactions as cleared or uncleared. If the selected transaction hasn't been previously marked as cleared, the ninth command on the Edit menu appears as Mark As Cleared. Choosing this command displays the letter *C* in the C-column of the Account Book. If the selected transaction was previously marked cleared, the Edit menu contains the command Mark As Uncleared, which removes the *C* from the C-column.

Edit	
Undo	Ctrl+Z
Cut	Ctrl+X
Copy	Ctrl+C
Paste	Ctrl+V
Delete Transaction	
Void Transaction	
Split Transaction...	**Ctrl+S**
Schedule in Future...	Ctrl+E
Mark as Cleared	Ctrl+M
Find...	Ctrl+F

Figure 5-5.
The Edit menu adds a command for marking transactions as cleared or uncleared when you're reconciling accounts.

11. When you've marked all the cleared transactions that appear on the bank statement, the Cleared Balance should equal the Statement Balance. These two fields, along with the difference between the balances, appear in the lower right-hand corner of the reconciliation version of the Account Book window. (See Figure 5-6.)

12. If the Cleared Balance and Statement Balance aren't equal, you need to add a missing transaction, correct a cleared or uncleared transaction, or remove an extraneous transaction. You can make changes to displayed transactions right in the Balance dialog box, or you can choose the Postpone command to return to the regular Account Book window and make your changes there. To return to the Balance dialog box after making any needed changes, choose Balance Account from the Options menu.

13. When the Balance dialog box for the account is displayed, choose Continue; you can also choose the Finish command button in the Account Book window, in which case Microsoft Money displays the Account Didn't Balance message box. (See Figure 5-7.) This message box suggests possible reasons why the account won't balance. It also provides two special tools for balancing your account.

14. Select the Go Back To Reconciling The Account option button and choose OK to return to the Balance dialog box. Select the option button called

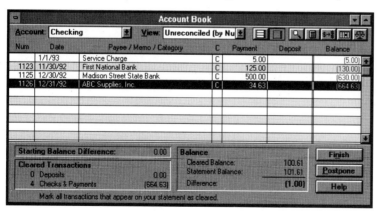

Figure 5-6.
When you've marked all the cleared transactions, the Cleared Balance should equal the Statement Balance. (If that doesn't happen, as in this figure, see step 12 above.)

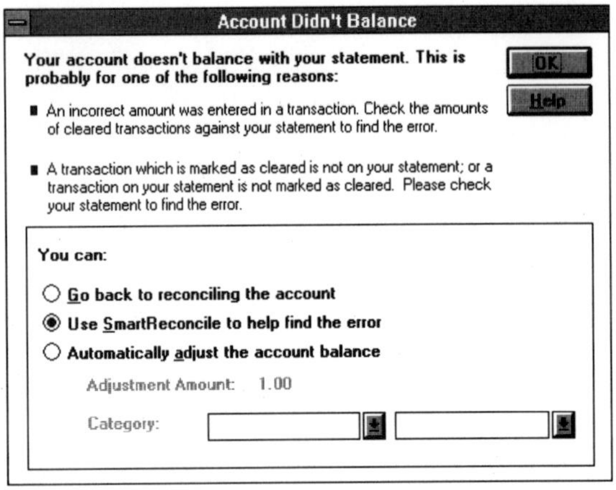

Figure 5-7.
The Account Didn't Balance message box.

Use SmartReconcile To Help Find The Error to tell Microsoft Money to look for an error. Select the Automatically Adjust The Account Balance option button to tell Microsoft Money to add a cleared transaction that makes the cleared balance equal to the statement balance.

> **MICROSOFT MONEY TIP:** *SmartReconcile can find several types of errors in the way you enter or edit transactions. It can find a transaction entered backwards, a transaction with transposed numbers, and one incorrectly marked as cleared or uncleared. However, SmartReconcile won't find multiple erroneous transactions, even if they are all errors of a type it recognizes. It can only locate the discrepancy when there is a single cause.*

15. When the Cleared Balance and the Statement Balance agree, choose the Finish command button. When you do, Microsoft Money changes all the C's to R's, for reconciled, redisplays the regular Account Book window, and displays a message notifying you that your account balances. Figure 5-8 shows the message box.

If you want to take a break from reconciling your account, you can choose the Postpone command button.

Figure 5-8.
The Balance Account message.

What to Do When an Account Won't Reconcile

If, after you complete step 11, the Cleared Balance still doesn't equal the Statement Balance, either you've made a mistake in marking cleared transactions, the Account Book is missing one or more transactions, or either you or the bank has incorrectly recorded a transaction. If you find yourself in this predicament, your best bet is first to be sure that your Account Book isn't missing a transaction. You can do this by using SmartReconcile or by being sure that every transaction that appears on the bank statement also appears in the Account Book. When you're sure that's the case, verify that each of the transactions you've recorded as cleared has, in fact, cleared. Finally, compare the transaction amounts shown in your register with the transaction amounts shown on your bank statement.

Remember, too, that in setting up your accounts you need to begin with an accurate, preferably just-reconciled balance. If you don't, you might not be able to reconcile the account because your starting balance is wrong.

Preventing Forgery and Embezzlement

You can take steps when you reconcile your account to protect against forgery and embezzlement. Although these tasks aren't part of the reconciliation process, it's easiest to perform them at the same time as you reconcile an account.

First of all, you should carefully review the face of each cancelled check to be sure you actually signed it and that someone else didn't fraudulently alter the check. (Check forgery, by the way, is defined as fraudulently altering or marking a check.) If you find evidence of forgery, report your discovery to the bank immediately. Usually, if you alert the bank immediately, you won't have to absorb the loss. However, if you procrastinate for a few weeks or months, you might forfeit all or most of your right to recover the stolen funds from the bank.

Errors Reconciliation Won't Catch

The main reason you should reconcile bank accounts is to find errors you or the bank made in recording account transactions. However, there are some bookkeeping errors that a reconciliation won't catch.

Uncleared Transactions You Forget to Record

One such error is a transaction that you've forgotten to record in your Account Book and that hasn't yet cleared the bank. Obviously, because neither your Account Book nor the bank statement includes the transaction, it can't be the reason for a difference between the two accounts. If the missing transaction is a check, however—and this is most likely, as you usually have more checks than deposits—you think you have more money in your checking account than you actually do. Unfortunately, the only thing to do to avoid this error is to be especially diligent about recording your transactions.

Fictitious Transactions

Another type of error a reconciliation won't catch is a fictitious transaction you inadvertently recorded. Because the transaction is fictitious, it never shows up on a bank statement and so is always listed as outstanding. Although this possibility might seem extreme, it might occur, for example, when you're using Microsoft Money's Future Transactions feature if you automatically record transactions you never complete. You might, for example, record a weekly check to your daughter's piano teacher without actually printing out the check.

BUSINESS NOTE: Embezzlement isn't much of a problem for individuals, but business users should use the reconciliation process to be sure that checks being written by employees actually go to firms they do business with. A common method of embezzling is to write a check to a fictitious business or employee. Then the embezzler, pretending to be the fictitious business or employee, simply cashes the check.

Fictitious transactions have the opposite effect on your account balance from uncleared transactions that you have forgotten to record: A fictitious check erroneously decreases the account balance, and a fictitious deposit erroneously increases the account balance. To prevent this error, you simply need to be careful not to record transactions until they occur.

Conclusion

This is a short chapter, but it covers an important topic: the steps for reconciling any checking accounts for which you use Microsoft Money. Fortunately, Microsoft Money provides tools that eliminate most and perhaps all of the drudgery and tediousness of this task.

Chapter 6

MANAGING FILES

The financial records you create using Microsoft Money are stored in files on your hard disk. You don't need to know much about these files to operate Microsoft Money in the most basic way. Even then, however, there are one or two areas you'll want to understand. For example, all users should learn how to back up and restore files, and former users of the Quicken checkbook program may want to transfer to Microsoft Money the information stored in Quicken registers.

Some users will want to work with files more extensively, perhaps to create archive copies. Others, such as the self-employed using Microsoft Money both at home and in business, might want to work with more than one set of files. This chapter describes how to accomplish all these tasks.

Backing Up and Restoring Microsoft Money Files

I don't need to tell you why it's important to back up your files. In fact, if you're like most people, the thought of a hard-disk failure or an accidental erasure of your Microsoft Money data files sends shivers down your spine. And well it should. Few things are more important than your personal or business financial records. The first thing you need to know about Microsoft Money's files is how to back them up and, should the unthinkable happen, how to restore them.

Backing Up Files

Backing up files is easy in Microsoft Money, which provides a special File menu command, Backup, precisely for this purpose. I want to share some suggestions about backup strategies and how to make the task as easy as possible.

Mechanically, backing up Money data files is simple and straightforward. You first label and format the floppy disk you'll use as your backup disk. Then you copy the Money data file from your hard disk to the backup disk by using the File Backup command.

Hands-On: Creating a Backup Disk

To create a backup disk, follow these steps.

1. Locate either a new floppy disk or an old disk that contains data you no longer need.

2. Label the disk with an appropriate description, such as Money Backup.

3. Insert the disk in the A or B floppy drive.

4. Start the Windows File Manager by displaying the Main program group window (see Figure 6-1) and double-clicking on the File Manager icon. (You do not need to exit from Microsoft Money to display the Main program group window. You can activate the Control menu and choose the Switch To command to display it.)

5. With the File Manager window displayed (see Figure 6-2), activate the Disk menu by clicking on the menu name.

6. With the Disk menu displayed (see Figure 6-3), choose the Format Diskette command. When you do, Windows displays the Format Diskette dialog box with the drop-down list box showing A as the drive in which you want to format the disk. (See Figure 6-4.) If you want to format a disk in the B drive, type in *b* or select B from the drop-down list box.

7. Choose OK. The File Manager displays a message box warning you that formatting will erase all the data on the disk and asks if you want to continue. If you do, choose Format. The File Manager next displays the dialog box shown in Figure 6-5, which simply asks for formatting instructions.

8. If the disk you're going to format is a high-density or quad-density disk, be sure the High Capacity check box is marked, as in Figure 6-5.

9. If you want the backup disk to be a system disk—one you can use to boot your computer—be sure the Make System Disk check box is marked.

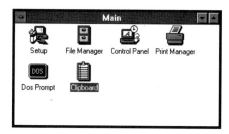

Figure 6-1.
The Main program group window.

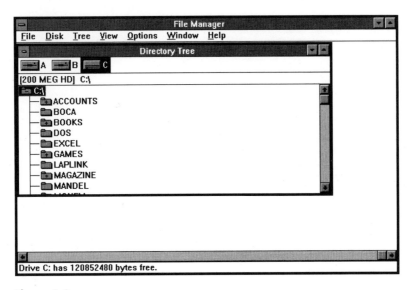

Figure 6-2.
The File Manager window.

Figure 6-3.
The File Manager Disk menu.

10. When you've finished giving the instructions for formatting, choose OK. Next the File Manager displays a message box telling you that it is formatting the disk and that you can choose Cancel (or press Esc) to cancel the formatting. It also displays the percentage of the disk that has been formatted.

11. When the format is complete, the File Manager displays another message box asking if you want to format another disk. Choose Yes if you do, No if you don't.

Figure 6-4.
The Format Diskette dialog box.

Figure 6-5.
The Format Diskette dialog box used to give formatting instructions to the File Manager.

After you've formatted a disk for storing the backup copy of the data file, you're ready to back up the Microsoft Money data file.

Hands-On: Backing Up a Microsoft Money Data File

To back up, start Microsoft Money, and follow these steps.

1. Place the backup disk in the A drive.

2. Activate the File menu (see Figure 6-6), and choose the Backup command. When you do, Microsoft Money displays the Backup dialog box shown in Figure 6-7.

3. To use a name other than the default filename, enter a new filename in the Backup File To text box. Remember to include the path description *a:* or *b:* and the file extension *bak*, preceded by a period.

Figure 6-6.
The File menu.

Figure 6-7.
The Backup dialog box.

MICROSOFT MONEY TIP: *You must follow DOS naming conventions when entering a new filename. Under these rules, a filename can be up to eight characters in length and cannot include spaces. Some of the special symbols that can also be used are: ~ ! @ # $ % ^ & ( ) _ - { } ' and '.*

The filename extensions BAK and MNY are treated differently by Microsoft Money; be sure to use BAK for backup files and MNY for data files.

4. When the Backup File To text box displays the filename and extension you want to use for the backup, choose Yes. Microsoft Money copies the currently open data file to the disk in the A drive and renames it as you specify. If there's another file with the same name on the disk—such as a copy of the file created by a previous backup operation—Microsoft Money displays a message box warning that it's about to overwrite the old file and giving you a chance to abort the backup.

Restoring Files to the Hard Disk

With luck, you will not have to restore a Microsoft Money data file very often. But when you do, follow these steps.

Hands-On: Restoring a Microsoft Money File

1. Insert a backup copy of the file in the A or B floppy drive.

2. Choose the Open command from the File menu. When you do, Money displays the Open dialog box shown in Figure 6-8.

3. Activate the Drives drop-down list box by clicking on the arrow to the right of the box. When you do, Money displays a list of the hard drives and floppy drives connected to your computer. (See Figure 6-9.)

4. Select the A or B floppy drive from the Drives drop-down list box.

5. Activate the List Files Of Type drop-down list box by clicking on the arrow to the right of the text box. (See Figure 6-10.) When you do, Money

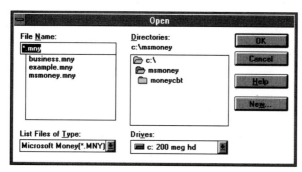

Figure 6-8.
The Open dialog box.

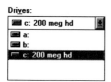

Figure 6-9.
The Drives drop-down list box.

List Files of Type:

Microsoft Money(*.MNY)
Microsoft Money(*.MNY)
Backups (*.BAK)
All Files (*.*)

Figure 6-10.
The List Files of Type drop-down list box.

displays the three groups of files you can select to display in the File Name list box: Microsoft Money (*.MNY), Backups (*.BAK), and All Files (*.*).

6. Select the Backups (*.BAK) item from the List Files Of Type drop-down list box. When you do, the Open dialog box's File Name list shows all the Microsoft Money backup files stored on the drive selected in step 4.

7. Identify the backup file you want to restore by selecting it from the File Name list. When you do, Microsoft Money enters the filename for you in the File Name text box.

8. Choose OK to open the backup file. If you checked Reminder To Backup in the Options menu's Settings dialog box, Microsoft Money will ask if you want to back up the currently open file, using the Backup dialog box shown in Figure 6-7. If you want to do so, follow the steps described earlier in the chapter.

 WARNING: *Be careful at this point that you don't inadvertently back up the currently open but corrupted Microsoft Money data file and in so doing overwrite your backup copy of the file. This could happen if, for example, you decide to back up the current file and then use the same filename and extension as those used for the existing backup file.*

9. Microsoft Money displays the Restore Backup dialog box shown in Figure 6-11 but won't let you open a backup file directly. First you need to change the filename extension to MNY. You can also put the file on a different disk or in a different directory or even rename the file.

10. To rename the file, enter the new filename and filename extension in the File Name text box.

11. To put the new file on a disk in a different drive, activate the Drives drop-down list box by clicking on the arrow to the right of the Drives box.

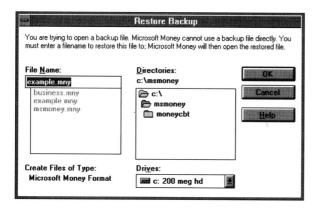

Figure 6-11.
The Restore Backup dialog box.

When you do, Microsoft Money displays a list of the drives exactly like the one shown in Figure 6-9.

12. Identify the drive you want to put the new file in by selecting it in the Drives drop-down list box.

13. To put the new file in a different directory, activate the Directories list by double-clicking on the Drive icon in the Directories list box. When you do, Money displays the directories in the selected drive's root directory.

14. Select one of these directories from the list. (To display the subdirectories in a directory, double-click on the directory.)

15. If the restored file doesn't contain your most recent transactions, re-enter the transactions you recorded between the time you backed up the file and the time you restored it as a Microsoft Money data file. A recent hard copy of the Microsoft Money Register Report will provide all the information organized by transaction, which should make re-entering transactions a snap. (Chapter 7, "Printing," describes how to print the Microsoft Money Register Report and other reports.)

Backup Strategies

Although the mechanics of backing up and restoring Microsoft Money files are simple, there's more to backup than formatting a few disks and choosing a series of command buttons. For example, you need to decide when and how often to back up your files. And some users might not want to use the backup and restore tools built into Microsoft Money, preferring to use a third-party backup utility such as PC Tools Deluxe or Fastback. Both scheduling backups and using third-party utilities deserve discussion.

Scheduling Backups

Two basic reasons exist for backing up your files. The first and most obvious is to protect your financial records in the event that your data file becomes corrupted—perhaps because of a hard-disk failure or a virus or through human error. The second, more specialized reason is to create a copy of the data file as it existed at a specific time—for example, the end-of-the-year file on which you base your income tax return.

The reason for backing up a Microsoft Money file determines when and how often you should do it. If your main concern is providing a backup file for use in recovering a corrupted file, you'll probably want to back up whenever the work of backing up seems insignificant compared to the work involved in re-creating your data file from scratch. Based on this general rule, you might want to back up daily if you record several dozen transactions every day, or you might choose to back up monthly if you record only a handful of transactions each month. Remember, too, that re-entering transactions can involve collecting the information necessary to record each transaction. If the half dozen or so pieces of data recorded with every transaction are extremely difficult to collect—because they were stored only in one place, the damaged Microsoft Money Account Book—it might take several minutes to record a single transaction. In that case, it might make sense to back up the data file every time you exit Microsoft Money. (Every time you exit the program or open a new file, Microsoft Money gives you the option of backing up the data file by displaying the Backup dialog box shown in Figure 6-7.)

You'll probably want to keep multiple backup copies of the Microsoft Money file or files. Suppose you back up your files on a daily basis, and on Friday you suddenly discover that the Microsoft Money file has been damaged. Perhaps someone unfamiliar with the program—a new employee or your young child—inadvertently and randomly deleted a series of transactions. As long as the damage occurred on Friday, you will be fine with only one backup copy.

But suppose the damage also occurred on Thursday and perhaps even Wednesday? What you would really want would be not the most recent backup but the backup before that or even the backup before that. The usual rule of thumb—sometimes referred to as the grandfather-father-son scheme—is to keep your three most recent backups. If the most recent backup copy, or son, is damaged, you have two other backups: the father and, as a last resort, the grandfather. You don't have to use a grandfather-father-son backup scheme, but it's a safety precaution you'll want to consider.

Using Third-Party Backup Utilities

If you're currently using a third-party backup utility such as PC Tools Deluxe Backup for Windows, you don't have to use the Microsoft Money Backup and Open commands to back up and restore the data file or files. You can use your own utility instead. In this case, you need to remember to back up the Microsoft Money data files by using the file specification C:\MSMONEY*.MNY, because Microsoft Money data files use the extension MNY and are stored in the Microsoft Money directory of your hard disk. Don't, by the way, back up the entire contents of the Money directory by using the *.* file specification. The Money directory contains not only data files but also Microsoft Money program files.

Archiving a Money File

As I noted earlier in this chapter, there is a second reason to make copies of your Microsoft Money data file: to have a copy of your financial records as they existed at a certain point in time. For example, you might want to have a copy of the Microsoft Money data file you used to prepare your annual tax return. If you later had questions about the data used to prepare the return—questions you couldn't answer with the current copy of the data file—you could return to this historical copy of the data file. Microsoft Money calls this file an archive copy, and the process by which you create such files is called archiving.

Within Microsoft Money, archiving serves another purpose. It allows you to remove old, unneeded transactions to keep your files at a manageable size. For example, as you start a new year, you could use Microsoft Money's archiving feature to remove any unneeded transactions from the previous year.

Hands-On: Archiving a File

Procedurally, archiving a file is quite simple. To do it, you follow these steps.

1. Activate the File menu and choose the Archive command. When you do, Money displays the Archive dialog box shown in Figure 6-12.

2. If you want to create a historical copy of the current file—and you probably do—mark the check box called Create A Backup Of The Current File For Recordkeeping Purposes.

3. To remove old, cleared transactions from the current file and thereby reduce its size, mark the check box called Remove Transactions From Current File Which Are Before, and enter a date in the text box.

MICROSOFT MONEY TIP: *The Archive command doesn't remove transactions that haven't been marked as cleared because you need to maintain these transactions in order to reconcile your bank account. Reconciliation justifies the difference between your Account Book balance and the bank statement balance by comparing that difference to the total uncleared transactions in the Account Book. If the difference between the two balances equals the total of all uncleared transactions, then your account balances. To perform this calculation, you need to keep old transactions that haven't cleared the bank. (Chapter 5, "Reconciling Your Bank Account," describes the reconciliation process in more detail.)*

4. When the Archive dialog box's option buttons are correctly marked and the text box filled, choose OK.

5. If you marked the Create A Backup Of The Current File For Recordkeeping Purposes check box, Microsoft Money next displays the Backup dialog box (refer to Figure 6-7), which you complete for archiving in the same way you do for backing up a file.

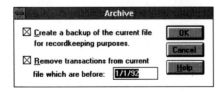

Figure 6-12.
The Archive dialog box.

6. Activate the Drives drop-down list box by clicking on the arrow to the right of the Drives text box. When you do, Microsoft Money displays a list of the hard drives and floppy drives connected to the computer. Figure 6-9 shows the Drives drop-down list box.

7. Select the drive you want from the Drives drop-down list box.

8. To put the new file in a directory other than the selected drive's root directory, activate the Directories list by double-clicking on the Drive icon in the Directories list box. When you do, Microsoft Money displays the directories in the selected drive's root directory.

9. Identify one of these directories by selecting it from the list. (To display subdirectories, double-click on a directory.)

10. Enter the name you want to use for the archive file copy in the File Name text box. Be sure to use the MNY filename extension and not the BAK, or backup, filename extension. Files that have the MNY filename extension can be opened directly without first being renamed.

11. Choose OK to create the archive file copy. When you do, Microsoft Money displays a message box that says the program is in the process of removing any old, unneeded transactions from the file. The message also says that the process might take several minutes if your file is large.

Importing Quicken Data

If you've used Quicken, the popular checkbook program created by Intuit, you can import your Quicken data into Microsoft Money. You want to be able to use the Quicken data, particularly if you're converting from Quicken to Microsoft Money at some time other than the very beginning of a new year. Even at the beginning of the year, converting your old Quicken data to Microsoft Money data files lets you use Microsoft Money's Report menu options to summarize the data collected with Quicken. Fortunately, importing data from Quicken isn't difficult.

Preparing the Quicken Data

You need to take several preliminary steps before choosing the Import command from the Microsoft Money File menu. The process for importing Quicken data begins in the Quicken program.

Hands-On: Preparing Quicken Data for Export

To prepare the Quicken data to be imported by Microsoft Money, you follow these steps.

1. Choose the Change Settings command from Quicken's Main Menu. When you do, Quicken displays the Change Settings menu.

2. Choose the Account Group Activities command from the Change Settings menu. When you do, Quicken displays the Account Group Activities menu.

3. Choose the Select/Set Up Account Group command from the Account Group Activities menu. When you do, Quicken displays the Select/Set Up Account Group screen, which lists the Quicken account groups you've created.

4. Using the Up and Down direction keys, highlight the Quicken account group from which you want to import data into Microsoft Money. Then press Enter. When you do, Quicken displays the Register screen showing the last account you used in the account group.

5. Press F2 to activate and display the Acct/Print menu.

6. Choose the Select/Set Up Account command. When you do, Quicken displays the Select Account To Use screen. Using the Up and Down direction keys, highlight the Quicken account whose data you want to import. Then press Enter.

7. Choose the Export command from the Acct/Print menu by typing the number 5. When you do, Quicken displays the Export Transactions To QIF File dialog box.

8. The Quicken Export command creates a QIF file that holds all the Quicken data in the selected account group. (QIF stands for Quicken Interchange Format, but you don't need to know anything about the file format to use it.) Simply enter the path and filename you want used in the File field. For example, you might want to store the QIF file in the Money directory and name it by using the Quicken account group name. If the Quicken account group was named QDATA, for example, and the Money directory is in your C hard drive, you would enter the path and filename *c:\msmoney\qdata.qif.*

9. Enter the range of transaction dates you want exported in the From and To fields. For example, if it's the middle of 1992 and you want to export only transactions from January 1, 1992, through June 30, 1992, enter *1/1/92* as the From date and *6/30/92* as the To date.

10. To begin the actual export operation, press Enter when the Export Transactions To QIF File dialog box is complete. As Quicken writes the QIF file, it briefly displays a message on the screen that says "Creating file." When the export operation is complete, Quicken returns you to the register screen.

After Quicken creates the QIF file, you've finished preparing the Quicken data for Microsoft Money. Your next steps will be to set up the necessary accounts in Microsoft Money and then use the Microsoft Money Import command. At this point, if you're finished with Quicken, exit the Quicken program and return to Microsoft Money.

Importing the Data

You need a new Microsoft Money account for each of your old Quicken accounts. Microsoft Money, like Quicken, uses accounts to record the transactions you enter. So if you created a Quicken account to record credit card spending, you need to create a credit card account in Microsoft Money into which you can import Quicken credit card transactions. (If you need help setting up new accounts, refer to the section on setting up accounts in Chapter 2.) Once you create the accounts you need in Microsoft Money, you can import the Quicken data stored in the QIF file into them.

Hands-On: Importing a QIF File

To import the data stored in a QIF file, follow these steps.

1. Choose the Import command from the File menu. When you do, Microsoft Money displays the Import dialog box shown in Figure 6-13.

2. Activate the Drives drop-down list box by clicking on the arrow to the right of the Drives text box. When you do, Microsoft Money displays a list of the hard drives and floppy drives connected to your computer. (Refer to Figure 6-9 for the Drives drop-down list box.)

3. Select the drive in which you stored the QIF file from the Drives drop-down list box.

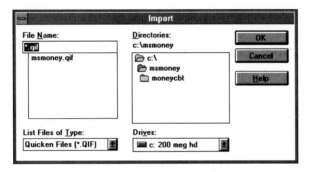

Figure 6-13.
The Import dialog box.

4. Identify the directory in which the QIF file is located, using the Directories list. To do so, activate the Directories list by double-clicking on the Drive icon in the Directories list box. When you do, Microsoft Money displays the directories in the selected drive's root directory. Identify one of these directories by selecting it from the list. (To display subdirectories, double-click on a directory.)

5. Activate the List Files Of Type drop-down list box by clicking on the arrow to the right of its text box. When you do, Money displays the two groups of files you can choose to display in the File Name list box: Quicken Files (*.QIF) and All Files (*.*).

6. Select Quicken Files from the List Files Of Type drop-down list box. When you do, the Open dialog box's File Name list displays all the Quicken QIF files in the selected directory in the selected drive.

7. Select the QIF file you want to import from the File Name list. When you do, Microsoft Money enters the filename in the File Name text box.

8. Choose OK to import the QIF file. Next Microsoft Money displays the Select Import Account dialog box shown in Figure 6-14.

9. To identify the Microsoft Money account into which you want to import the transactions stored in the QIF file, select an account from the Account List box.

10. If a transaction involves a transfer between two accounts, you can choose to record the transaction only in the current account by marking

Figure 6-14.
The Select Import Account dialog box.

the Import Only One Side Of Transfers check box. To record the transaction in both of the accounts involved in a transfer, leave the check box unmarked.

11. Choose Continue. Microsoft Money begins reading the QIF file.

12. Besides storing transaction data, the QIF file also identifies transactions by their Quicken accounts. Every time Microsoft Money encounters a new account, it displays the Assign Import Account dialog box, shown in Figure 6-15. You use the Assign Import Account dialog box to indicate which Microsoft Money accounts are equivalent to the Quicken accounts from which you're importing transactions. Microsoft Money identifies the account name. If an equivalent Microsoft Money account exists, select it from the Account List box, and choose the Assign command button. If an equivalent Microsoft Money account doesn't already exist, choose the Create command button to display the Set Up New Account dialog box. (Refer to the section of Chapter 2 entitled Setting Up Accounts for help using the Set Up New Account dialog box.)

You will need to repeat steps 11 and 12 several times if the imported QIF file contains transactions from several Quicken accounts. When Microsoft Money finishes importing the data, it displays the Microsoft Money Account Book window showing the transactions imported from Quicken.

Assign Import Account

Please select a corresponding account in Microsoft Money or choose the Create button to create a Microsoft Money account with that name.

Account List

Checking
Residence
Savings

Assign

Create

Help

Figure 6-15.
The Assign Import Account dialog box.

Exporting Data to a QIF File

Microsoft Money also lets you export data to a QIF file.

Hands-On: Exporting a Microsoft Money File

To export the Money data to a QIF file, follow these steps.

1. Choose the Export command from the File menu. When you do, Microsoft Money displays the Export dialog box shown in Figure 6-16.

2. By default, Microsoft Money gives the export file the same name as the data file, with the file extension QIF. Microsoft Money also places the export file in the current Microsoft Money directory—probably MSMONEY. If you want, you can change the filename. You can also include a pathname in the Export File To text box to place the new file somewhere besides the Microsoft Money directory. You might, for example, want to place the QIF file in the Quicken directory.

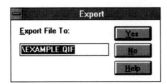

Export

Export File To:

\EXAMPLE.QIF

Yes

No

Help

Figure 6-16.
The Export dialog box.

3. When the filename and, optionally, the pathname are correct, choose Yes to initiate the export operation. Microsoft Money creates the QIF file. When it finishes, it displays a message box that says the export is complete.

Once you've created the QIF file, exit Microsoft Money and start Quicken. Quicken's Acct/Print menu provides an Import menu command. When you choose this command, Quicken displays a dialog box that prompts you for the pathname and filename of the QIF file. Enter the pathname and filename, and then press Enter. (For more information on importing a QIF file into Quicken, refer either to the Quicken user's manual or to one of the popular tutorials on using Quicken.)

Working with More than One Set of Files

Thus far, this book has assumed that you want to work with a single Microsoft Money data file. You should know, however, that you have the option of working with more than one data file. There are several reasons to do this. Using multiple files provides a way to segregate your data. For example, you might want to keep the data from different businesses—particularly those with different owners—in separate files. You might also want to segregate personal financial records from business financial records so that the two sets of records don't get mixed up.

As you might remember from Chapter 4, "Supercharging Your Checkbook," you can use a password to control access to a single file. If you wanted other family members to have access to personal financial records but not to business financial records, you could set up two files, each with a separate password.

There are, however, some disadvantages to segregating your data in different files. You can't transfer money between accounts in two different files, so when a transfer occurs, you have to record the transaction separately in each account. You also can't create reports summarizing information in more than one file.

In spite of these disadvantages, you might want to create separate data files. To do so, you need to know how to do three things: create new files, identify the file you want to work with, and consolidate multiple files into a single file.

Creating a New File

Once you decide to work with multiple data files, your first task is to create the new data file. Many of the steps you take to do so should seem familiar because you carried them out when you first started the Microsoft Money program.

Hands-On: Creating a New File

To create a new file, follow these steps.

1. Choose the New command on the File menu. When you choose this command, Microsoft Money displays the New dialog box shown in Figure 6-17.

2. Activate the Drives drop-down list box by clicking on the arrow to the right of the Drives text box. When you do, Microsoft Money displays a list of the hard drives and floppy drives connected to your computer. (Refer to Figure 6-9 for an example of the Drives drop-down list box.)

3. Select the drive in which you want the new file to be located.

4. To put the new file in a directory other than the selected drive's root directory, activate the Directories list by double-clicking on the Drive icon in the Directories list box. When you do, Microsoft Money displays the directories in the selected drive's root directory.

5. Identify one of these directories by selecting it from the list. (To display subdirectories, double-click on a directory.)

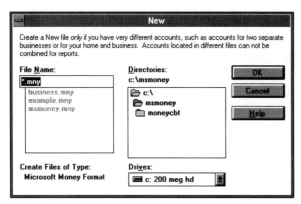

Figure 6-17.
The New dialog box.

6. Enter the name you want to use for the new file in the File Name text box. You don't need to enter the filename extension MNY because Microsoft Money will do it for you. If you do enter a filename extension, however, be sure to use the MNY filename extension and not BAK, or backup. The MNY filename extension identifies the new file as a regular data file.

7. Choose OK to create a new file. When you do, Money displays the Setup New File dialog box shown in Figure 6-18.

8. In the Setup New File dialog box, tell Microsoft Money whether you want the new file to use the predefined lists of categories. Mark the option button for the categories you want to use: Home, Business, Both Home And Business, or None.

9. When the Setup New File dialog box is complete, choose OK. Microsoft Money next displays a message box telling you to create an account. When you choose OK to continue creating the new file, it displays the Create New Account dialog box as shown in Figure 6-19.

10. Type the name you want to use for the account, such as *Checking* or *Visa.*

11. Click on the option button for the type of account you're setting up— Bank Account, Credit Card Account, Cash Or Other Account, Asset Account, or Liability Account—and choose OK.

12. When Microsoft Money asks for the account's starting balance, enter it in the Opening Balance dialog box (see Figure 6-20), and choose OK.

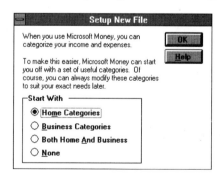

Figure 6-18.
The Setup New File dialog box.

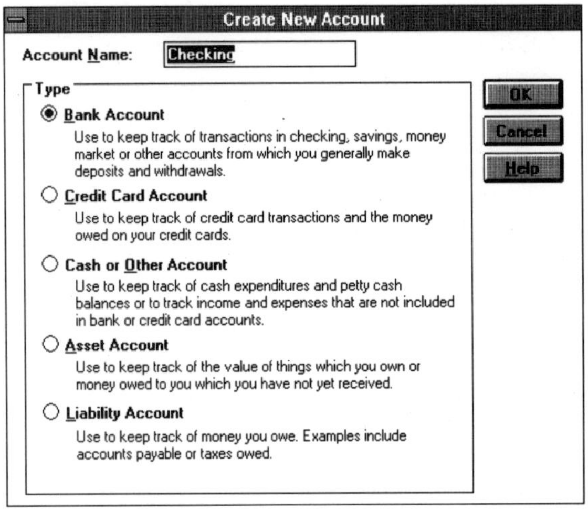

Figure 6-19.
The Create New Account dialog box.

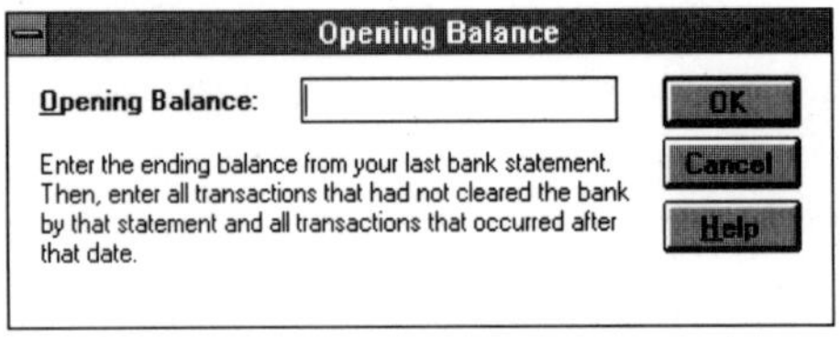

Figure 6-20.
The Opening Balance dialog box.

You're finished creating the new file, although you might need to create additional accounts. (Refer to Chapter 2, "Preparing to Use Microsoft Money," if you have questions about the steps for creating new accounts.)

Identifying the File You Want

Of course, once you start working with more than one Microsoft Money data file, you need a way to choose the file into which you want to enter transactions — the open file. By default, Microsoft Money opens the file you used last; to access another file, you need to use the File menu's Open command.

If you have created only one data file, Microsoft Money does not explicitly display the filename. When you have more than one data file, however,

Microsoft Money changes the appearance of the title bar; the name of the data file is appended to the name of the program. For example, instead of Microsoft Money, you might see

Microsoft Money - C:\MSMONEY\EXAMPLE.MNY

Hands-On: Choosing the File You Want to Use

To open a file, follow these steps.

1. Choose the Open command from the File menu. When you do, Money displays the Open dialog box. (Refer to Figure 6-8.)

2. Activate the Drives drop-down list box by clicking on the arrow to the right of the Drives text box. When you do, Microsoft Money displays a list of the hard drives and floppy drives connected to your computer. (See Figure 6-9 for an example of the Drives drop-down list box.)

3. Select the drive in which the file is stored from the Drives drop-down list box.

4. Verify that the List Files Of Type box displays the file type Microsoft Money (*.MNY). If it doesn't, activate the List Files Of Type drop-down list box by clicking on the arrow to the right of the List Files Of Type text box. (Refer to Figure 6-10 for an example of the List Files Of Type drop-down list box.) When you do, Microsoft Money displays the three groups of files you can choose to display in the File Name list box: Microsoft Money Files (*.MNY), Backups (*.BAK), and All Files (*.*). Choose the first file type, Microsoft Money (*.MNY).

5. If the file is located in a directory other than the selected drive's root directory, activate the Directories list by double-clicking on the Drive icon in the Directories list box. When you do, Microsoft Money displays the directories in the selected drive's root directory. Identify one of these directories by selecting it from the list. (To display subdirectories, double-click on a directory.)

6. After you identify the drive, directory, and file type, the Open dialog box's File Name list shows all Microsoft Money data files in the selected directory in the selected drive. Select the file you want to use from the File Name list. When you do, Microsoft Money enters the filename in the File Name text box.

7. Choose OK to open the Microsoft Money file. Microsoft Money then displays the familiar Backup dialog box (refer to Figure 6-7) to ask if you want to back up the open data file. If you do, choose Yes and follow the usual backup procedures. If you don't, choose No.

Consolidating Multiple Files

If you create more than one set of files and later decide that you want a single file after all, you can consolidate files by using the Import and Export commands. Here's what you do: Export all transactions from the first file to one QIF file; then export all transactions from the second file to a second QIF file. Then simply create a third file, and import the two QIF files into it. If you have questions about the mechanics of using the Import and Export commands, refer to the discussion of these commands earlier in this chapter.

Conclusion

Every user should learn how to back up, restore, and archive files. Many users—particularly former Quicken users—will find it helpful to know how to import and export data. And, finally, a handful of users will want to work with more than one data file. All the topics covered in this chapter will help you safeguard your financial records and use Microsoft Money efficiently.

Chapter 7

PRINTING

Knowing how to print is essential to using Microsoft Money. Even if you don't want to print checks, a reasonable decision, you still need to know how to produce reports, if only to create a paper copy of the Microsoft Money Account Book register.

Printing Checks

One of Microsoft Money's time-saving features is check printing. If you decide to use check printing, you'll no longer need to spend time writing out checks by hand but will be able to print checks with your computer, saving time and minimizing errors. To do so, you'll find it helpful to follow the step-by-step instructions for at least the first time or two you print. Before proceeding to that information, it makes sense to discuss a few other aspects of check printing first.

For example, if you still haven't decided whether you want to print checks, I can help you make that decision. If you decide to do so, I'll offer some pointers to help you pick the best type of check form to use with Microsoft Money.

Deciding to Print Checks

If you've already decided to print checks and have purchased your check forms, you can skip to the section How to Print Checks. If you haven't yet decided or picked your check forms, let me share a few thoughts about printing checks.

Should You Even Print Checks?

There are advantages and disadvantages to printing checks with Microsoft Money. The first disadvantage is that computer check forms are quite expensive. Before you dismiss this point as the penny-pinching complaint of a conservative accountant, let me review a few numbers. If you buy 200 checks from your bank, you pay somewhere between $8 and $10, depending on the type of checks you order and your bank. Computer check forms will cost roughly $40 to $60 plus a few dollars for shipping for 250 checks. Instead of paying $.04 to $.05 per check, you pay $.16 to $.24 per check. That might be only pennies, but if you use a couple of hundred checks a year, you'll probably spend $35 to $50 more for computer check forms.

That $35 to $50 might be money well spent, considering the potential time savings you'll enjoy by printing your checks automatically. Let me point out, however, another disadvantage of printing checks using Microsoft Money or any checkbook program. Although the actual time spent printing checks is much reduced—because Microsoft Money uses information you've already entered to print the check—you'll spend some time loading the check forms into the printer.

If you have an impact printer, for example, you'll first unload the paper that's in it and then fiddle around with the check forms. If you have a laser printer, you'll need to pull out the paper tray and stick in as many check forms as you need. After you finish printing, you'll reverse the process. Once you get good at it—and you will, if you print checks frequently—the procedure won't take much time. Even so, the time you thought you were saving can quickly be eaten up loading and unloading check forms.

Check forms aren't all bad, however. In fact, they provide three major advantages compared to handwritten or typewritten checks. One advantage is obvious: If you print large numbers of checks—say, several hundred a month—the time savings can be huge. If you can batch all your check writing and print checks only once or twice a month, you can save several hours each month.

Another advantage to computer-printed checks is that the final products—neat, computer-printed checks—are more professional looking than hand-written ones. For some individuals, and, especially, for businesses, appearance might be very important. Spending extra money to look more professional might be a wise investment if you're trying to build credibility among your business contacts.

The third advantage to computer-printed checks is that some check forms provide stubs, or vouchers, which Microsoft Money can use to describe a check. If you use Microsoft Money to produce a check to pay several invoices, for example, you can use the voucher to identify the purchases or note the invoice numbers. If you use Microsoft Money to produce payroll checks, you can use it to describe employees' gross pay and deductions.

How do the advantages and disadvantages of computer-printed checks stack up? It depends on your specific needs. My guess is that most home users, and even many small businesses, won't find many reasons to use computer-printed checks; the time savings won't justify the extra cost. On the other hand, any business with more than a few dozen checks to write each month will probably benefit from the time saved and the usefulness of the vouchers.

Choosing the Right Check Form

If you decide to print checks with Microsoft Money, you can choose from among three check forms for impact printers and two forms for laser printers.

Impact printers let you print wallet-size, standard, and voucher checks. Wallet check forms (see Figure 7-1) make the most sense for home users and home-based businesses. Here's why: Wallet check forms are smaller than standard checks—just 2.83 inches by 6 inches—so they can be easily slipped into shirt pocket or wallet for a trip to the grocery store or your favorite restaurant. And, as Figure 7-1 indicates, they have a 2.5 inch stub and a total form width of 8.5 inches. This stub makes it easier to load the form into your printer. In addition, wallet-size check forms are less expensive than other choices.

Standard- and voucher-size checks are good choices for businesses simply because they are larger. (See Figures 7-2 and 7-3.) In both forms, the check is 3.5 inches by 8.5 inches. The only difference between them is that the voucher check has an attached 3.5-inch-by-8.5-inch voucher or check stub. Because Microsoft Money prints split-transaction information on the voucher, any information you enter in the Split Transaction window to describe the check appears on the voucher.

If you're using a laser printer, you can choose between two check forms—laser standard and laser voucher—which resemble their impact-printer cousins.

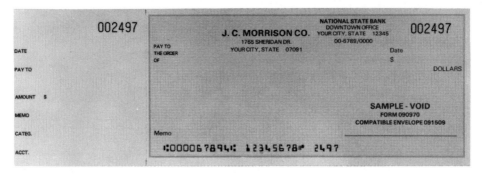

Figure 7-1.
A sample wallet check form.

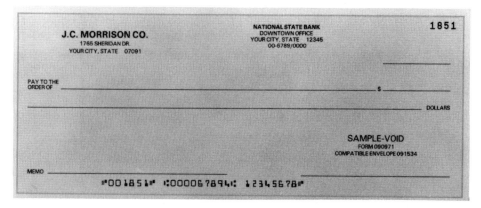

Figure 7-2.
A sample standard check form.

Figure 7-4 shows a laser standard check form, and Figure 7-5 shows a laser voucher check form.

Which laser check form you choose depends on whether you use check vouchers. If you need the space provided by the voucher to describe either the reason for the check or the way the check amount was calculated, order the laser voucher check form. If you don't need the space, order the less expensive laser standard form.

How to Print Checks

When you're ready to print checks, simply describe the check form you've selected and follow a simple sequence of steps.

Hands-On: Describing the Check Form and Check Printer

Before you can print your first check, you need to tell Microsoft Money which check form you've selected and which printer you'll use. As long as you don't change your printer or check forms, you need to perform this task only once.

To describe the check form and the printer you'll use to print the check, follow these steps.

1. Activate the File menu, and choose the Print Setup command. When you do, Microsoft Money displays the Print Setup dialog box shown in Figure 7-6.

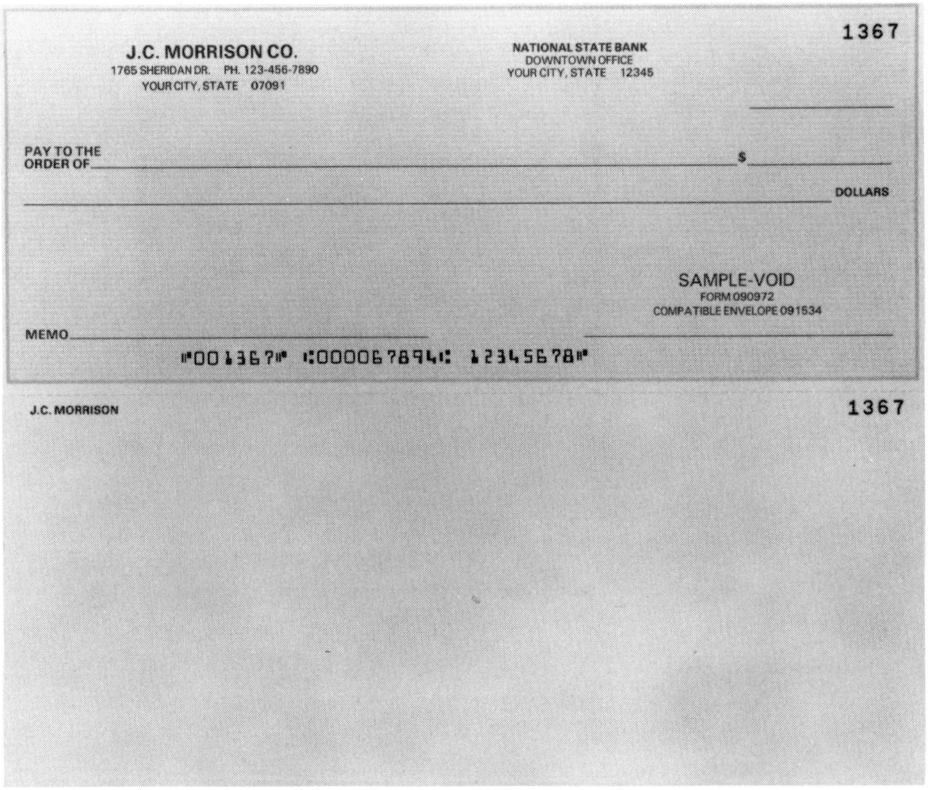
1367

J.C. MORRISON CO.
1765 SHERIDAN DR. PH. 123-456-7890
YOUR CITY, STATE 07091

NATIONAL STATE BANK
DOWNTOWN OFFICE
YOUR CITY, STATE 12345

PAY TO THE
ORDER OF $

DOLLARS

SAMPLE-VOID
FORM 090972
COMPATIBLE ENVELOPE 091534

MEMO

⑈001367⑈ ⑆000067894⑆ 12345678⑈

J.C. MORRISON 1367

Figure 7-3.
A sample voucher check form.

2. Because you're defining the Print Setup for checks, select the Setup For: Check Printing option button. When it is selected, the Print Setup dialog box on your screen should include the Check Type and Check Source drop-down list boxes in the lower right-hand corner of the dialog box, as shown in Figure 7-6.

3. If you use more than one printer with your computer, activate the Specific Printer drop-down list box by clicking on the down arrow at the far right of the Specific Printer text box. Then select the printer you'll use for check printing. Figure 7-7 shows the Specific Printer drop-down list box. (If you use a single printer, you needn't worry about this step because Microsoft Money can use the default printer.)

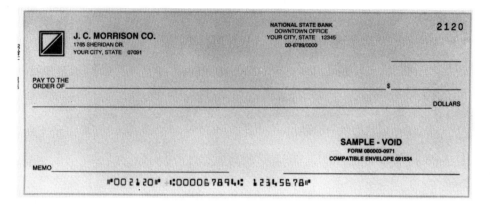

Figure 7-4.
A sample laser standard check form.

4. If you are using a laser printer, select the Orientation Portrait option button.

5. Activate the Check Type drop-down list box, and select the type of check form—Wallet, Standard, Voucher, Laser Standard, or Laser Voucher—you will use.

6. If you have a multiple-tray laser printer, activate the Check Source drop-down list box, and select the paper tray you will use.

7. When the Print Setup dialog box correctly describes the printer and check forms you will use, choose OK.

MICROSOFT MONEY TIP: *The Options command button displays a standard Windows dialog box in which you can change any of the Windows print-option settings. You should not need to use this dialog box, however. All the print-option settings required for printing checks appear on the Print Setup dialog box. If you choose the Options command button from the Print Setup dialog box and have questions, refer to the Windows user documentation or to one of the popular Windows tutorials.*

Hands-On: Printing Checks

After you've identified the printer and form type you will use for printing checks, you're ready to begin printing.

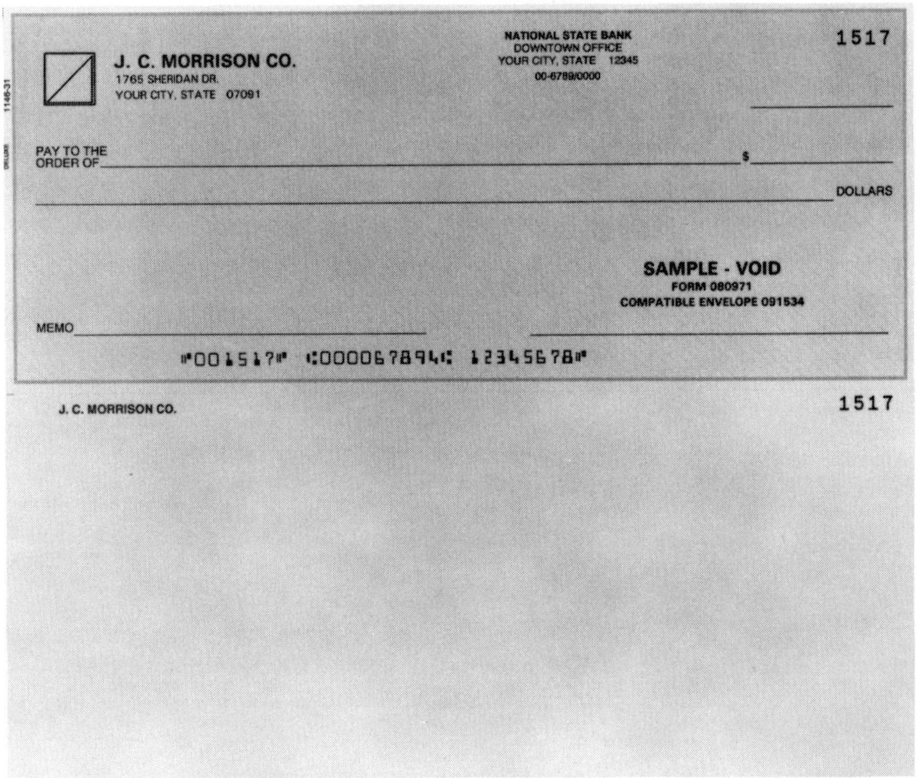

NATIONAL STATE BANK
DOWNTOWN OFFICE
YOUR CITY, STATE 12345
00-6789/0000

1517

J. C. MORRISON CO.
1765 SHERIDAN DR.
YOUR CITY, STATE 07091

PAY TO THE
ORDER OF_____ $_____

_____ DOLLARS

SAMPLE - VOID
FORM 080971
COMPATIBLE ENVELOPE 091534

MEMO_____

⑈0⑈1517⑈ ⑆00006789⑆⑈ ⑈12345678⑈

J. C. MORRISON CO.   1517

Figure 7-5.
A sample laser voucher check form.

To print checks, follow these steps.

1. Load the check forms into the printer.

2. Choose the Print Checks command from the File menu. When you do, Money displays the Print Checks dialog box shown in Figure 7-8.

3. Verify that the printer, check form, and account displayed in the top left-hand corner of the dialog box are correct. If they aren't, choose Cancel and make the necessary changes. For example, if the account is incorrect, use the Account List command on the List menu to change the current account. If you need to change the printer or check form, use the Print Setup command described earlier in this chapter.

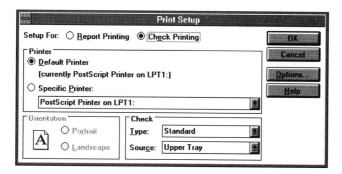

Figure 7-6.
The Print Setup dialog box.

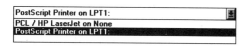

Figure 7-7.
The Specific Printer drop-down list box.

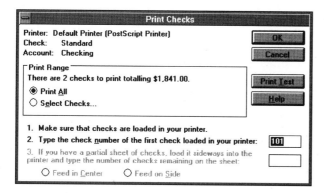

Figure 7-8.
The Print Checks dialog box (for a laser printer).

4. The Print Range portion of the Print Checks dialog box tells you how many checks are set up for printing (those for which you entered print instead of a check number in the Checks & Forms window) and the total amount of these checks. If you want to print all the checks set up for printing, select the Print All option button. Then, skip to step 6.

5. If you don't want to print all the checks set up for printing, select the Select Checks option button. When you do, Microsoft Money displays the Select Checks dialog box (see Figure 7-9), which lists the checks set up for printing. With the mouse, click on each check you want to print, or use the cursor keys to highlight each check and press the Spacebar. When you've selected all the checks you want to print, choose OK to return to the Print Checks dialog box.

6. In the text box labeled Type The Check Number Of The First Check Loaded In Your Printer, type the preprinted check number of the first check form loaded in your printer if you have a rear-feed-tractor or laser printer; if you have a top-feed-tractor printer, type the preprinted number on the second form. Microsoft Money needs this information to update the check number fields in the Account Book.

MICROSOFT MONEY TIP: *If you're printing laser check forms, you can print partial sheets of check forms. To do so, load the check forms sideways in the printer, enter the number of check forms on the sheet, and mark the Feed In Center or Feed On Side option button to describe how you're aligning the check forms in the printer.*

7. If you want to print a sample check, choose the Print Test command button. Microsoft Money briefly displays a message box telling you that it's printing a test check and then displays another message box telling you to adjust your printer as needed.

MICROSOFT MONEY TIP: *Printing test checks is a good idea the first few times if you use an impact printer. If you use a laser printer, you don't need to do this because a laser printer takes care of forms alignment for you.*

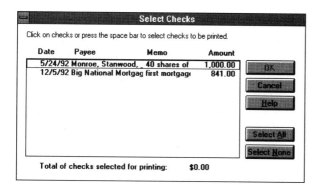

Figure 7-9.
The Select Checks dialog box.

8. To print the checks, choose OK. Microsoft Money begins printing checks. As it prints each check, it updates the Num field in the Account Book, replacing the word *print* with the actual check form number.

9. When Microsoft Money finishes printing the checks, it displays a message box asking you to review the checks to make sure they are printed correctly. (See Figure 7-10.) You might also want to sign them at this time.

10. If the printed checks are correct, choose Continue; when you do, Microsoft Money returns you to the window you were using before choosing the Print Checks command. You're now finished printing checks.

If, however, your review of the checks identifies printing problems, choose Reprint and complete steps 11 through 13.

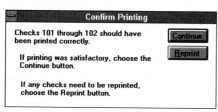

Figure 7-10.
The message box telling you Microsoft Money has finished printing checks and asking you to review the printed checks.

11. When you choose Reprint, Microsoft Money displays the Select Checks To Reprint dialog box (see Figure 7-11), in which you identify the checks you want to reprint. To reprint all the checks, choose the Select All command button. To reprint only some of them, either click on each check with the mouse, or highlight it by using the cursor keys and then pressing the Spacebar.

12. After you've identified the checks you want to reprint, enter the appropriate check number on the form for the first reprinted check in the Begin Reprinting Checks At Check Number text box.

13. Choose OK to begin reprinting checks. When Microsoft Money finishes printing the checks, it displays a message box that again asks you to review the checks. (Refer to Figure 7-10.) If the reprinted checks are correct, choose Continue. If the reprinted checks are incorrect, choose Reprint and repeat steps 11 through 13.

Figure 7-12 shows an example of a printed check.

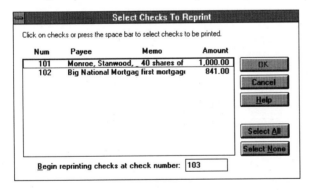

Figure 7-11.
The Select Checks To Reprint dialog box.

Producing Reports

Microsoft Money's reports let you extract and, optionally, summarize the financial information stored in the Microsoft Money Account Book. To print reports, you use the Report menu shown in Figure 7-13. Although producing reports using the Report menu commands isn't difficult, understanding the steps for producing any report and knowing about the six basic reports Microsoft Money produces will make it very easy.

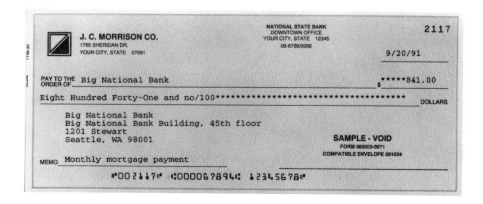

Figure 7-12.
A sample printed check.

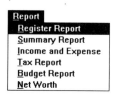

Figure 7-13.
The Report menu.

Some people, of course, will want to do more than simply produce standard versions of the Microsoft Money reports. So, after covering the basics, I'll describe how to export a report to a disk file so that you can import it into another application program, such as a spreadsheet. I'll also describe how to change the appearance of any of the six reports.

The Basics of Printing Reports

Microsoft Money produces six reports: the Register Report, the Summary Report, the Income and Expense Report, the Tax Report, the Budget Report, and the Net Worth Report. Although each report extracts and summarizes different information from the Microsoft Money Account Books, use the same sequence of steps to produce and print all the reports.

Hands-On: Print Setup for Reports

1. Activate the File menu and choose the Print Setup command. When you do, Money displays the Print Setup dialog box. (See Figure 7-14.)

2. Select the Setup For Report Printing option button. When you do, the Print Setup dialog box on your screen includes the Paper Size and Paper Source drop-down list boxes in the lower right-hand corner of the dialog box, as in Figure 7-14.

3. If you use more than one printer with your computer, activate the Specific Printer drop-down list box by clicking on the down arrow at the far right of the Specific Printer text box. Then select the printer you'll use for report printing from the list box. (Refer to Figure 7-7 for an example of the Specific Printer drop-down list box.)

4. If you have a laser printer, select the appropriate Orientation option button, Portrait or Landscape.

5. If you have a laser printer, activate the Paper Size drop-down list box, and select the paper size you want.

6. If you have a multiple-tray laser printer, activate the Paper Source drop-down list box, and select the paper tray you will use.

7. When the Print Setup dialog box describes the printer and paper you want to use, choose OK.

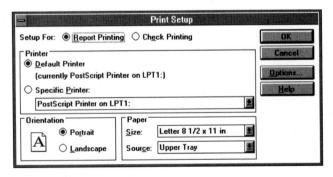

Figure 7-14.
The Print Setup dialog box.

MICROSOFT MONEY TIP: *As mentioned earlier in the chapter, choosing the Print Setup dialog box's Options command button displays a standard Windows dialog box in which you can change any of the Windows print-option settings. You should not, however, need to use this dialog box. All the print-option settings for printing reports appear on the Print Setup dialog box. If you have questions about the Options command button, refer to the* Microsoft Windows Users Guide *or to a Windows tutorial.*

Once you describe the printer and the paper you want to use, you're ready to begin producing reports.

Hands-On: Producing and Printing a Report

To produce and optionally print a Microsoft Money report, follow these steps.

1. Choose the Report menu command corresponding to the report you want to produce. (Refer to Figure 7-13 for the Report menu with its list of available reports.) When you do, Microsoft Money displays a window with an on-screen version of the report based on its default settings. (Figure 7-15 shows the Register Report.) Typically, a report is several pages long, so it won't all fit inside the window. You can use the horizontal and vertical scroll bars to view different pages of the report.

2. If you don't want to print the report, choose the Close command button to remove the report window.

3. If you want to print the report, choose the Print command button, which appears in upper right-hand corner of the report window. (See Figure 7-15.) When you do, Microsoft Money displays the Print Report dialog box. (See Figure 7-16.)

4. If you want to print the entire report, select the Print Range All option button. If you want to print only a portion of the report, select the Print Range Pages option button, and then enter the numbers of the first and last pages you want printed in the From and To text boxes.

5. If your printer is capable of varying print quality, activate the Print Quality drop-down list box, and select the print quality you want to use for the report. The quality you choose will affect printing speed: Lower-quality reports print faster but don't look as crisp, and higher-quality reports look

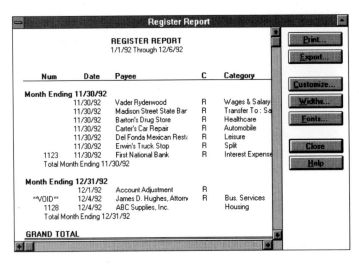

Figure 7-15.
A Register Report displayed in a window.

Figure 7-16.
The Print Report dialog box.

sharp but take longer to print. Figure 7-17 shows an example of a Print
Quality drop-down list box. The list box you see will depend on your
printer.

Print **Q**uality:

Figure 7-17.
The Print Quality drop-down list box.

6. By default, Microsoft Money prints a single copy of each report. If you want more than one copy, enter the number of copies in the Copies text box.

 MICROSOFT MONEY TIP: *By default, Microsoft Money collates report pages when you print multiple copies. That is, Microsoft Money prints the pages of the first report, then the pages of the second report, then the pages of the third report, and so on. You might not want to print collated reports, because they take more time to print than uncollated reports. If you don't want Microsoft Money to collate, remove the mark in the Collate Copies check box.*

7. When the Print Report dialog box is complete, choose OK. Microsoft Money starts printing your report and also displays a message box that tells you the report is printing and which page of the report is printing.

Reviewing the Microsoft Money Reports

Each of Microsoft Money's six reports conveys different information and serves a different purpose. As a result, you might not be sure—particularly when you're first working with Microsoft Money—which report you want in a given situation.

To address this initial confusion, Table 7-1 summarizes the six reports. The table describes the information each report contains and the way the report can be used, along with providing a brief description of how it can be modified. (I furnish detailed steps for modifying each report later in the chapter in the section entitled Changing Report Appearance.)

Report	Description	Purpose	Modifications possible
Register Report	Summarizes transactions entered in an Account Book (essentially equivalent to the check register or transaction list you probably now maintain by hand)	To print a Register Report each time you enter transactions—at the end of the month and at the end of the year—as a permanent hard-copy record of account transactions	Customize by specifying a report title, information to be included, range of transaction dates, and accounts to be included; use a different subtotaling method
Summary Report	Subtotals Account Book transactions by payee	To summarize payments to different businesses or individuals for budgeting or (in business) for completing IRS 1099 forms	Customize by specifying a report title, particular transaction data to be included in subtotals, different subtotals to be calculated, and range of transaction dates and accounts to be included
Income and Expense Report	Subtotals transactions in an Account Book by income and expense category	To monitor actual income and expenses, e.g., for monitoring business profitability	Customize by specifying a report title, particular transaction data to be used in subtotals, different subtotals to be calculated, and range of transaction dates and accounts to be included; also control appearance of account transfers

Table 7-1.
The six Microsoft Money reports.

(continued)

Table 7-1. *continued*

Report	Description	Purpose	Modifications possible
Tax Report	Subtotals transactions using categories marked as tax-related	To monitor annual taxable income and tax deductions for tax planning; to prepare income tax returns	Customize by specifying a report title, particular transactions to be included, transaction data to be included in subtotals, different subtotals to be calculated, and range of transaction dates and accounts to be included
Budget Report	Summarizes transactions by income and expense category (like the Income and Expense Report) and compares category subtotals to budgeted amounts	When the Microsoft Money budgeting feature is used, to compare actual with budgeted spending on a frequent, perhaps monthly, basis	Customize by specifying a report title, particular transaction data to be included in subtotals, different subtotals to be calculated, and range of transaction dates and accounts to be included
Net Worth Report	Shows current account balance for each account (bank, credit card, cash, asset, liability)	To summarize all bank account and credit card balances in one place; to calculate net worth	Customize by specifying a report title, date on which to measure account balances, and accounts to be included

Figures 7-18 through 7-23 on the following pages show sample pages from each of the reports. Notice that all the information doesn't always fit on the page. In a later section in this chapter entitled Changing Report Appearance, I'll describe how to make everything fit.

REGISTER REPORT
1/1/93 Through 12/31/93

Num	Date	Payee	C	Category	Amount
Month Ending 1/31/93					
	1/30/93	Jumbo Jet Manufacturing		Wages & Salary : Gross	1,000.00
201	1/30/93	Ronald Silvera Properties		Housing : Rent	(350.00)
202	1/31/93	Shawmanns Deli		Food : Groceries	(245.93)
203	1/31/93	Erwin's Truck Stop		Split	(195.95)
204	1/31/93	Del Fonda's Mexican Re:		Food : Dining Out	(97.52)
	Total Month Ending 1/31/93				110.60
Month Ending 2/28/93					
	2/25/93	Shawmanns Deli		Food : Groceries	(245.93)
	2/25/93	Erwin's Truck Stop		Split	(195.95)
	2/28/93	Del Fonda's Mexican Re:		Food : Dining Out	(97.52)
	2/28/93	Jumbo Jet Manufacturing		Wages & Salary : Gross	1,000.00
	2/28/93	Ronald Silvera Properties		Housing : Rent	(350.00)
	Total Month Ending 2/28/93				110.60
Month Ending 3/31/93					
	3/25/93	Shawmanns Deli		Food : Groceries	(245.93)
	3/25/93	Erwin's Truck Stop		Split	(195.95)
	3/31/93	Jumbo Jet Manufacturing		Wages & Salary : Gross	1,000.00
	3/31/93	Ronald Silvera Properties		Housing : Rent	(350.00)
	3/31/93	Del Fonda's Mexican Re:		Food : Dining Out	(97.52)
	Total Month Ending 3/31/93				110.60
Month Ending 4/30/93					
	4/25/93	Erwin's Truck Stop		Split	(195.95)
	4/25/93	Shawmanns Deli		Food : Groceries	(245.93)
	4/30/93	Del Fonda's Mexican Re:		Food : Dining Out	(97.52)
	4/30/93	Ronald Silvera Properties		Housing : Rent	(350.00)
	4/30/93	Jumbo Jet Manufacturing		Wages & Salary : Gross	1,000.00
	Total Month Ending 4/30/93				110.60
Month Ending 5/31/93					
	5/25/93	Shawmanns Deli		Food : Groceries	(245.93)
	5/25/93	Erwin's Truck Stop		Split	(195.95)
	5/31/93	Del Fonda's Mexican Re:		Food : Dining Out	(97.52)
	5/31/93	Ronald Silvera Properties		Housing : Rent	(350.00)
	5/31/93	Jumbo Jet Manufacturing		Wages & Salary : Gross	1,000.00
	Total Month Ending 5/31/93				110.60
Month Ending 6/30/93					
	6/25/93	Shawmanns Deli		Food : Groceries	(245.93)
	6/25/93	Erwin's Truck Stop		Split	(195.95)
	6/30/93	Jumbo Jet Manufacturing		Wages & Salary : Gross	1,000.00
	6/30/93	Del Fonda's Mexican Re:		Food : Dining Out	(97.52)
	6/30/93	Ronald Silvera Properties		Housing : Rent	(350.00)
	Total Month Ending 6/30/93				110.60
Month Ending 7/31/93					
	7/25/93	Erwin's Truck Stop		Split	(195.95)
	7/25/93	Shawmanns Deli		Food : Groceries	(245.93)
	7/31/93	Del Fonda's Mexican Re:		Food : Dining Out	(97.52)
	7/31/93	Ronald Silvera Properties		Housing : Rent	(350.00)
	7/31/93	Jumbo Jet Manufacturing		Wages & Salary : Gross	1,000.00
	Total Month Ending 7/31/93				110.60
Month Ending 8/31/93					
	8/25/93	Erwin's Truck Stop		Split	(195.95)
	8/25/93	Shawmanns Deli		Food : Groceries	(245.93)
	8/31/93	Del Fonda's Mexican Re:		Food : Dining Out	(97.52)
	8/31/93	Ronald Silvera Properties		Housing : Rent	(350.00)
	8/31/93	Jumbo Jet Manufacturing		Wages & Salary : Gross	1,000.00
	Total Month Ending 8/31/93				110.60
Month Ending 9/30/93					
	9/25/93	Erwin's Truck Stop		Split	(195.95)
	9/25/93	Shawmanns Deli		Food : Groceries	(245.93)
	9/30/93	Del Fonda's Mexican Re:		Food : Dining Out	(97.52)
	9/30/93	Ronald Silvera Properties		Housing : Rent	(350.00)
	9/30/93	Jumbo Jet Manufacturing		Wages & Salary : Gross	1,000.00
	Total Month Ending 9/30/93				110.60

Figure 7-18.

A page from a sample Register Report.

SUMMARY REPORT
1/1/92 Through 12/6/92

Payee	Total
1991 IRA Contribution	0.00
Apex Swimming Pools, I	0.00
Big National Mortgage, I	(792.00)
Del Fonda's Mexican Re	(104.26)
Erwin's Truck Stop	(66.15)
Initial mortgage balance	(100,000.00)
Jumbo Jet Manufacturing	2,500.00
Monroe, Stanwood, & Ar	0.00
Ronald Silvera Propertie	(1,500.00)
Shawmanns Deli	(161.34)
Stereo Equipment	1,320.00
Wall Street Money Marke	5,000.00
GRAND TOTAL	(93,803.75)

Figure 7-19.

A page from a sample Summary Report.

Exporting Reports

You may have noticed the Export command button on the Register Report window in Figure 7-15. This command lets you create disk files that store the information that appears in any printed report. You can import these disk files into applications such as Microsoft Works for Windows, Lotus 1-2-3, or Borland's Quattro Pro. First, of course, you need to display the report you want in a report window.

Hands-On: Exporting a Report

To export a report displayed in the report window, follow these steps.

1. Choose the Export command button. When you do, Microsoft Money displays the Export dialog box. (See Figure 7-24.)

2. Activate the Drives drop-down list box by clicking on the arrow to the right of the Drives text box. When you do, Microsoft Money displays a list of the hard drives and floppy drives connected to your computer.

3. Select the drive in which you want to store the exported file.

4. Activate the Directories drop-down list box by clicking on the arrow to the right of the Directories text box. When you do, Microsoft Money displays a list of the directories on the selected drive. (To display subdirectories, double-click on a directory.)

5. Select the directory in which you want to store the exported file.

INCOME AND EXPENSE REPORT
1/1/92 Through 12/6/92

Subcategory	Total
INCOME	
Wages & Salary	
Gross Pay	2,500.00
Total Wages & Salary	2,500.00
Income - Unassigned	6,320.00
TOTAL INCOME	8,820.00
EXPENSES	
Automobile	
Gasoline	46.15
Maintenance	20.00
Total Automobile	66.15
Food	
Dining Out	69.65
Groceries	161.34
Food - Unassigned	34.61
Total Food	265.60
Housing	
Rent	1,500.00
Total Housing	1,500.00
Interest Expense	
Interest Expense - Unass	792.00
Total Interest Expense	792.00
Expense - Unassigned	100,000.00
TOTAL EXPENSES	102,623.75
TRANSFERS	
House	(20,000.00)
IRA	(2,000.00)
Mortgage	49.00
Phoenix Mutual Fund	(1,000.00)
TOTAL TRANSFERS	(23,049.00)
INCOME LESS EXPENSES	(116,852.75)

Figure 7-20.

A page from a sample Income and Expense Report.

6. Enter the filename you want to use for the exported file in the File Name text box.

7. Choose OK.

Later, to import the exported report file into another application, follow the instructions in that application's user documentation. In general, importing tab-delimited files (files in which the fields in each record are separated by a tab character), such as Microsoft Money creates, isn't difficult. In Microsoft Excel,

TAX REPORT
1/1/92 Through 12/31/92

Subcategory	Total
INCOME CATEGORIES	
Bond discount	1.98
Investment Income	
Investment Income - Una	240.00
Total Investment Incom	240.00
Wages & Salary	
Gross Pay	2,500.00
Total Wages & Salary	2,500.00
Income - Unassigned	41,270.00
TOTAL INCOME CATEGORI	44,011.98
EXPENSE CATEGORIES	
Bond Premium	3.56
Charitable Donations	100.00
Taxes	
Property Tax	1,200.00
Total Taxes	1,200.00
TOTAL EXPENSE CATEGOI	1,303.56
GRAND TOTAL	42,708.42

Figure 7-21.
A page from a sample Tax Report.

for example, you open a tab-delimited file the same way you open a regular spreadsheet file. In Microsoft Word for Windows, you open a tab-delimited file the same way you open a text file. In both cases, you need to specify the complete filename and extension.

Changing Report Appearance

Many people will never need reporting features beyond those I've already described. Even if you're one of them, however, you should know that you can change the way each of the six reports looks by using the Customize, Widths, and Fonts command buttons that appear in the report windows. (Refer to Figure 7-15.) By using the Customize command button, for example, you can control the information appearing in a report and the way it's arranged. With the Widths command button, you can alter the horizontal dimension of the report. Finally, if your printer supports multiple fonts, you can use the Fonts command button to control the type style and size used to print your reports.

BUDGET REPORT
1/1/92 Through 12/6/92

Subcategory	1/1/92 Actual	Through Budget	1/31/92 Difference	2/1/92 Actual	Through Budget
INCOME CATEGORIES					
Wages & Salary					
Gross Pay		1,000.00	(1,000.00)	2,500.00	1,000.00
Total Wages & Salary		1,000.00	(1,000.00)	2,500.00	1,000.00
Income - Unassigned					
TOTAL INCOME CATEGORI		1,000.00	(1,000.00)	2,500.00	1,000.00
EXPENSE CATEGORIES					
Automobile					
Gasoline		35.00	(35.00)		35.00
Maintenance	20.00	0.00	20.00		
Payments		165.00	(165.00)		165.00
Total Automobile	20.00	200.00	(180.00)		200.00
Charitable Donations	100.00	0.00	100.00		
Food					
Dining Out	23.83	75.00	(51.17)		75.00
Groceries		250.00	(250.00)	75.92	250.00
Food - Unassigned					
Total Food	23.83	325.00	(301.17)	75.92	325.00
Housing					
Rent	750.00	350.00	400.00		350.00
Total Housing	750.00	350.00	400.00		350.00
Interest Expense					
Interest Expense - Unass					
Total Interest Expense					
Taxes					
Property Tax	1,200.00	0.00	1,200.00		
Total Taxes	1,200.00	0.00	1,200.00		
Expense - Unassigned					
TOTAL EXPENSE CATEGOI	2,093.83	875.00	1,218.83	75.92	875.00
GRAND TOTAL	(2,093.83)	125.00	(2,218.83)	2,424.08	125.00

Figure 7-22.
A page from a sample Budget Report.

Using the Customize Command Button

Because the Customize command button works differently for each of the six reports, I'll describe separately the step-by-step process of customizing each report. This approach unavoidably involves a certain amount of repetition.

The first step, no matter which report you're customizing and what changes you make, is to choose the Customize command button from the report window. When you do, Microsoft Money displays the Customize dialog box for

```
                    NET WORTH REPORT
                       As of 12/6/92


        ASSETS                      Total

        Bank and Cash Accounts
        Checking                   1,061.86
              Total Bank and Cash A  1,061.86

        Other Assets
        Dewclaw,Inc. Bond          1,043.82
        House                    122,000.00
        Investments                5,000.00
        IRA                        4,100.00
        Personal Property          1,320.00
        Phoenix Mutual Fund        2,100.00
        Rawlters Corp. Bond          953.61
              Total Other Assets   136,517.43

        TOTAL ASSETS              137,579.29


        LIABILITIES                 Total

        Credit Cards
        VISA                          34.61
              Total Credit Cards      34.61

        Other Liabilities
        Home Equity Loan          20,000.00
        Mortgage                  99,951.00
              Total Other Liabilities 119,951.00

        TOTAL LIABILITIES         119,985.61


        NET WORTH                  17,593.68
```

Figure 7-23.
A page from a sample Net Worth Report.

that report. You indicate the changes you want in the dialog box and then choose the View command button to return to the report window and see your changes.

Customizing the Register Report
Choose the Customize button in the Register Report window to display the Customize Register Report dialog box. (See Figure 7-25.)

Report titles. Microsoft Money gives each report a generic, descriptive title. In this case, the default title is Register Report. If you want to use a different title, type it in the Title text box.

Optional transaction data. The basic Register Report (refer to Figure 7-18) includes the transaction number (Num), Date, Payee, and Amount. By default, two optional pieces of information also appear: the cleared flag (C) and the

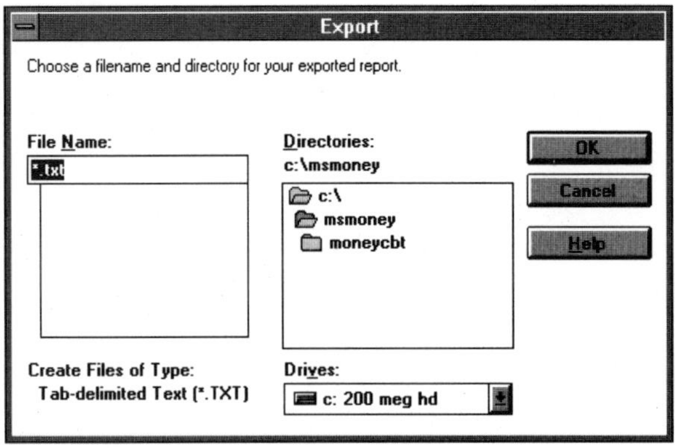

Figure 7-24.
The Export dialog box.

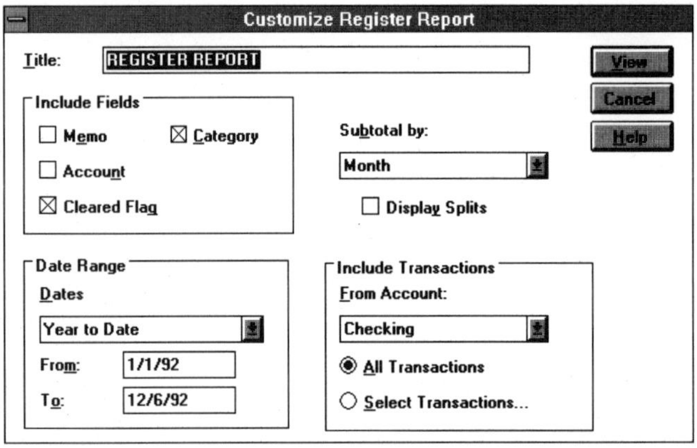

Figure 7-25.
The Customize Register Report dialog box.

Category. Two other optional items are Memo and Account. You control the optional data by marking the Include Fields check boxes for the fields you want to include.

Hands-On: changing Register Report subtotaling. By default, the Register Report subtotals the Register transactions by account. To change this, follow these two steps.

1. Activate the Subtotal By drop-down list box (see Figure 7-26) by clicking on the down arrow to the right of the Subtotal By text box.

2. Select the subtotaling method you want to use—None, Account, Payee, Category, Subcategory, Week, or Month.

Split-transaction information. As you probably know, Microsoft Money transactions can be split into two or more income or expense categories. A check written to pay a credit card bill, for example, might be split into $50 for entertainment, $75 for auto expenses, $25 for interest charges, and so on. To include split-transaction information on the Register Report, mark the Display Splits check box.

Hands-On: including transactions within a date range. By default, the Register Report lists transactions from the beginning of the year through the current date. You can change this date range by using one of two methods. The easiest way is as follows:

1. Activate the Dates drop-down list box. (See Figure 7-27.)

2. Select the range of dates you want, such as Month To Date or Last 30 Days. (Microsoft Money uses the current system date to identify what constitutes the previous year, previous month, current year, and so on.)

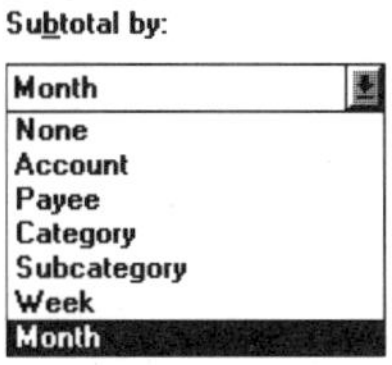

Figure 7-26.
The Subtotal By drop-down list box.

Figure 7-27.
The Dates drop-down list box.

To include a more specific range of transactions on a Register Report, you use the From and To text boxes. To do so, follow these steps.

1. Enter the first date for which you want to report transactions in the From text box.

2. Enter the last date for which you want to show transactions in the To text box.

Hands-On: specifying the account. By default, the Register Report includes only transactions from the current account. You can change the Register Report to include a different account, or even to include multiple accounts, by following these steps.

1. Activate the From Account drop-down list box. (See Figure 7-28.)

2. If you want a single account, simply select the account you want from the drop-down list box.

3. If you want every account's transactions to appear on the Register Report, scroll down to and select All Accounts.

4. If you want a group of accounts to appear, scroll down to and select the Multiple Accounts item from the drop-down list box. When you do, Microsoft Money displays the Select Accounts dialog box. (See Figure 7-29.)

5. To identify the accounts you want to include, click on each one with the mouse, or highlight each account by using the cursor keys and pressing the Spacebar.

Hands-On: limiting the transactions that appear on a Register Report. Typically, a Register Report includes all the transactions from the selected accounts. You can, however, limit those that appear by following these steps.

Erom Account:

Checking
Checking
Dewclaw,Inc. Bond
Home Equity Loan
House
Investments
IRA
Mortgage
Personal Property

Figure 7-28.
The From Account drop-down list box.

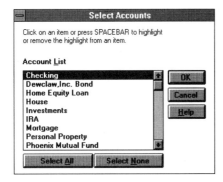

Figure 7-29.
The Select Accounts dialog box.

1. Select the Select Transactions option button. When you do, Microsoft Money displays the Select Transactions dialog box. (See Figure 7-30.)

2. To limit transactions appearing on the Register Report to those of a certain type, activate the Type drop-down list box (see Figure 7-31), and select the transaction type you want, such as Payments, Deposits, or Transfers.

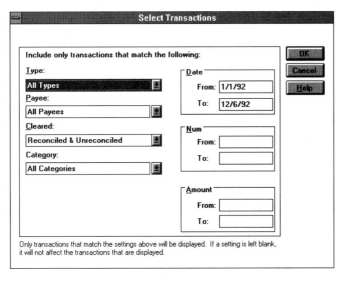

Figure 7-30.
The Select Transactions dialog box.

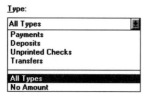

Figure 7-31.
The Type drop-down list box.

3. To limit transactions appearing on the Register Report to those with a specific payee, activate the Payee drop-down list box, which lists all your payees (see Figure 7-32), and select the payee name you want.

4. To limit transactions to those that are reconciled or those that are unreconciled, activate the Cleared drop-down list box, and select Unreconciled Transactions, Reconciled Transactions, or Reconciled & Unreconciled Transactions.

5. To limit transactions to those of a certain category or type of category, activate the Category drop-down list box (see Figure 7-33), and select the category or type of category you want. As Figure 7-33 shows, the Category drop-down list box includes items describing groups of categories, including All Categories, Income Categories, Expense Categories, Tax Categories, Blank Category, and even Select Multiple Categories. As you might guess, Select Multiple Categories displays another dialog box, Select Categories, which lists all your income and expense categories.

6. To limit transactions to those falling within a certain date range, type the first date for which you want to see transactions in the Date From text box and the last date for which you want to see transactions in the Date To text

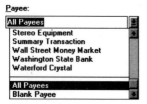

Figure 7-32.
The Payee drop-down list box.

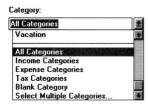

Figure 7-33.
The Category drop-down list box.

box. (You can also use the Date Range From and Date Range To fields on the Customize Register Report dialog box to limit the date range.)

7. To limit transactions to those with transaction numbers falling within a specified range, type the first number of the transaction number range in the Num From text box and the last number of the transaction number range in the Num To text box.

8. To limit transactions to those with amounts falling within a specified range, type the starting amount of the range in the Amount From text box and the ending amount of the range in the Amount To text box.

If you have defined a classification, Microsoft Money adds a drop-down list box to the Select Transactions dialog box so that you can create reports that include only transactions falling under that classification. This drop-down list box works in the same way as others in the Select Transactions dialog box.

 MICROSOFT MONEY TIP: *If you leave a text box blank or a drop-down list box unchanged in the Select Transactions dialog box, it has no effect on the transactions included in the report.*

Customizing the Summary Report

Choose the Customize command button from the Summary Report window to display the Customize Summary Report dialog box. (See Figure 7-34.)

Report titles. The default title is Summary Report. If you want to change it, type a new title in the Title text box.

Hands-On: changing Summary Report subtotaling. By default, the Summary Report subtotals the transactions by payee and prints each payee subtotal on a separate line. You can choose another subtotaling scheme, however, or even use dual subtotaling. For example, you can subtotal by both payees and

```
┌─────────────────────────────────────────────────────────────┐
│  ─    │         Customize Summary Report          │          │
├─────────────────────────────────────────────────────────────┤
│  Title:   [SUMMARY REPORT                    ]    ┌───────┐   │
│                                                   │ View  │   │
│  Row for Every:    [Payee              ▼]         └───────┘   │
│  Column for Every: [None               ▼]         ┌───────┐   │
│                                                   │Cancel │   │
│  ☐ Display Shortcuts                              └───────┘   │
│                                                   ┌───────┐   │
│  ┌─ Date Range ──────────┐ ┌─ Include Transactions─┤ Help │  │
│  │ Dates                 │ │ From Account:        └───────┘  │
│  │ [Year to Date    ▼]   │ │ [All Accounts      ▼]          │
│  │                       │ │                                │
│  │ From:  [1/1/92   ]    │ │ ⦿ All Transactions            │
│  │ To:    [12/6/92  ]    │ │ ○ Select Transactions...      │
│  └───────────────────────┘ └───────────────────────────────┘│
└─────────────────────────────────────────────────────────────┘
```

Figure 7-34.
The Customize Summary Report dialog box.

months, arranging the payee subtotals by row and the month subtotals by columns.

To change the subtotaling scheme, simply follow these steps.

1. Activate the Row For Every drop-down list box (see Figure 7-35) by clicking on the down arrow to the right of the text box.

2. Select the new subtotaling method you want to use, for which subtotals should appear on each row. For example, if you select Payee, payee subtotals will appear on each row of the Summary Report.

3. Activate the Column For Every drop-down list box by clicking on the down arrow to the right of the text box. (The Column For Every drop-down list box closely resembles the Row For Every drop-down list box.)

```
Row for Every:   [Payee               ▼]
                 ┌─────────────────────┐
                 │ None                │
                 │ Account             │
                 │ Payee               │
                 │ Category            │
                 │ Subcategory         │
                 │ Week                │
                 │ Month               │
                 └─────────────────────┘
```

Figure 7-35.
The Row For Every drop-down list box.

4. Select the new subtotaling method you want to use, for which subtotals should appear in each column. For example, if you select Month, monthly subtotals appear in each column of the Summary Report.

Hands-On: including transactions within a date range. Like other reports, the Summary Report, by default, summarizes transactions from the beginning of the year through the current date. You can change this date range by one of two methods. The easiest way is as follows:

1. Activate the Dates drop-down list box. (Refer to Figure 7-27.)

2. Select the range of dates you want.

To include a more specific range of transactions in a Summary Report, use the From and To text boxes. To do this, follow these steps.

1. Enter the first date for which you want to see transactions in the From text box.

2. Enter the last date for which you want to see transactions in the To text box.

Hands-On: specifying the account. By default, a Summary Report includes transactions from all your accounts. However, you can also create a Summary Report using only a single account or a group of accounts. To do so, follow these steps.

1. Activate the From Account drop-down list box. (Refer to Figure 7-28.)

2. If you want a single account, select the account you want from the drop-down list box.

3. If you want to summarize every account's transactions, scroll down to and select the All Accounts item from the drop-down list box.

4. If you want a group of accounts to appear, scroll down to and select Multiple Accounts from the drop-down list box. When you do, Microsoft Money displays the Select Accounts dialog box. (Refer to Figure 7-29.)

5. Identify the accounts you want by clicking on each one with the mouse or highlighting each account by using the cursor keys and then pressing the Spacebar.

Hands-On: limiting the transactions included in a Summary Report. To limit the transactions included on a Summary Report, follow these steps.

1. Select the Select Transactions option button. When you do, Microsoft Money displays the Select Transactions dialog box. (Refer to Figure 7-30.)

2. To limit transactions to those of a certain type, activate the Type drop-down list box (refer to Figure 7-31), and then select the transaction type you want.

3. To limit transactions to those with a specific payee, activate the Payee drop-down list box (refer to Figure 7-32), and select the payee name you want.

4. To limit transactions to either reconciled or unreconciled transactions, activate the Cleared drop-down list box, and then select one of the listed choices.

5. To limit transactions to those of a certain category or type of category, activate the Category drop-down list box (refer to Figure 7-33), and then select the wanted category or type of category. If you want to include multiple categories, select the Select Multiple Categories item, which displays another dialog box listing all the income and expense categories.

6. To limit transactions to those falling within a certain date range, type the first date for which you want to see transactions in the Date From text box and the last date for which you want to see transactions in the Date To text box. (You can also use the Date Range From and Date Range To fields on the Customize Summary Report dialog box to accomplish this task.)

7. To limit transactions to those with transaction numbers falling within a specified range, enter the first number of the range in the Num From text box and the last number of the range in the Num To text box.

8. To limit transactions to those with transaction amounts falling within a specified range, enter the starting amount of the range in the Amount From text box and the ending amount of the range in the Amount To text box.

If you have defined a classification, Microsoft Money adds a drop-down list box to the Select Transactions dialog box so that you can create reports that include only transactions falling under that classification. This drop-down list box works in the same way as others in the Select Transactions dialog box.

Customizing the Income and Expense Report

Select the Customize command button from the Income and Expense Report window. When you do, Microsoft Money displays the Customize Income and Expense Report dialog box, shown in Figure 7-36.

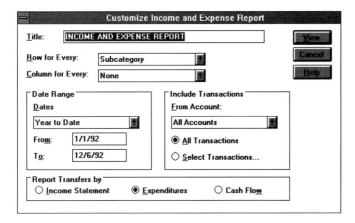

Figure 7-36.
The Customize Income and Expense Report dialog box.

Report titles. The default title is Income and Expense Report. To use a different report title, simply type it in the Title text box.

Hands-On: changing subtotaling. By default, the Income and Expense Report
subtotals transactions by category and prints each category subtotal on a separate line. You can choose another subtotaling scheme or even use dual subtotaling. For example, you can subtotal both by category and month,
arranging category subtotals by row and month subtotals by column.

To use another subtotaling scheme, simply follow these steps.

1. Activate the Row For Every drop-down list box by clicking on the down
   arrow to the right of the text box. (Refer to Figure 7-35.)

2. Select the new subtotaling method you want to use, for which subtotals
   should appear on each row. For example, if you choose Category, category
   subtotals appear on each row of the Income and Expense Report.

3. Activate the Column For Every drop-down list box by clicking on the down
   arrow to the right of the text box.

4. Select the new subtotaling method you want to use, for which subtotals
   should appear in each column. For example, if you choose Month, monthly
   subtotals appear in each column of the Income and Expense Report.

Hands-On: including transactions within a date range. Like other reports, the Income and Expense Report summarizes transactions from the beginning of the year through the current date. You can change this date range by using one of two methods. The easiest way to do so is as follows:

1. Activate the Dates drop-down list box. (Refer to Figure 7-27.)

2. Select the range of dates you want.

To include a more specific range of transactions in an Income and Expense Report, use the From and To text boxes. To do so, follow these steps:

1. Enter the first date for which you want to see transactions in the From text box.

2. Enter the last date for which you want to see transactions in the To text box.

Hands-On: specifying the account. By default, an Income and Expense Report includes transactions from all your accounts. You can also create an Income and Expense Report that uses only a single account or a group of accounts. To do so, follow these steps.

1. Activate the From Account drop-down list box. (Refer to Figure 7-28.)

2. If you want a single account, simply select the account you want from the drop-down list box.

3. If you want all account transactions to be summarized, scroll down to and select the All Accounts item from the drop-down list box.

4. If you want a group of accounts to appear, scroll down to and select Multiple Accounts from the drop-down list box. When you do, Microsoft Money displays the Select Accounts dialog box. (Refer to Figure 7-29.)

5. Identify the accounts you want by clicking on each one with the mouse or highlighting each account by using the cursor keys and pressing the Spacebar.

Hands-On: limiting the transactions included in an Income and Expense Report.
As with other Microsoft Money reports, you can limit the transactions included on an Income and Expense Report. To do so, follow these steps.

1. Select the Select Transactions option button. When you do, Microsoft Money displays the Select Transactions dialog box. (Refer to Figure 7-30.)

2. To limit transactions included in the Income and Expense Report to those of a certain type, activate the Type drop-down list box (refer to Figure 7-31), and then select the transaction type you want.

3. To limit transactions to those with a specific payee, activate the Payee drop-down list box (refer to Figure 7-32), and then select the payee name you want.

4. To limit transactions to reconciled or unreconciled transactions, activate the Cleared drop-down list box, and select one of the listed choices.

5. To limit transactions to those assigned to a certain category or type of category, activate the Category drop-down list box (refer to Figure 7-33), and then select the category or type of category you want. To include more than one category, select the Select Multiple Categories item, which lists all income and expense categories.

6. To limit the transactions to those falling within a certain date range, use the Select Transactions dialog box; type the first date for which you want to see transactions in the Date From text box and the last date for which you want to see transactions in the Date To text box. (You can also use the Date Range From and Date Range To fields on the Customize Income and Expense Report dialog box.)

7. To limit transactions to those with transaction numbers falling within a specified range, enter the first number of the range in the Num From text box and the last number of the range in the Num To text box.

8. To limit transactions to only those with transaction amounts falling within a specified range, type the starting amount of the range in the Amount From text box and the ending amount of the range in the Amount To text box.

If you have defined a classification, Microsoft Money adds a drop-down list box to the Select Transactions dialog box so that you can create reports that include only transactions falling under that classification. This drop-down list box works in the same way as others in the Select Transactions dialog box.

Specifying how transfers should be treated. A sticky problem with regard to the Income and Expense Report is how account transfers should be treated. The Report Transfers By option buttons let you control how account transfers should be treated. Select Income Statement if you don't want to include transfers in the Income and Expense Report. Select Expenditures if you want to include transfers in a special report section on account changes. (Expenditures is the default setting.) Select Cash Flow if you want transfers into the account recorded as a separate line in the income section of the report and transfers out of the account recorded as a separate line in the expense section.

Customizing the Tax Report

Customizing the Tax Report is very similar to customizing the Summary or the Income and Expense Report. If you've read through the previous sections, you'll probably want to read closely only the paragraph headed Choosing the Report Type.

To start, choose the Customize command button from the Tax Report window. When you do, Microsoft Money displays the Customize Tax Report dialog box. (See Figure 7-37.)

Report titles. The default title is Tax Report. To use a more descriptive title, such as Report on 1992 Income Tax Deductions, type it in the Title text box.

Choosing the report type. Microsoft Money produces two types of tax reports. One type, called a Tax Summary Report, shows only the category totals. The other type, called a Tax Transactions Report, shows the category totals and individual transactions that add up to produce the totals. Select the option button that corresponds to the type of tax report you want.

```
┌─────────────────────────────────────────────────────────┐
│                    Customize Tax Report                   │
├─────────────────────────────────────────────────────────┤
│ Title:   [TAX REPORT                        ]    [ View ] │
│ ┌─Report Type──────────────────────────────┐    [Cancel] │
│ │  ◉ Tax Summary      ○ Tax Transactions   │    [ Help ] │
│ └───────────────────────────────────────────┘            │
│ Row for Every:   [Subcategory      ▼]  □ Display Shortcuts│
│ Column for Every:[None             ▼]                    │
│ ┌─Date Range──────────┐  ┌─Include Transactions─────────┐│
│ │ Dates               │  │ From Account:                ││
│ │ [Previous Year    ▼]│  │ [All Accounts            ▼]  ││
│ │ From:  [1/1/91   ]  │  │ ○ All Transactions           ││
│ │ To:    [12/31/91 ]  │  │ ◉ Select Transactions...     ││
│ └─────────────────────┘  └──────────────────────────────┘│
└─────────────────────────────────────────────────────────┘
```

Figure 7-37.
The Customize Tax Report dialog box.

Hands-On: subtotaling. By default, the Tax Report subtotals transactions by sub-category and prints each subcategory subtotal on a separate line. You can choose another subtotaling scheme or have Microsoft Money calculate more than one set of subtotals.

To use another subtotaling scheme, simply follow these steps.

1. Activate the Row For Every drop-down list box by clicking on the down arrow to the right of the text box. (Refer to Figure 7-35.)

2. Select the new subtotaling method you want to use, for which subtotals should appear on each row. For example, if you choose Category, category subtotals appear on each row of the Tax Report.

3. Activate the Column For Every drop-down list box by clicking on the down arrow to the right of the Column For Every text box.

4. Select the new subtotaling method you want to use and which subtotals should appear in each column.

Hands-On: including transactions within a date range. By default, the Tax Report summarizes transactions from the previous year. You can change this date range by using one of two methods. The easiest way to do so is as follows:

1. Activate the Dates drop-down list box. (Refer to Figure 7-27.)

2. Select the range of dates you want.

To include a more specific range of transactions in a Tax Report, use the From and To text boxes. To do so, follow these steps.

1. Enter the first date for which you want to see transactions in the From text box.

2. Enter the last date for which you want to see transactions in the To text box.

PERSONAL FINANCIAL TIP: If you collect income tax data using Microsoft Money, be sure to print out at least one copy of the Tax Transactions Report and store it with your annual income tax return. Should you be audited—an unlikely but time-consuming event—you'll need a Tax Transactions Report to explain how you arrived at your income tax deduction amounts.

Hands-On: specifying the account. By default, a Tax Report includes transactions from all your accounts. You can also create a Tax Report using only a single account or group of accounts. (Although this capability is provided, it's unlikely you'll use it unless you maintain different accounts to track different taxable entities.)

To specify a particular account or accounts, follow these steps.

1. Activate the From Account drop-down list box. (Refer to Figure 7-28.)

2. If you want a single account, simply select the relevant account from the drop-down list box.

3. If you want to summarize every account's transactions, scroll down to and select the All Accounts item from the drop-down list box.

4. If you want only a group of accounts to appear, scroll down to and select Multiple Accounts from the drop-down list box. When you do, Microsoft Money displays the Select Accounts dialog box. (Refer to Figure 7-29.)

5. Identify the accounts you want by clicking on each one with the mouse or highlighting each account by using the cursor keys and then pressing the Spacebar.

Hands-On: limiting the transactions included in a Tax Report. As with other Microsoft Money reports, you can limit the transactions included in a Tax Report. To do so, follow these steps.

1. Select the Select Transactions option button. When you do, Microsoft Money displays the Select Transactions dialog box. (Refer to Figure 7-30.)

2. To limit transactions to those of a certain type, activate the Type drop-down list box (refer to Figure 7-31), and select the transaction type you want.

3. To limit transactions to those with a specific payee, activate the Payee drop-down list box (refer to Figure 7-32), and select the payee name you want.

4. To limit transactions to reconciled or unreconciled transactions, activate the Cleared drop-down list box, and select one of the listed choices.

5. To limit transactions to those assigned to a certain category or type of category, activate the Category drop-down list box (refer to Figure 7-33), and select the category or type of category you want. Before you make this

change, however, remember that the feature that differentiates a Tax Report from a regular Summary Report is the inclusion of categories marked as tax-related.

6. To limit transactions included in the Tax Report to those falling within a certain date range, use the Select Transactions dialog box; type the first date for which you want to see transactions in the Date From text box and the last date for which you want to see transactions in the Date To text box. (You can also use the Date Range From and Date Range To fields on the Customize Tax Report dialog box.)

7. To limit transactions to those with transaction numbers falling within a specified range, type the first number of the range in the Num From text box and the last number of the range in the Num To text box.

8. To limit the transactions to those with transaction amounts falling within a specified range, type the starting amount of the range in the Amount From text box and the ending amount of the range in the Amount To text box.

If you have defined a classification, Microsoft Money adds a drop-down list box to the Select Transactions dialog box so that you can create reports that include only transactions falling under that classification. This drop-down list box works in the same way as others in the Select Transactions dialog box.

Customizing the Budget Report

The steps for modifying the Budget Report are almost identical to those for modifying the Summary Report. In fact, there's only a minor mechanical difference, which relates to the treatment of empty categories. If you've read everything in this chapter up to this point, you can skip everything but the paragraph headed Dealing with Empty Categories.

To begin making changes to the Budget Report, choose the Customize command button from the Budget Report window. When you do, Microsoft Money displays the Customize Budget Report dialog box shown in Figure 7-38.

Report titles. The default title is Budget Report. To use a more descriptive and meaningful title, such as Rashad Family Budget 1993 or James Hughes, Inc., Business Plan 1993, type it in the Title text box.

Hands-On: subtotaling. By default, the Budget Report is set to subtotal transactions by subcategory and print each subcategory subtotal on a separate line.

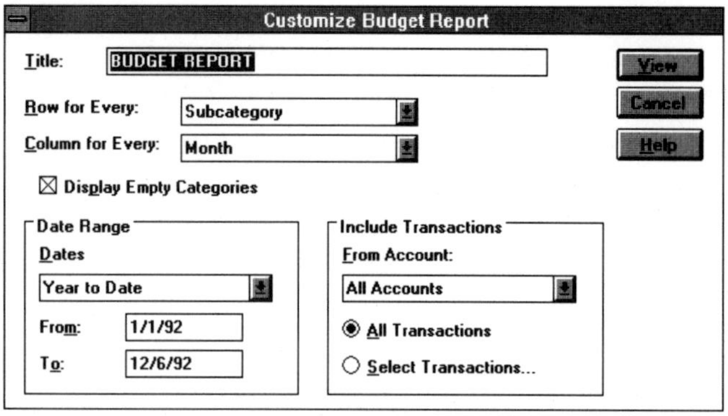

Figure 7-38.
The Customize Budget Report dialog box.

You can, however, choose a different way to subtotal, such as by category. Or you can use a second subtotal; for example, you can subtotal by both category and month.

To use a different subtotaling scheme, simply follow these steps.

1. Activate the Row For Every drop-down list box by clicking on the down arrow to the right of the text box. Because you budget by category and sub-category, the drop-down list box will show only two items: Category and Subcategory.

2. Select the new subtotaling method you want to use, for which subtotals should appear on each row. For example, when you select Category, category subtotals appear on each row of the Budget Report.

3. Activate the Column For Every drop-down list box by clicking on the down arrow to the right of the Column For Every text box.

4. Select the new subtotaling method you want to use, for which subtotals should appear in each column. For example, when you select Month, monthly subtotals appear in each column of the Budget Report.

Dealing with empty categories. The Microsoft Money reports summarize factual data from your Account Books; just because you've budgeted for some income or expense item doesn't mean it actually occurs. When there isn't any data to summarize, marking the Display Empty Categories check box tells

Microsoft Money to display a zero subtotal for a category or subcategory for which no transactions are recorded. If you don't want zero subtotals appearing on your report, unmark the Display Empty Categories check box.

Hands-On: including transactions within a date range. By default, the Budget Report summarizes transactions from the beginning of the year through the current date. You can change this date range by using one of two methods. The easiest way to change the date range is as follows:

1. Activate the Dates drop-down list box. (Refer to Figure 7-27).

2. Select the range of dates you want.

To include a more specific range of transactions, you can use the From and To text boxes. To do so, follow these steps:

1. Enter the first date for which you want to see transactions in the From text box.

2. Enter the last date for which you want to see transactions in the To text box.

Hands-On: specifying the account. A Budget Report usually includes transactions from all of your accounts. Because there are situations in which that isn't appropriate — suppose you and your spouse keep separate budgets but share some accounts — you can also create a Budget Report that summarizes a single account or a group of accounts.

To do so, follow these steps.

1. Activate the From Account drop-down list box. (Refer to Figure 7-28.)

2. If you want a single account, simply select the account you want from the drop-down list box.

3. If you want all account transactions to be included, scroll down to and select the All Accounts item from the drop-down list box.

4. If you want a group of accounts to appear, scroll down to and select Multiple Accounts from the drop-down list box. When you do, Microsoft Money displays the Select Accounts dialog box. (Refer to Figure 7-29.)

5. Identify the accounts you want by clicking on each one with the mouse or highlighting each account by using the cursor keys and then pressing the Spacebar.

Hands-On: limiting the transactions included in a Budget Report. You can also limit the transactions included in a Budget Report, although you wouldn't be likely to do so. If you did, however, you would follow these steps:

1. Select the Select Transactions option button. When you do, Microsoft Money displays the Select Transactions dialog box. (Refer to Figure 7-30.)

2. To limit transactions included in the Budget Report to those of a certain type, activate the Type drop-down list box (refer to Figure 7-31), and select the appropriate transaction type.

3. To limit transactions to those with a specific payee, activate the Payee drop-down list box (refer to Figure 7-32), and select the payee name you want.

4. To limit transactions to reconciled or unreconciled transactions, activate the Cleared drop-down list box, and select one of the listed choices.

5. To limit transactions to those in a certain category or type of category, activate the Category drop-down list box (refer to Figure 7-33), and select the category or type of category you want.

6. To limit transactions to those falling within a certain date range, use the Select Transactions dialog box; type the first date for which you want to see transactions in the Date From text box and the last date for which you want to see transactions in the Date To text box. (You can also use the Date Range From and Date Range To fields on the Customize Budget Report dialog box.)

7. To limit transactions to those with transaction numbers falling within a specified range, enter the first number of the range in the Num From text box and the last number of the range in the Num To text box.

8. To limit transactions to those with transaction amounts falling within a specified range, enter the starting amount of the range in the Amount From text box and the ending amount of the range in the Amount To text box.

If you have defined a classification, Microsoft Money adds a drop-down list box to the Select Transactions dialog box so that you can create reports that include only transactions falling under that classification. This drop-down list box works in the same way as others in the Select Transactions dialog box.

Customizing the Net Worth Report

The Net Worth Report is probably the simplest to customize because there's not much you can do to it. To begin making changes to the Net Worth Report, choose the Customize command button from the Net Worth Report window. When you do, Microsoft Money displays the Customize Net Worth Report dialog box shown in Figure 7-39.

Report titles. The default title is Net Worth Report. To use a more descriptive title, such as Gonzalez Brothers—Net Worth Estimate, type it in the Title text box.

Specifying the net worth measurement date. A Net Worth Report shows the account balances on a specific date. By default, the date Microsoft Money uses is the current system date. You can use some other measurement date by entering it in the Show Balances As Of text box.

Specifying the account. Normally, a Net Worth Report includes all your accounts. If you prepare a Net Worth Report for your business, however, you usually don't include personal accounts. Similarly, if you prepare a personal Net Worth Report, you probably don't want to include all your business accounts. Follow these steps to specify the accounts you want included in the Net Worth Report.

1. Select the Select Accounts option button. When you do, Microsoft Money displays the Select Accounts dialog box, which lists all your accounts. (Refer to Figure 7-29.)

2. To identify an account you want included in the Net Worth Report, simply click on it with the mouse, or highlight the account by using the cursor keys and then pressing the Spacebar.

Figure 7-39.
The Customize Net Worth Report dialog box.

Using the Widths Command Button

All Microsoft Money report windows provide a Widths command button that controls the width of the report displayed in the report window and the width of the printed report. When you choose the Widths button, Microsoft Money displays the Report Column Width dialog box. (See Figure 7-40.) If the width allotted to a column is too large for the information it holds, choose a narrower column width. If there isn't enough room in a column to display all the information in a field—for example, if payee names are being truncated—choose a wider column. (Most of the time, you'll want to increase report width rather than decrease it.)

Using the Fonts Command Button

Each Microsoft Money report window also provides a Fonts command button that controls which font (type style) and character size are used for printing. When you choose the Fonts command button, Microsoft Money displays the Select Font dialog box shown in Figure 7-41. Select the font you want from

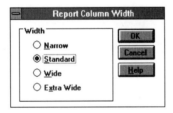

Figure 7-40.
The Report Column Width dialog box.

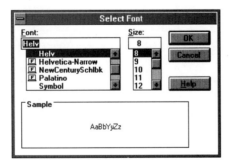

Figure 7-41.
The Select Font dialog box.

the list box. To use a different character size, select it from the Size drop down list box. (The fonts and sizes listed in your Select Font dialog box depend on your printer.) Microsoft Money then displays a bit of sample text in the selected font and size in the Sample box. When you finish, choose OK.

Conclusion

Most of the material covered in this long chapter isn't all that difficult. Printing checks, as you by now know, is a simple matter of choosing a check form, telling Microsoft Money which check form you're using, and following a simple sequence of steps. Likewise, producing Microsoft Money reports is easy, and the process of customizing reports is made even easier because the steps you take for each report are so similar.

Chapter 8

USING MICROSOFT MONEY AT HOME

This chapter and the next aren't about the mechanics of using a particular menu command or working with a specific window. They're about using Microsoft Money as a financial-management tool. This chapter covers several personal accounting and record-keeping tasks you might perform at home. If you're using Microsoft Money principally as a business accounting tool, you might want to skip ahead to the next chapter, which covers business applications.

This chapter assumes that you already know the basics of using Microsoft Money. It covers how to use the program to track your investments, track your credit card spending and balances, keep records of real estate, and keep insurance records. At the end of the chapter, I'll describe how to use Microsoft Money to measure your net worth.

Tracking Investments

One popular home accounting application of Microsoft Money is tracking investments. You might, for example, want to keep records of money market accounts, certificates of deposit, savings bonds, mutual funds, stocks, 401(k) plans, or individual retirement accounts. The following paragraphs describe how to track each of these investments.

Money Market Accounts

Money market accounts are similar to checking accounts with variable interest rates. The interest rate varies because it is based on the earnings of the money market fund's investments.

Generally, you own a certain number of shares in a money market fund, and each share's value is maintained at $1.00. Although the accounts aren't insured by the federal government—as most regular bank accounts are—they almost never have fluctuations in principal, and the per share value remains constant at $1.00.

Given the characteristics of money market accounts, you can take two approaches in your record keeping. You can simply treat your money market account as a regular checking account, setting up an account for it and recording withdrawals and deposits as they occur. If you take this approach, you should reconcile the account on a monthly basis when you receive the monthly money market account statement, just as you do with a regular checking account.

A second, more expeditious approach is to create an asset account called something like Investments and to enter the current money market balance as a transaction in the account. You would also use this account to manage other investments—in fact, this Investments account would be simply a list of the values of all your investments.

The problem with this approach is that it doesn't create a record of transactions that explains the changes to each investment. In the case of your money market account, for example, these transactions might include checks written on the account, additional deposits, and monthly interest credited to the account. The absence of a record of these transactions means you can't reconcile the money market account and won't track income and expenses that flow through the account. Instead, every time the money market account balance changes, no matter what the reason, you'll simply update the transaction representing the money market account.

Figure 8-1 shows a single-line view of an Account Book that simply lists investments. If you're tracking only account balances, you don't need to see category and subcategory fields.

How should you decide between these two approaches? If you want to reconcile the money market account or track the income and expenses that flow through an account, you need to treat a money market account like a regular checking account.

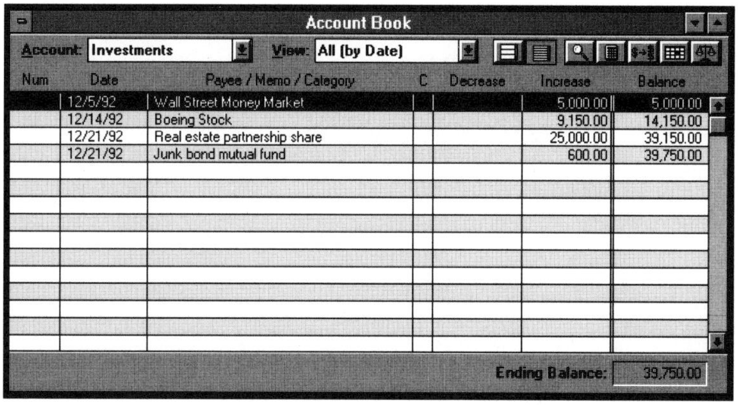

Figure 8-1.
A sample Account Book listing current investment balances.

If your money market account has few transactions, however, you might not want to bother to track its income and expenses. For example, if the only change in your money market account most months is the interest income added to the account, you probably don't need to reconcile it. You also don't need to track the only income flowing through the account—the interest income—because the money market fund manager tracks it for you.

Certificates of Deposit

A certificate of deposit is simply an agreement you make with a bank in which you deposit a certain sum of money; on a specified future date, called the maturity date, the bank repays the money plus a specified amount of interest. The simplest way to keep records of certificates of deposit is to create an asset or bank account called Investments or Certificates and enter each certificate of deposit as a transaction. Using this approach, the Account Book becomes a list of your certificates of deposit, and the account balance is the total value of your certificates.

If a certificate matures and you renew it at the same bank, you can edit the transaction amount to show the new certificate's account balance, including the interest earned. If a certificate matures and you don't renew it, you simply delete the transaction representing the certificate.

If it's important for you to monitor maturity dates, you can include this information in one of the input fields, such as the Memo text box. You can then look for maturing certificates of deposit periodically, using the Account Book window or one of Microsoft Money's reports. Remember, too, that you can use the report customization feature to create reports that list transactions based on the contents of the Date or Memo text box.

If you buy and sell negotiable certificates of deposit, you can also treat them like bonds. In that case, you might want to refer to the section headed Other Bonds later in this chapter.

United States Savings Bonds

You can keep records of your United States Savings Bonds the same way you keep track of certificates of deposit: You create an account called, say, Investments and enter each savings bond as a transaction. The Account Book becomes a list of your savings bonds, and the account balance is the total value of your savings.

There is a record-keeping challenge involved in tracking savings bonds, however. The interest income the bond earns isn't paid to you directly but is added to the value of the bond. As the bond's value increases each year, it earns more interest. For example, when you buy a $50 savings bond, you actually pay something like $25 for it. When it matures, you get back $50. The difference between $25 and $50 represents the interest income the bond earns over the years you hold it. If the bond's interest rate is 6 percent, it earns 6 percent of $25.00, or $1.50 the first year. This increases the bond's value at the end of the first year to $26.50. The second year, at the interest rate of 6 percent, the bond will earn 6 percent of $26.50, or $1.59. This interest, in turn, increases the bond's value at the end of the second year to $28.09. Over the years, the interest added to the bond's value eventually pushes the value to the dollar amount shown on the face of the actual bond.

How should you treat these increases in the bond's value and the interest income earned? As the preceding discussion shows, it's quite a bit of work to track these two items year by year. For this reason, federal tax laws allow you to wait until a savings bond matures to report the interest earned over the bond's entire life. Given this provision and the fact that the amounts earned are usually quite small, it usually makes sense to ignore the year-to-year changes in the bond values as well as the annual interest.

Other Bonds

A bond is simply an agreement you make with a borrower such as the federal government or a corporation. The agreement typically works like this: You lend money to the borrower by buying a certain number of bonds, which the borrower repays by buying back the bonds on a specified future date, called the maturity date. As long as you hold the bond, the borrower pays you interest, usually on a semiannual basis.

Although bonds resemble certificates of deposit, keeping records of them is a little more difficult because a bond's redemption value usually isn't the same as its purchase price. So you not only have to record the interest earned as income, you also have to record as income or expense the difference between the purchase price and the redemption value.

Accounting for Bond Premiums

If you buy a bond for more than the borrower will redeem it for, the extra amount you pay is called a premium. Why would you and other investors pay more for a bond than the borrower will redeem it for? Because the borrower agrees to pay a higher rate of interest than the current rate. For example, imagine that a borrower issues $1,000 bonds that pay 6.6 percent interest, or $66. Subsequent to the issue of the bonds, investors like you decide that 6 percent is the going bond interest rate; a bond that pays $66 is therefore worth more than just $1,000, because $66 is 6 percent of $1,100, not $1,000.

Bond premiums present an accounting problem. In effect, the $100 is an expense, or loss, because although you might pay $1,100 for the bond described in the preceding paragraph, you'll only receive $1,000 when you redeem it. What you should do is spread the $100 bond premium as an expense over the years until the borrower redeems the bond. This is called amortization. To amortize the bond premium, you multiply the effective interest rate the bond earns by its purchase price and then subtract this amount from the actual interest the bond pays for the year. The difference is the bond premium expense that you will record for the first year. (The effective interest rate is simply the total yield, from purchase to maturity—a figure you'll learn when you purchase the bond.)

In the years that follow, you make only one minor modification in this bond-premium allocation formula. Instead of multiplying the effective interest rate the bond earns by the bond purchase price, you multiply the effective interest rate by the bond purchase price minus the bond premium amounts you've already allocated.

Suppose, for example, that you purchase a $1,050 bond that pays an effective interest rate, or yield to maturity, of 6 percent. Further suppose that the bond annually pays $66 in interest. Given these facts, the bond premium charged as expense the first year would be calculated as

$66 − (6\% * \$1,050) = \$3$

During the second year, the bond premium charged to expense would be calculated as

$66 − [6\% * (\$1,050 − \$3)] = \$3.18$

Because you record allocations of bond premiums as expenses, you need to set up an account for each bond you own. You record bond-premium allocations as reductions in the bond account balance and assign the transactions to an expense category called something like Premium or Bond Premiums. (See Figure 8-2.)

Because the ending account balance equals the bond purchase price minus all the bond premiums already allocated, you can simply multiply the effective interest rate by the account ending balance and then subtract this figure from the annual interest actually paid to calculate the next year's allocation of bond premium. In Figure 8-2, I use the Memo text box to document the premium amortization calculation.

Accounting for Bond Discounts

Accounting for bond discounts works much like accounting for bond premiums. As you might have guessed, bond discounts arise when you buy a bond for less than the borrower will redeem it for. The difference between the purchase price and the redemption price is called the discount. The reason for a bond discount mirrors the reason for a bond premium: Whereas a premium indicates that the borrower is paying more than investors require, a discount indicates that the borrower is paying a lower interest rate than investors require.

Suppose, for example, that a borrower issues $1,000 worth of bonds at 6 percent interest, or $60, and that subsequent to the issue investors like you decide that 6.66 percent should be the going rate. In this case, a bond that

Num	Date	Payee / Memo / Category	C	Decrease	Increase	Balance
	1/1/90	Monroe, Stanwood, & Arlington			1,050.00	1,050.00
		initial purchase price				
		Transfer From : Checking				
	12/31/90	Amortization of bond premium		3.00		1,047.00
		$66 minus $1,050 times 6% yield				
		premium				
	12/31/91	Amortization of bond premium		3.18		1,043.82
		$66 minus $1,047 times 6% yield				
		premium				
	12/31/92	Amortization of bond premium		3.56		1,040.26
		$66 minus $1,043.82 times 6%				
		premium				
		Ending Balance:				1,040.26

Figure 8-2.
An Account Book window showing annual amortization of a bond premium as expenses.

pays $60 is worth less than $1,000, because $60 is 6.66 percent of $900, not $1,000.

As you might guess, the $100 difference is income because although you might pay $900 for the bond described in the preceding paragraph, you'll receive $1,000 when you redeem it. You should, therefore, treat the $100 bond discount you receive as income and spread it over the years between purchase and redemption.

To make this discount allocation, you follow a procedure similar to that for allocating a bond premium. You multiply the effective interest rate the bond earns by the bond purchase price and then subtract from this figure the actual interest the bond paid for the year. The difference is the bond discount income to record for the year. As noted earlier, the effective interest rate is simply the yield to maturity—a figure you'll obtain when you purchase the bond.

In the following years, you make only one minor modification in this bond-discount allocation formula. Instead of multiplying the effective interest rate the bond earns by the bond purchase price, you multiply the effective interest rate by the bond purchase price plus the bond discount amounts already allocated in earlier years.

Here's an example of how to deal with a bond discount. Suppose that you purchase a $950 bond that pays an effective interest rate, or yield to maturity, of 6.5 percent. Further suppose that the bond annually pays $60 in interest. Given these facts, the bond discount allocated as income the first year would be calculated as

$$(6.5\% * \$950) - \$60 = \$1.75$$

During the second year, the bond premium charged to expense would be calculated as

$$[6.5\% * (\$950 + \$1.75)] - \$60 = \$1.86$$

Bond discounts, like bond premiums, require you to set up an account for each bond. You then record the bond-discount allocations as increases in the bond account balance and assign the transactions to an income category called something like Discount or Bond Discounts. (Figure 8-3 shows an Account Book window filled out to show the amortization of a bond discount.)

Because the ending account balance equals the bond purchase price plus all the bond discounts already allocated, you can calculate the next year's

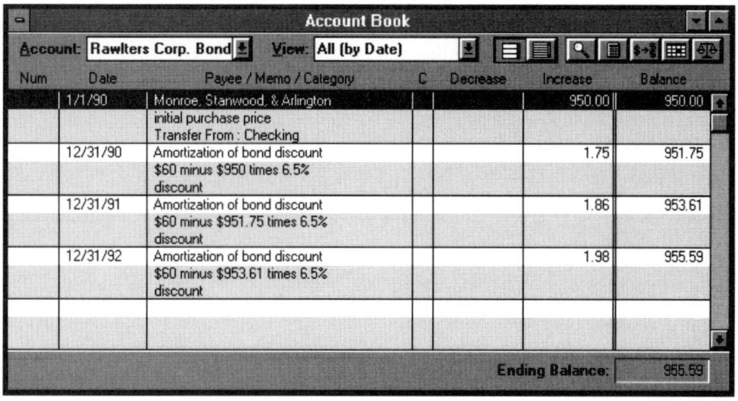

Figure 8-3.
An Account Book window showing annual allocations of a bond discount as income.

allocation of the bond discount by multiplying the effective interest rate by the account's ending balance and then subtracting from this figure the annual interest actually paid.

Reviewing Income Tax Rules
Concerning Discounts and Premiums

At this point, you might be shaking your head over the complexities inherent in dealing with bond premiums and discounts. Before you resign yourself to an annual ritual of calculating the appropriate amount of bond premium or bond discount to allocate as income or expense, you should know that you aren't required to allocate bond premiums. You can simply charge the bond premium as an expense in the year you sell the bond. This approach, however, is not without cost: In the meantime, you pay income taxes on the premium. Eventually, because you are entitled to deduct the bond premium as an expense in the year you sell, you'll get back your overpayment—but that might be 10 or 20 years away. Typically, people want to accelerate income tax deductions, not delay them.

You are required to allocate bond discounts as income, however, unless the effect of doing so is very, very small. Currently, for example, the basic rule is that if the difference between the effective interest rate and the stated interest rate is less than 0.25 percent, or one-fourth of a percent, you don't have to allocate the discount. The stated interest rate is the rate shown on the face of the actual bond. (Consult your tax advisor for up-to-date information on allocating bond discounts and premiums.)

Calculating Gains and Losses on Sales and Redemptions

If you use the approaches described in the preceding paragraphs, calculating the gain or loss on the sale or redemption of a bond is easy. You simply subtract the ending account balance from the sales price. If the difference is a positive amount, you have a gain. If the difference is a negative amount, you have a loss.

Tracking Bond Market Values

The record keeping required by the income tax laws determines how you account for bonds. As a result, you don't record the market values of bonds in your Account Books. If you absolutely must have a report that shows the current market values of your bond investments, you can do so by following these steps. First set up a separate file for storing the market value information of your investments. Then set up an account called Investments, and list each investment as a transaction, showing a transaction amount equal to the investment's market value. (The steps for creating such a separate file are covered in Chapter 6, "Managing Files.")

Mutual Funds

Mutual funds pool the funds of a great number of individuals and then invest the pooled money on behalf of those individuals. Different funds have different purposes, and, accordingly, they invest in different types of securities. For example, there are mutual funds that invest solely in low-grade bonds, high-grade bonds, stocks of domestic companies, stocks of foreign companies, and so forth.

When you purchase shares in a mutual fund, the share price you pay is based on the underlying value of the securities the mutual fund holds. Because the mutual share price fluctuates, the value of your investment fluctuates.

Accounting for mutual fund investments isn't as complicated as accounting for bonds—even if the mutual fund actually invests in bonds. You simply set up an account for each mutual fund and then record each purchase of fund shares—including any reinvestment of dividends—as a transaction. Typically, when you purchase fund shares using money from, say, your checking account, you won't use a category but will instead record the transaction as a transfer from your checking account to the mutual fund. However, when the fund reinvests dividends by purchasing additional shares, you will use an income category to record the fact that you have received dividend income.

The only complicating factor about mutual fund shares crops up when you sell the shares. For income tax purposes, you need to assume that the oldest shares you own are the ones you sell first. For this reason, you need to be sure to record each purchase of shares as a separate transaction in the register. What's more, because you won't always sell the exact number of shares acquired in the oldest purchase transaction, be sure to record both the number of shares and the share price somewhere in the transaction, such as in the Memo field, so you can accurately calculate the gain or loss on the sale. Figure 8-4 shows an Account Book window summarizing purchases of a mutual fund.

Stocks

For the most part, record keeping for stocks works like record keeping for mutual funds, so I will refer you to the preceding section instead of repeating the description. However, stocks do have one unique feature you should consider. For income tax purposes, brokerage commissions aren't tax-deductible expenses. Instead, they are adjustments to purchase and sales prices. Suppose,

Num	Date	Payee / Memo / Category	C	Decrease	Increase	Balance
	2/3/91	Monroe, Stanwood, & Arlington			1,000.00	1,000.00
		76 shares of Phoenix at $13.16				
		Transfer From : Checking				
	12/31/91	Reinvested dividend			100.00	1,100.00
		5 shares of Phoenix at $20.00				
		Investment Income				
	5/24/92	Monroe, Stanwood, & Arlington			1,000.00	2,100.00
		40 shares of Phoenix at $25.00				
		Transfer From : Checking				
	12/31/92	Reinvested dividend			240.00	2,340.00
		8 shares of Phoenix at $30.00				
		Investment Income				
					Ending Balance:	2,340.00

Figure 8-4.
An example of how you might keep records for a mutual fund.

for example, that you purchase $10,000 worth of some company's stock and pay a $100 brokerage commission. Further suppose that you later sell the stock for $12,000 and pay a $150 commission. To calculate the gain, you would subtract the adjusted purchase cost of $10,100 (calculated as the stock purchase price plus the brokerage commission) from the adjusted sales price of $11,850 (calculated as the sales price of the stock minus the brokerage commission paid to sell the stock). The actual gain would be $1,750.

Given the requirement to include brokerage commissions as adjustments to the purchase or sales price, you should usually include them as part of the transaction you record in the register.

401(k) Plans

With 401(k) plans, your record keeping doesn't need to be complicated because the plan trustee does the hard work for you. However, if you're tracking investments and want the value of your 401(k) to appear on reports, you can create an account named something like Investments and enter your 401(k) account balance as a transaction. If you've already created an Investments account, simply include your 401(k) as a transaction in that register. This is the same approach illustrated in Figure 8-1.

To update the transaction amount, either because of additional contributions made to the account or because of account earnings, you simply edit the transaction amount. Typically, trustees prepare account statements on a monthly or quarterly basis; you can use these statements to gather information on the account's current value.

Individual Retirement Accounts

If your individual retirement account (IRA) doesn't include nondeductible contributions, you can use the approach for your 401(k) outlined in the preceding section. If your IRA includes nondeductible contributions, however, you need

 PERSONAL FINANCIAL TIP: You don't need to track the income your 401(k) earns because the income taxes on it are deferred until you actually begin withdrawing the money from the account—usually when you retire.

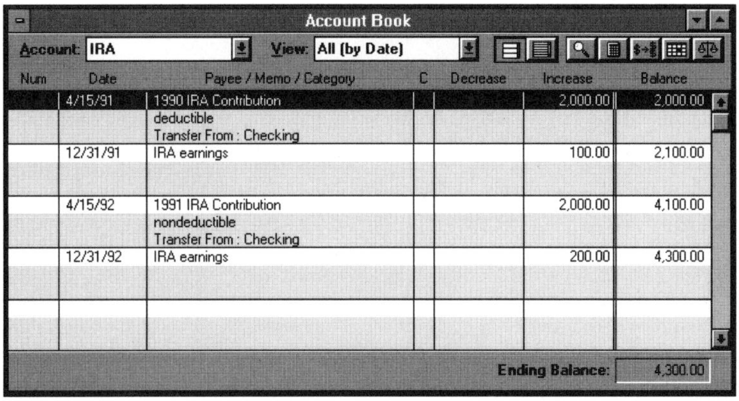

Figure 8-5.
An Account Book tracking deductible and nondeductible IRA contributions and earnings.

to keep track of them because when you ultimately withdraw money from the IRA, you won't pay income taxes on these contributions. You'll pay income taxes only on your deductible contributions and on the earnings of the IRA.

The easiest way to keep track of your nondeductible contributions is to set up an account called something like Individual Retirement Account and then record as a separate transaction each deductible contribution, each nondeductible contribution, and each increase in the account from earnings. Figure 8-5 shows an Account Book window completed to do exactly this.

Credit and Debit Cards

Microsoft Money lets you easily track credit card and debit card spending as well as card balances. Despite the outward similarities of credit and debit cards, however, you use different approaches for each.

Credit Cards

Whether you realize it or not, you already know how to track credit card balances and credit card spending because the process for doing so closely resembles keeping your checkbook. All you do is set up an account for each credit card and begin recording credit card spending and payments. Figure 8-6 shows an Account Book window filled out to record credit card spending.

		Account Book					
Account: VISA		View: All (by Date)					
Num	Date	Payee / Memo / Category	C	Charge	Credit	Balance	
	12/5/92	Del Fonda's Mexican Restaurant		34.61		34.61	
		Food					
	12/10/92	Erwin's Truck Stop		18.92		53.53	
		gas for sedan					
		Automobile					
	12/22/92	Erwin's Truck Stop		25.75		79.28	
		oil change for station wagon					
		Automobile					
					Ending Balance:	79.28	

Figure 8-6.
An Account Book window recording credit card purchases.

Before you go to the trouble of setting up an account for each of your credit cards, you might consider whether they're really necessary. If you always pay off your credit card balance in full at the end of the month, you don't actually need an account for it. When you record the check that pays off the credit card balance in full, you can summarize your credit card spending.

Debit Cards

Debit cards work like credit cards, but instead of maintaining a credit balance that you borrow against, you pay an amount in advance and then spend it by using the debit card. Despite the similarities between credit cards and debit cards, you don't account for them in the same way because debit card balances are assets, just as checking account balances are. Credit card balances, on the other hand, are liabilities. For this reason, you should treat debit cards the same way you treat checking accounts, setting up an account for each debit card and recording the debit card balance as the starting account balance. When you use the debit card, record your spending as a withdrawal and record payments to increase or replenish the debit card balance as deposits. You can use the Balance Accounts command to reconcile your monthly account statement with your records, following the same procedures described in Chapter 5, "Reconciling Your Bank Account."

Real Estate

For many individuals, real estate ownership has a major financial impact on net worth. A home is often a person's single largest asset, and the mortgage used to buy a home is often a person's single largest liability. Home equity credit lines and loans are popular vehicles used to tap the financial wealth a home represents. All these items can complicate your personal finances—especially when it comes to record keeping.

You can use Microsoft Money to simplify the financial record keeping associated with owning real estate. In the next few paragraphs, I describe how to use Microsoft Money to keep financial records of your home's purchase price and the cost of improvements to it, how to account for your mortgage, and how to treat home equity credit lines and loans and seller-financed mortgages.

Personal Residence

The historical appreciation of real estate makes it tempting to track the fair market value of a home. However, it makes more sense to track the original cost of the home as well as the cost of home improvements. The reason for this is that, in general, the gains you realize when you sell a house are taxed as income. There are two exceptions to this rule. You don't have to pay income tax on the gain if you purchase another home of equal or greater value within 24 months of selling the home. And taxpayers age 55 or older are allowed to ignore, once, up to $125,000 of gain on the sale of a primary residence.

Even if you think that one of the two exceptions might apply to you, it makes sense to keep a record of your home's cost as well as the cost of improvements to it. There's no harm in doing so, the work is extremely minimal, and you may save a lot of money.

To keep a record of a home's cost and the cost of improvements, you first set up an asset account named something like Home or Residence. In this account, you record as transactions the original cost of the home as well as associated purchase costs such as escrow fees and title insurance. In the future, whenever you spend money to improve the home, you transfer the money from your checking account to the asset account set up for your home. Figure 8-7 shows an Account Book window filled in with transactions that track the total cost of a home and improvements to it.

Num.	Date	Payee / Memo / Category	C	Decrease	Increase	Balance
	12/5/90	Initial purchase price			100,000.00	100,000.00
		from escrow statement				
	4/15/91	Plants R Us			2,000.00	102,000.00
		front yard landscaping				
		Transfer From : Checking				
	7/17/92	Apex Swimming Pools, Inc.			20,000.00	122,000.00
		swimming pool				
		Transfer From : Checking				

Ending Balance: 122,000.00

Figure 8-7.
A sample Account Book recording the cost of a home and improvements to it.

What qualifies as an improvement? Anything that adds to the value of the home or to its useful life. For example, adding a swimming pool, finishing the basement, and landscaping the site all qualify as improvements. However, such maintenance costs as those for painting the interior or exterior, repairing a leaky roof, or fixing faulty electrical wiring wouldn't qualify as improvements.

Home Mortgage

You can use Microsoft Money to track a home mortgage and the interest and principal portions of mortgage payments. First, you'll need to acquire an amortization schedule, which shows the interest and principal portions of each mortgage payment as well as the mortgage principal balance after each payment. If you know how to use a spreadsheet such as Lotus 1-2-3, Microsoft Excel, Microsoft Works, or Borland's Quattro Pro, you can easily construct an amortization schedule yourself. Figure 8-8 shows the first page of an amortization schedule I built using Microsoft Excel. If you don't know how to use a spreadsheet, you can get an amortization schedule from the mortgage lenders—although they might charge you a few dollars.

As you can see from Figure 8-8, each row of the amortization schedule shows the total mortgage payment, the interest component, the principal portion, and the resulting principal balance after the payment has been credited.

Fixed Interest Rate Amortization Inputs	
Principal	$100,000
Debt Term	360
Amortize Term	360
Interest Rate	0.79%

Home Mortgage Amortization Schedule				
Month Number	Total Payment	Interest Component	Principal Component	Principal Balance
1	$841	$792	$49	$99,951
2	841	791	50	99,901
3	841	791	50	99,851
4	841	790	50	99,801
5	841	790	51	99,750
6	841	790	51	99,699
7	841	789	52	99,647
8	841	789	52	99,595
9	841	788	52	99,543
10	841	788	53	99,490
11	841	788	53	99,437
12	841	787	54	99,383
13	841	787	54	99,329
14	841	786	54	99,275
15	841	786	55	99,220
16	841	785	55	99,164
17	841	785	56	99,109
18	841	785	56	99,052
19	841	784	57	98,996
20	841	784	57	98,939

Figure 8-8.
An amortization schedule.

After you acquire or construct the amortization schedule, you'll need to set up a liability account for the mortgage, setting the starting balance as the current principal balance. When you've done so, you're ready to record the checks you write to pay the mortgage. When you record the check, you simply split the transaction between a transfer to the mortgage liability account and an assignment to the interest expense category. To determine how to record the split, look at the row of the amortization table corresponding to the payment you're making. Figure 8-9 shows how the Split Transaction screen looks when the first mortgage payment shown on the amortization schedule in Figure 8-8 is recorded.

Split Transaction		
Category	Description	Amount
Interest Expense	first mortgage loan payment	792.00
Transfer To : Mortgage	first mortgage loan payment	49.00

| Done | Cancel | Help | Unassigned Amount: | 0.00 |

Figure 8-9.
Splitting a mortgage payment transaction between principal and interest.

You'll need to do one other thing to track your mortgage balances with Microsoft Money. At the end of the year, you'll receive a statement from the mortgage holder reporting the interest and principal paid over the year and the ending mortgage principal balance. When you get this statement, adjust the ending balance shown on the mortgage account to equal the amount the mortgage lender says you owe, categorizing any difference as interest expense.

There will probably be some difference between the figures shown by the amortization schedule and the bank's mortgage statement. The amortization schedule usually assumes that you pay your mortgage on exactly the same day each month and that every month has the same number of days. In actuality, you're unlikely to pay the mortgage on the exact same day each month—and, of course, not all months have the same number of days. These factors cause minor errors in the amortization schedule's allocation of mortgage payments between principal and interest.

Home Equity Lines of Credit and Home Equity Loans

You can also use Microsoft Money to track home equity lines of credit and home equity loans. To track home equity lines of credit, follow the approach described earlier for credit cards. To track home equity loans, follow the approach described in the preceding paragraphs for home mortgages.

Seller-Financed Mortgages

It's possible that you'll sell a house by acting as the mortgage lender. In this case, you can use Microsoft Money to track mortgage balances and interest. First set up an asset account for the mortgage with the starting balance set as the beginning mortgage amount. Every time you deposit a mortgage check into your checking account, you split the transaction between interest income and the mortgage principal. You usually won't use an amortization schedule for the split; instead, you'll calculate the actual interest income. For example, suppose that the borrower last paid you 30 days ago, that the monthly payment is $1,000, that the annual interest rate is 12 percent, and that the mortgage principal balance at the time of the last mortgage payment was $100,000. To calculate the interest income earned since the last payment, you would make the following calculation:

12% annual rate / 365 days a year * 30 days * $100,000

The result of this calculation is $986.10 of interest income. That leaves $13.90 of the monthly payment of $1,000 to apply to principal. In the Split Transaction dialog box, then, you would categorize $986.10 as interest income and transfer $13.90 to the Mortgage asset account.

Insurance

Although you don't really need to keep financial records of your insurance coverage, there are a few related issues Microsoft Money can help you handle. For example, some life insurance policies contain an investment component; and annuities, another life insurance company product, are themselves investments that you may want to account for. It's also not a bad idea to maintain records of property insurance policies for the assets you own.

Whole and Universal Life Insurance Policies

Both whole and universal life insurance policies contain an investment component. A portion of the premium goes into a savings account. Over time, the savings account grows as portions of your premium payments continue to be added to the savings account and the savings account itself earns interest. This savings account is an investment, and you can treat it as such. Because you don't need to track the income the savings account earns, you don't need to do anything fancy. The simplest approach is set up an account for Investments, if you haven't already done so, and enter as a transaction the cash surrender value of the life insurance policy. (This same approach is described for tracking 401[k] investments and illustrated in Figure 8-1.)

To update the cash surrender value to reflect premium additions or earnings on the account, you simply edit the transaction amount to correspond to the current cash surrender value shown on the insurance company's annual policy statement.

Annuities

At least in terms of financial record keeping, annuities work exactly like deductible individual retirement accounts and 401(k) accounts. You can create an account named something like Investments and enter the annuity purchase price as a transaction in the Account Book. If you've already created an Investment account, you could include the annuity as a transaction in that register. To update the transaction amount to reflect either additional contributions made to the annuity or the annuity's earnings, edit the transaction amount. Don't worry about tracking the income that the annuity earns. Income taxes on annuity earnings, like those on IRAs and 401(k)s, are deferred until you actually begin withdrawing the money. (This same approach is illustrated in Figure 8-1.)

Asset Lists for Property and Casualty Insurance

One other insurance record-keeping task for which you should consider using Microsoft Money is maintaining lists of personal property you've insured. The reason is probably clear: If disaster strikes, a list of the insured items can make claim reports and collections easier and more complete.

 PERSONAL FINANCIAL TIP: It's obvious, but I should point out that this list won't do you much good if your computer and all your backup disks are lost in a fire or flood, along with everything else. For this reason, you should keep an up-to-date copy of your asset list in a secure place such as a safety deposit box.

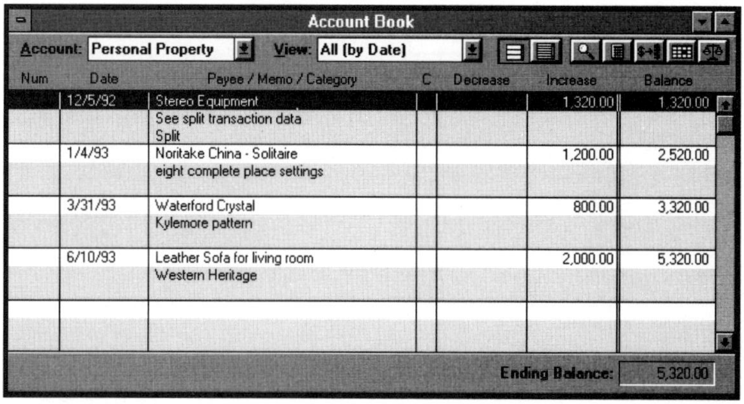

Figure 8-10.
A sample asset list for property or casualty insurance purposes.

To create such an asset list, set up an account called something like Personal Property and carefully list all assets you've insured. As you purchase major items in the future, remember to add them to the list. The more information on your list, the better. If possible, include information like model numbers and original costs. Remember that you can use the Split Transaction dialog box to store additional data. Figure 8-10 shows a sample asset list you might maintain for property or casualty insurance purposes.

A Few Words on Measuring Your Net Worth

The preceding paragraphs of this chapter describe how to use Microsoft Money to track individual assets and liabilities. If you track all your assets and liabilities, you can also track your net worth. This possibility raises three issues that I'll briefly discuss before concluding the chapter.

Most of the techniques I've described don't provide market-value estimates of your assets and liabilities. Instead, they focus on what you need to do for income tax accounting. (For most people, saving money on their income taxes and making tax return preparation easier is more important than knowing their net worth.) As a result, the Net Worth Report that Microsoft Money produces might not accurately measure your net worth. If there are differences between the ending account balances and the market values of your assets and liabilities, the net worth that Microsoft Money calculates will be wrong.

A second issue concerns the organization of the file in which you store account information. Specifically, you need to store all accounts relating to a particular person in the same file if you want to measure that person's net worth. To measure your own net worth, therefore, you shouldn't include accounts that really belong to the business you own, to your spouse, or to one of your children. These accounts should be stored in their own, independent files.

A third and final issue related to measuring your net worth is that, in most cases, not all your assets should be counted as part of your net worth. The reason is that the actual market value of certain assets is quite low or is temporary. For example, furniture doesn't belong in your calculation of net worth, even if you have very nice furniture for which you spent a lot of money. Similarly, your wedding china usually doesn't belong, nor your skiing equipment or stereo gear. If you'll be tracking these kinds of assets with Microsoft Money, perhaps for property and casualty insurance purposes, you might want to set up a separate file for these accounts.

Conclusion

This chapter covers the whole range of personal financial record-keeping tasks you can perform with Microsoft Money. You obviously won't want to use Microsoft Money for every task described in the chapter. But for those you do undertake, the suggestions and ideas here should make using Microsoft Money easier and more convenient.

Chapter 9

USING MICROSOFT MONEY IN A BUSINESS

You can use Microsoft Money for business accounting, but because it isn't specifically designed for such work, you'll have to resort to a few tricks. This chapter describes these tricks, as well as the techniques you'll employ to perform all the standard business accounting tasks: payroll, inventory, accounts receivable, liabilities, and fixed assets. At the end of the chapter, I discuss some advanced accounting issues, such as owners' equity accounting and multiple-state accounting and describe important month-end and year-end procedures.

However, you don't necessarily need to study this chapter from front to back. Simply read the sections that apply to financial record-keeping tasks you want to automate using Microsoft Money. And don't mistake the inclusion of a topic here as evidence that you, too, should be using Microsoft Money for that particular purpose. The general rule is to automate a task only if doing so will save you time and make running your business easier—and you're the best judge of that.

Payroll

Although Microsoft Money doesn't provide a payroll feature as such, it can print checks and so can easily be used to print payroll checks. The mechanics of check printing are covered in Chapter 7; here, I will simply describe how to calculate and record payroll deductions and taxes.

Preparing Checks

To prepare payroll checks, you need to set up several new liability accounts and expense categories. You need liability accounts to record the money you owe the federal government for employer payroll taxes, to account for employee social security, to keep track of medicare taxes, and to monitor employees' federal income tax withholdings. You also need to define the following expense categories: gross pay, employer's social security and medicare tax, and federal unemployment tax. I'll demonstrate only the federal payroll taxes; you follow the same procedure for state payroll taxes.

Suppose you have an employee to whom you pay $600 twice a month. Further suppose that, based on the employee's W-4 form and the current Circular E Employer's Tax Guide, you're supposed to withhold $70 per pay period for federal income taxes; that the employee's social security withholdings amount to $37.20 per pay period and his or her medicare taxes come to $8.70 per period; that you must match the employee's social security and medicare taxes; and, finally, that you must pay $10 in federal unemployment tax. Given this information, you would enter the employee's semimonthly payroll information in the Split Transaction dialog box as shown in Figure 9-1.

The Split Transaction dialog box shows four transfers: the first transfer records the liability stemming from the federal unemployment tax; the second recognizes the liability resulting from the employee's social security withholding and from the employer's matching social security withholding; the third recognizes the liability that stems from the employee's medicare taxes withheld and the employer's matching medicare taxes; and the fourth recognizes the liability that stems from the federal income taxes withheld from the employee's check. The Split Transaction dialog box also shows four expense categories, one for the employee's gross pay, one for the employer's social security taxes, one for the employer's medicare taxes, and one for the federal unemployment tax.

The net amount of the payroll check is $484.10, which is the sum of all the expenses categorized as well as the funds transferred in the Split Transaction dialog box. If you've performed the arithmetic correctly, however, the payroll check amount should also equal the gross pay amount minus the employee's social security and medicare withholdings and the federal income tax withheld.

In Figure 9-1, all the expense categories and transfer accounts are grouped together to show on the sample screen. The social security and medicare Transfer From amounts, for example, combine both the employee's deduction and

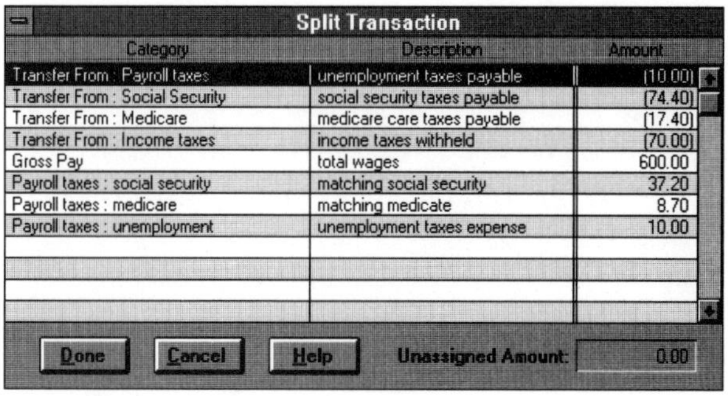

Category	Description	Amount
Transfer From : Payroll taxes	unemployment taxes payable	(10.00)
Transfer From : Social Security	social security taxes payable	(74.40)
Transfer From : Medicare	medicare care taxes payable	(17.40)
Transfer From : Income taxes	income taxes withheld	(70.00)
Gross Pay	total wages	600.00
Payroll taxes : social security	matching social security	37.20
Payroll taxes : medicare	matching medicate	8.70
Payroll taxes : unemployment	unemployment taxes expense	10.00

Split Transaction

Done   Cancel   Help   Unassigned Amount: 0.00

Figure 9-1.
A sample payroll check's Split Transaction dialog box.

the employer's matching liability. You will probably want to separate out the portions of the Transfer From amounts that stem from these two sources.

You might also want to segregate those pieces of the transaction that affect only the employer from those that affect the employee. For example, the Transfer From amounts that relate to the employer's matching of social security and medicare deductions, the unemployment tax expense, and the unemployment tax liability could appear together. (You could, for example, put these pieces of the transaction several lines below the expense category and transfer accounts that apply to the employee.)

Making Tax Deposits

On a periodic basis, you must pay the federal government the amounts you owe it, based on the federal unemployment taxes you've calculated, your matching of social security and medicare contributions, and the money withheld from the employee's gross pay for social security, medicare, and income taxes. How often you have to pay depends on how much money you owe; you'll find this information in the current Circular E Employer's Tax Guide. However, you can learn how much you owe simply by totaling the payroll tax liability accounts. The combined total ending balances of these accounts equal the payroll tax deposit you owe. (A convenient way to calculate this amount is to use the Net Worth Report described in Chapter 7.)

Suppose that you use the payroll tax liability accounts shown in Figure 9-1 and that the transaction shown is the only one to affect payroll tax liability. When you write the check paying the tax deposit, you will split the transaction between the four accounts shown: $10 to the unemployment taxes payable account, $74.40 to the social security taxes payable account, $17.40 to the medicare taxes payable account, and $70 to the income taxes withheld account. After you record the check, each of the four payroll tax liability accounts will have a zero ending balance.

Filing Quarterly and Annual Payroll Tax Returns

Employers need to complete a 941 or 942 payroll tax return on a quarterly basis. It requires employers to report the total wages paid, calculate and report social security and medicare taxes, and report federal income tax withheld. You calculate social security and medicare payments by multiplying their tax percentages by the total gross pay. To figure out how much federal income tax was withheld, look at the liability account for federal income taxes withheld.

There is one potential problem with the approach described in the preceding paragraph. Employees pay social security and medicare taxes only on wages below ceiling amounts. For example, in 1991, employees paid social security taxes of 6.2 percent only on wages up to $53,400 and medicare taxes of 1.45 percent only on wages up to $125,000. These ceiling amounts increase every year based on inflation. If you have employees who make more than the ceiling amounts, you won't be able to print out a report that summarizes the total Gross Pay expense category, because social security and medicare taxes won't be owed on the entire amount.

To get around this problem, print a Net Worth Report that provides the account balances for the social security and medicare tax liability accounts. Assuming you've figured these amounts correctly, you can then calculate wages subject to social security based on the social security taxes owed. For example, if you owe $6,200 of social security, you know that half of the $6,200 is social security taxes employees paid on their wages, because employers must match employee deductions for social security and medicare. If the social security tax percentage is 6.2 percent, the total wages subject to social security is $3,100 divided by 6.2 percent, or $50,000. Similarly, you can calculate the wages subject to medicare tax based on the medicare taxes owed. If you owe $1,450 of medicare, half of the $1,450, or $725, is medicare taxes the employees paid on their wages. If the medicare tax percentage is 1.45 percent, the total wages subject to medicare is $725 divided by 1.45 percent, or $50,000.

Preparing W-2s and the W-3

The one other payroll task you must complete is the annual preparation of W-2 forms and the W-3 form. You complete a W-2 for each employee to summarize the gross pay earned over the year, the social security and medicare taxes withheld, and the federal income taxes withheld. You also complete a W3 form, which summarizes the W2s. Although you won't be able to use Microsoft Money to print these forms, you can use it to calculate the needed summary information. Simply print a report that summarizes your payroll transactions by employee, or payee, and that gives subtotals for the expense categories and transfer accounts used to split the transactions. (For information on how to print reports, refer to Chapter 7, "Printing.")

Inventory Accounting

Manufacturing, wholesale, and retail businesses have a unique record-keeping requirement: inventory accounting. Inventory record keeping should do two things: tell you how much inventory you're currently holding, in dollars and in units, and tell you how much inventory you've sold, in dollars and in units, over a given period, such as the last month or the last year.

Because Microsoft Money tracks only dollars, you won't be able to track the units of inventory you're holding or the units of inventory you've sold. However, there are two accounting techniques you can use to calculate, or at least estimate, the dollar value of inventory held and sold: They're called the periodic inventory method and the gross margin method.

The Periodic Method

The periodic inventory system gets its name from the fact that you measure your inventory only periodically. But every time you do so, you end up with a fairly accurate accounting of what you're holding as well as a reasonable estimate of the inventory sold since you last measured it.

Suppose, for example, that you started your business a year ago. Further suppose that at that time you held $12,000 worth of inventory and that over the ensuing year you purchased $35,000 worth of inventory. If you physically count the inventory currently on the shelves of your store and find you're holding $7,000 of inventory, you will, of course, know both the dollar value and the number of units held. But you can also estimate the inventory you've sold over the last year by using the following formula.

Beginning inventory balance + inventory purchases over the year − ending inventory balance = inventory sold over the year

To use this system with Microsoft Money, you simply set up an account for your inventory with the starting balance set to your current holdings. Each time you purchase something for resale, you transfer the money spent to the inventory account. Then, on a periodic basis, say monthly or quarterly, you physically count the units and dollars of inventory and enter a transaction in the inventory Account Book to adjust the inventory account to the true balance. For the transaction's expense category, you use an account defined solely for tracking the cost of the inventory sold. It might have a name such as Cost of Goods Sold or Inventory Sold.

Figure 9-2 shows the Account Book window with transactions recording a beginning inventory of $12,000, $35,000 in inventory purchases over the year, and the final cost-of-goods-sold transaction that adjusts the ending inventory balance to the actual physical count of the inventory, $7,000.

A system like the one described is easy to use. It will periodically tell you how much inventory you hold and how much you've sold. However, such a system has some drawbacks.

The first problem is that every time you want to calculate how much inventory you hold and how much you've sold, you need to physically count your stock. Unfortunately, only when you perform this physical count do you know for sure what inventory you're holding and what you've sold since the last count. You can solve this problem by frequent physical counts, but that's a lot of work. In practice, you'll probably find it difficult to count inventory more than once or twice a year if your holdings are at all substantial.

A second problem with a periodic system is that it implicitly assumes that the only reason your inventory balances decrease is that you sell items. Unfortunately, that's usually not the case; employee theft, shoplifting, breakage, and spoilage all decrease inventory balances. A periodic system lumps together all

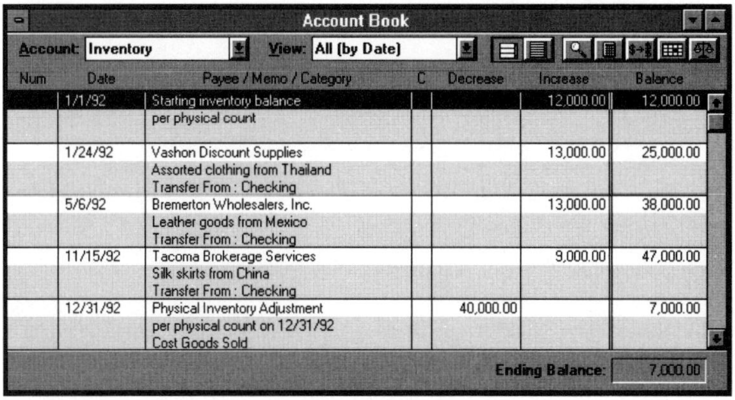

Num	Date	Payee / Memo / Category	C	Decrease	Increase	Balance
	1/1/92	Starting inventory balance per physical count			12,000.00	12,000.00
	1/24/92	Vashon Discount Supplies Assorted clothing from Thailand Transfer From : Checking			13,000.00	25,000.00
	5/6/92	Bremerton Wholesalers, Inc. Leather goods from Mexico Transfer From : Checking			13,000.00	38,000.00
	11/15/92	Tacoma Brokerage Services Silk skirts from China Transfer From : Checking			9,000.00	47,000.00
	12/31/92	Physical Inventory Adjustment per physical count on 12/31/92 Cost Goods Sold		40,000.00		7,000.00

Ending Balance: 7,000.00

Figure 9-2.
An Account Book window showing sample periodic system inventory transactions.

the reasons for inventory balance decreases, whereas it might be important to know how much of the decrease stems from sales and how much stems from other causes. For example, if you're a retailer and shoplifting becomes a significant reason for inventory balance decreases, you might want to install in-store surveillance cameras. If you're a food wholesaler and find you're losing a big chunk of your inventory through spoilage, you might want to consider creating special refrigerated storage areas.

The Gross Margin Method

Another inventory accounting technique you can use with Microsoft Money is a perpetual system based on the average cost of goods sold of the items you sell (that is, the gross margin). As with the periodic approach, you'll need to set up an account for tracking the inventory and enter the starting balance as the inventory you currently hold—for which you might need to perform a physical count of your inventory.

Next calculate your average cost of goods sold. For example, if half your business involves selling skis that cost you $40 for $100 and the other half of your business is selling ski boots that cost $60 for $100, here's how you would calculate your average cost of goods.

Skis at $40 / $100 * 50%	20%
Boots at $60 / $100 * 50%	30%
Average cost of goods sold	50%

Finally, every time you make a sale, you record a decrease in your inventory balance equal to the percentage of the average cost of goods sold times the sale amount. So, if you sell a pair of ski boots for $100, you record a $50 decrease (50 percent of $100) in the inventory balance account and categorize the transaction as a cost-of-goods-sold expense. Similarly, if you sell a pair of skis for $100, you record a $50 decrease (50 percent of $100) in the inventory balance account and again categorize the transaction as a cost-of-goods-sold expense.

Even with this system, you'll want to count the inventory you're holding periodically in order to correct for inaccuracies in the cost-of-goods-sold percentage and to account for other reasons your inventory balances decrease, such as theft or spoilage.

The average cost-of-goods-sold system isn't without fault. The major problem is that the average cost-of-goods-sold percentage is never precisely correct because, after all, it is only an average. If your actual sales don't match those assumed in your percentage calculation—50 percent skis and 50 percent ski boots in the preceding example—both your cost-of-goods-sold figure and your ending inventory balance will be incorrect. In general, these averaging errors cancel each other out—but not if you start selling many more skis than boots, or vice versa.

Accounts Receivable

Most businesses have receivables—amounts customers owe for products or services received but not yet paid for. Accurate, detailed records of these receivables are important because they usually represent a major business asset that needs to be carefully monitored. Customer payments on receivables are, after all, a business's primary source of cash.

You can use Microsoft Money to track these receivables, as well as the payments on them. This section will explain how to track receivables as well as how to age receivables and treat uncollectible amounts.

Tracking Unpaid Invoices and Customer Payments

The best approach to tracking unpaid customer invoices and the payments that customers make on these invoices is to set up each individual invoice as an account. For example, when you write invoice number 90-234 to Geronimo Manufacturing for $1,000 in consulting services, you create an asset account named something like Geronimo 90-234 and set the starting balance as 0. You then record a transaction to increase the account balance to $1,000 and assign the transaction to whatever category you've chosen to summarize your sales. Figure 9-3 shows an example of an Account Book window completed in this way.

> **TIP**
>
> **MICROSOFT MONEY TIP:** *Because invoices usually don't require special formatting, you can easily prepare an invoice using the Windows Write accessory program. Then using the Cut, Copy, and Paste commands that appear on the Edit menus in both the Write application and Microsoft Money, you can copy the invoice amount from an invoice created in Write to the Account Book.*

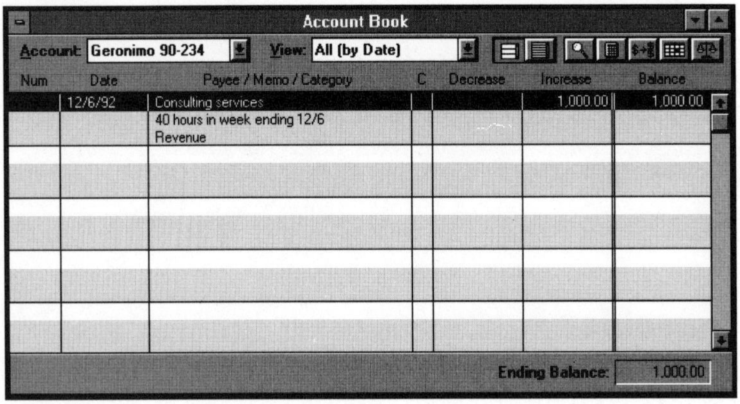

	Account Book	

Account: Geronimo 90-234   View: All (by Date)

Num	Date	Payee / Memo / Category	C	Decrease	Increase	Balance
	12/6/92	Consulting services			1,000.00	1,000.00
		40 hours in week ending 12/6				
		Revenue				

Ending Balance: 1,000.00

Figure 9-3.
The Account Book used to track unpaid customer receivables.

Later, when the customer pays the invoice, you record the deposit in your checking account. However, rather than assign the deposit to an income category, you should transfer it from the account you set up for the receivable. If the customer pays the total amount of the invoice, which is the usual case, the ending balance of the receivable account drops to zero. If a single check pays several receivables, you simply split the deposit transaction so that it reflects transfers from several accounts. Figure 9-4 shows the Account Book window after the transfer transaction is recorded.

The two purposes of tracking receivables are to keep track of how much money your customers owe you and to make sure you collect that money. Although you don't generally need to continue tracking the account after you collect on a receivable, you shouldn't delete the account. When you first enter the invoice in the receivables account, you are recording the sale. If you delete the account, you also delete the record of the sale.

If you absolutely must delete an account—perhaps because you've run out of disk space—edit the checking account deposit transaction that transferred money in from the receivable account so that it assigns the deposit to the appropriate income category.

Agings

Accounts-receivable agings group customer receivables by date. Usually, there are groupings for receivables less than a month old, more than a month old

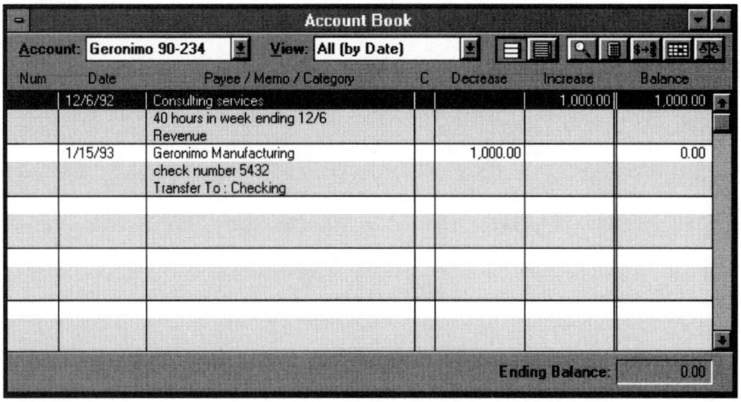

Figure 9-4.
A checking account deposit recorded as a transfer to the receivable account. The receivable balance is reduced by the amount of the deposit.

but less than two months old, and more than two months old. Receivable agings are useful tools because they highlight receivables that might require special effort to collect. (Usually the older a receivable gets, the more difficult it becomes to collect.)

To create an aging of receivables, you produce a Summary Report showing receivable amounts in rows and months in columns. Figure 9-5 is an example of an aging report shown in the Summary Report window.

Uncollectible Receivables and Bad Debts

If a receivable becomes uncollectible, you have two ways to account for it. You can simply delete the account. Because the sales amount is recorded in the receivable account, deleting the account removes the sale. The second method is to record a transaction decreasing the receivable account's ending balance and assigning the transaction to an expense category set up to track bad debts.

Accrual versus Cash Accounting

If you want to use the techniques outlined in the preceding paragraphs on receivables, you should know about the difference between accrual-based and cash-based accounting. Checkbook programs such as Microsoft Money use cash-based accounting. This simply means that when money flows into your

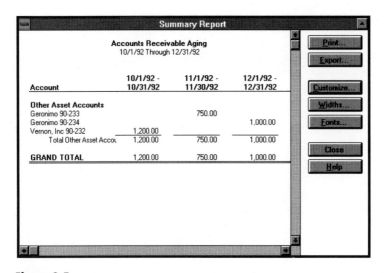

Figure 9-5.
A sample receivables aging report.

checking account, it's usually income, and when money flows out of your checking account, it's usually an expense. (The only exception is when you're actually transferring money between accounts, such as from savings to checking.) Cash-based accounting is convenient, and, in all likelihood, it's what you want to use to prepare your income tax return.

When you begin setting up receivables in their own accounts, however, you've actually taken a huge step in the direction of accrual-based accounting. With accrual-based accounting, you record a sale when it occurs, not when you collect the money. However, this also means that you record an expense when you incur it, not when you have to pay it. Accrual-based accounting is generally a better accounting system than cash-based accounting because it measures your profits more accurately and lets you keep detailed records of such items as your customer receivables. However, there is a practical problem with accrual-based accounting.

Because a checkbook program like Microsoft Money isn't designed to handle accrual-based accounting, it's easy to assign income and expense transactions to the wrong periods. For example, if you delete an account that records a receivable, thereby deleting the record of the sale, you need to adjust the deposit transaction to record the sale. (This procedure is described earlier in this chapter in the section headed Tracking Unpaid Invoices and Customer Payments.) However, if the date of the original transaction differs from the date of the deposit transaction—and they will differ—you've moved the date of the sale. This might seem innocuous, and many times it will be. But sometimes it isn't.

When you move a transaction from one month to another or from one year to another, you've changed the sales figures for the two months or for the two years. This means the old sales figures are wrong, as well as anything that's based on those figures. Unfortunately, you might already have prepared financial statements and tax returns based on the old sales figures. How should you deal with this problem? Just remember that, when you change a sale's transaction date, you might change your old sales figures for the month or year—which simply means you shouldn't use the old sales figures.

Liability Accounting

Liability accounting in a business works in essentially the same way it does for home record keeping. In fact, if you read the last chapter, you'll notice that credit lines work in roughly the same way as credit cards and that bank loans work in roughly the same way as home mortgages.

Credit Lines

Tracking credit-line balances and credit-line spending closely resembles keeping your checkbook. You set up a liability account for the credit line and then begin recording credit-line withdrawals and payments. Figure 9-6 shows an example of an Account Book window filled out to record a credit line withdrawal, an interest charge, and a payment.

Bank Loans

You can use Microsoft Money to track bank-loan balances as well as the interest and principal portions of the loan payments you make. But first you need to acquire an amortization schedule, which shows the interest and principal portions of each mortgage payment, as well as the mortgage principal balance after each payment. If you know how to use a spreadsheet such as Lotus 1-2-3, Microsoft Excel, Microsoft Works, or Borland's Quattro Pro, you can easily construct an amortization schedule yourself. Figure 9-7 shows an amortization schedule I built using Microsoft Excel. If you don't know how to use a spreadsheet or don't want to, you can also get a schedule from the bank.

		Account Book				▼ ▲
Account: Credit Line		View: All (by Date)				
Num	Date	Payee / Memo / Category	C	Increase	Decrease	Balance
	12/1/92	Draw for buying new delivery van		25,000.00		25,000.00
		Transfer To : Checking				
	12/31/92	Credit line interest for month		250.00		25,250.00
		1% interest on average balance				
		Interest Expense				
205	1/5/93	Washington State Bank			2,000.00	23,250.00
		pay down portion of line				
		Transfer From : Checking				
					Ending Balance:	23,250.00

Figure 9-6.
An Account Book window showing credit-line activity.

As you can see from Figure 9-7, each row of the amortization schedule shows the total loan payment, the interest component of the payment, the principal portion of the payment, and the resulting loan principal balance.

After you've acquired or constructed the amortization schedule, you need to establish a liability account for the bank loan, setting the current principal balance as the opening balance. At this point, you're ready to record the checks you write to the bank. When you record the check for the loan payment, you simply split the transaction between a transfer to the loan liability account and an assignment to the interest expense category. To determine how you should make the split, look at the row of the amortization table corresponding to the payment you're making. Figure 9-8 shows how the Split Transaction screen looks after you record the first payment shown on the amortization schedule in Figure 9-7.

Fixed Interest Rate Amortization Inputs	
Principal	$25,000
Debt Term	36
Amortize Term	36
Interest Rate	1.00%

Fixed Interest Rate Amortization Schedule				
Period	Total Payment	Interest Component	Principal Component	Principal Balance
1	$830	$250	$580	$24,420
2	830	244	586	23,833
3	830	238	592	23,241
4	830	232	598	22,644
5	830	226	604	22,040
6	830	220	610	21,430
7	830	214	616	20,814
8	830	208	622	20,191
9	830	202	628	19,563
10	830	196	635	18,928
11	830	189	641	18,287
12	830	183	647	17,640
13	830	176	654	16,986
14	830	170	661	16,325
15	830	163	667	15,658
16	830	157	674	14,984
17	830	150	681	14,304
18	830	143	687	13,616
19	830	136	694	12,922
20	830	129	701	12,221
21	830	122	708	11,513
22	830	115	715	10,798
23	830	108	722	10,075
24	830	101	730	9,346
25	830	93	737	8,609
26	830	86	744	7,865
27	830	79	752	7,113
28	830	71	759	6,354
29	830	64	767	5,587
30	830	56	774	4,812
31	830	48	782	4,030
32	830	40	790	3,240
33	830	32	798	2,442
34	830	24	806	1,636
35	830	16	814	822
36	830	8	822	0

Figure 9-7.
An amortization schedule.

Checks & Forms

Account: Checking   View: All (by Date)

Check | Deposit | Payment | Transfer

Transfer   # 206

From: Checking   Date: 12/6/92

To: Loan $ 830.00

Eight Hundred Thirty and no/100××× **Dollars**

Pay To: Washington State Bank

Memo: First payment on $25,000 loan

Ending Balance: [16,035.64]

Split Transaction

Category	Description	Amount
Transfer To : Loan	First payment on $25,000 loan	580.00
Interest Expense	First payment on $25,000 loan	250.00

Figure 9-8.
Splitting a loan payment transaction between principal and interest.

There is one other action you need to take when tracking loan balances with Microsoft Money. At the end of the year, you'll receive a statement from the lender reporting the interest and principal paid over the year and the ending loan balance. When you get this statement, adjust the Account Book's ending balance to equal the bank's ending balance. Categorize any difference as interest expense.

There will undoubtedly be differences between what the amortization schedule shows and what the bank's loan statement shows. The amortization schedule usually assumes that you make your loan payment on exactly the same day each month and that every month has the same number of days. In actuality, you're unlikely to make the payment on exactly the same day each month—and, of course, not all months have the same number of days. These two factors cause minor errors in the amortization schedule's allocation of loan payments between principal and interest.

Fixed Assets Accounting

Fixed assets—such as equipment, machinery, and furniture—can be tracked in a Microsoft Money Account Book. To do this, you create an account for each asset or asset group, setting the opening balance as the original purchase price. You might also want to enter as a transaction any depreciation you charge on the asset.

For example, suppose you purchase a truck for $200,000 that you expect to use for five years. At the end of the five years, you expect the truck to have no salvage value. In this case, you might choose to depreciate the truck's purchase price by allocating the $200,000 in even portions over the five years you plan to use it. This depreciation method is known as straight-line depreciation. Figure 9-9 shows how your Account Book might look if you chose this approach. (You can record the depreciation transactions all at once as long as you use as transaction dates the dates the depreciation is actually charged rather than the date you enter the transactions in the Account Book.)

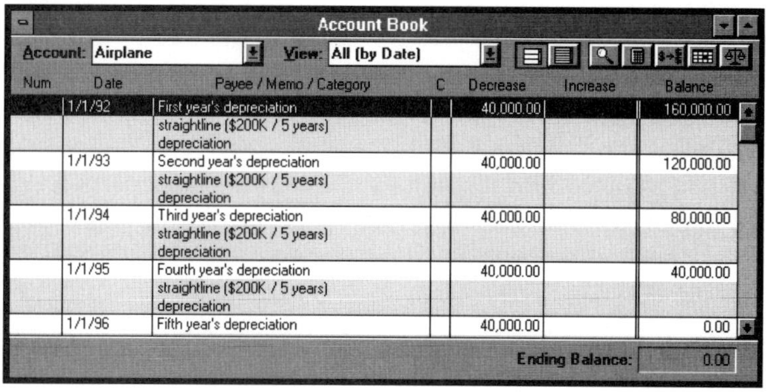

Num	Date	Payee / Memo / Category	C	Decrease	Increase	Balance
	1/1/92	First year's depreciation straightline ($200K / 5 years) depreciation		40,000.00		160,000.00
	1/1/93	Second year's depreciation straightline ($200K / 5 years) depreciation		40,000.00		120,000.00
	1/1/94	Third year's depreciation straightline ($200K / 5 years) depreciation		40,000.00		80,000.00
	1/1/95	Fourth year's depreciation straightline ($200K / 5 years) depreciation		40,000.00		40,000.00
	1/1/96	Fifth year's depreciation		40,000.00		0.00
					Ending Balance:	0.00

Account: Airplane   View: All (by Date)

Figure 9-9.
Recording fixed assets and depreciation on fixed assets in the Account Book.

Miscellaneous Accounting Issues

Other business accounting issues you might need to address using Microsoft Money include multiple-state accounting, multiple-company accounting, sales returns, and accounting for owners' equity. Any one of these issues can drastically complicate your use of Microsoft Money, so I'll briefly discuss each of them and make some suggestions that might save you time and frustration.

Multiple-State Accounting

If your firm transacts business in more than one state, you usually need to track the sales, and sometimes the expenses, associated with each state's activities. The way to do so is to set up State as a classification, with individual states as items. For example, if you sell your products in three states, California, Nevada, and Arizona, you create three items in the State classification. If you also need to track sales and expenses within a state, such as by county, you can use sub-items. (Chapter 4, "Supercharging Your Checkbook," describes how to use the Other Classification command on the List menu to create classifications, items, and sub-items.)

Multiple-Company Accounting

Multiple-company accounting generally means one of two things. It can mean that you keep records for more than one business. For example, if you are an accountant who performs financial record keeping for several business clients, you might use Microsoft Money for each client's records. A second type of multiple-company accounting involves keeping accounts for several related businesses owned by the same person or group. At some point, you will want to combine the sales and expenses for all the businesses to create a consolidated statement of income and a consolidated balance sheet. The appropriate technique for using Microsoft Money for multiple-company accounting depends on the specific situation.

To use Microsoft Money to perform financial record keeping for several unrelated business, as an accountant or bookkeeper might, you simply set up different files, one for each business. Suppose you want to use Microsoft Money for three businesses: Doctor Leslie's medical practice, Ben's Landscaping Service, and James Hughes, Attorney. You could set up three separate files: DRLESLIE, BENSLAND, and JHUGHES. (Chapter 6, "Managing Files," describes how to create and use different files.)

To use Microsoft Money to perform financial record keeping for several businesses with the same ownership, you'll need to use the Other Classification feature. You'll set up a Business classification with an item for each business and record the classification whenever you enter an income or expense transaction. Say, for example, that you own three businesses: a restaurant named Bud's, a janitorial service named Acme Cleaning, and a small herb farm named Herb's Herbs. You might create a Business class with three items: Bud's, Acme, and Herb's. To produce an income statement for a particular business, you would specify that only transactions falling into the relevant classification be included. (Chapter 4, "Supercharging Your Checkbook," describes how to use the Other Classification command on the List menu. Chapter 7, "Printing," describes producing reports that include only transactions falling into particular classifications.)

Accounting for Partnership and Corporation Owners' Equity

Owners' equity refers to the difference between a business's total assets and its total liabilities. This difference is also called a firm's net worth, and it is calculated and presented on Microsoft Money's Net Worth Report. For sole proprietorships—that is, businesses owned by a single person—this approach is usually perfectly adequate. For partnerships and corporations, however, each owner—whether a partner or corporate shareholder—wants to know what portion of the owners' equity belongs to him or her. This requirement presents some problems, but following the approach described below, you can construct a workable solution.

Partnerships

In the case of a partnership, a separate liability account should be set up for each partner. This account isn't really a liability account, because the partner isn't legally owed any money; rather, the account is the partner's capital, or owners' equity, account. The initial transaction to this account should record the original capital contributed by the partner; you wouldn't assign any income or expense transaction category. After you have set up all the partners' capital accounts, the total assets in them should equal what Microsoft Money labels as the total liabilities, and the net worth figure that Microsoft Money calculates on the net worth statement should equal zero. Suppose, for example, that three lawyers have just formed a new law partnership by contributing $10,000 each in cash. Figure 9-10 shows a sample Net Worth Report recording these transactions.

If a partner draws money out of the partnership, record the withdrawal as a transfer from his or her capital account. If a partner receives a share of the firm's profits, record that share as an increase in his or her capital account

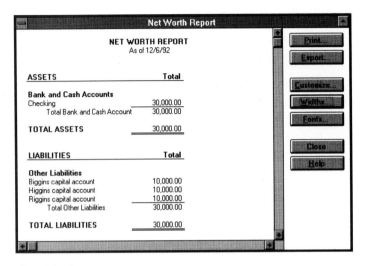

Figure 9-10.
The beginning Net Worth Report of a partnership.

without assigning any income or expense category. When the partnership profits are distributed among the partners, the amount to be distributed should equal the total profits earned since the last profit distribution. You can get this total profits figure from an Income and Expense Report summarizing the income and expenses since the last profit distribution. (If you correctly distribute 100 percent of the partnership profits, Microsoft Money shows the net worth figure on its Net Worth Report as zero.)

This might sound complicated, but an example should help to clear up any confusion. Suppose that the three-person law firm Biggins, Higgins, and Riggins makes $150,000 in profits, that each partner draws $40,000 over the year, and that the three partners share equally in the $150,000 of profits. Figure 9-11 shows the Account Book window for Biggins's capital account. Higgins's and Riggins's capital accounts would be identical. Figure 9-12 shows how the net worth statement would look at the end of the year after all partnership profits were distributed.

Corporations

Accounting for the owners' equity of a corporation is a little more work. However, the basic process is the same as for partnerships as long as you have only a few shareholders and your shareholders don't buy and sell shares.

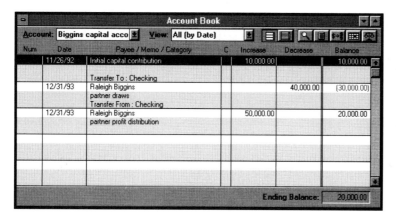

Figure 9-11.
Raleigh Biggins's capital account after he contributed $10,000, drew out $40,000, and received $50,000 as his share of partnership profits.

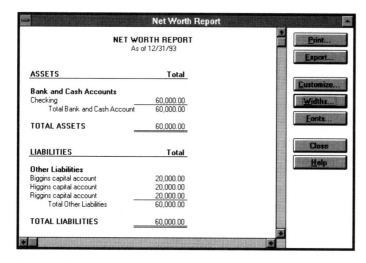

Figure 9-12.
The partnership's Net Worth Report after all partner withdrawals and profit distributions.

You set up a liability account for each shareholder, with the starting balance equal to the stock the investor purchases from the corporation. You then record dividends paid to the shareholder as transfers to the liability account and record the shareholder's share of corporate earnings as an increase in his or her account. As in a partnership, the transactions that record the shareholder's starting account balance or share of corporate earnings shouldn't be assigned to income or expense categories.

Some Problems

Using Microsoft Money for partnership or corporation owners' equity accounting is pushing the limits of what the program will do. As you've no doubt noticed, there are several problems with the only available approach.

One problem is that because you use liability accounts to track the owners' equity, the Microsoft Money Net Worth Report will always show your business's net worth as zero after you distribute the firm's profits. In truth, the real owners' equity, or net worth, is the sum of the partners' capital accounts or the shareholder accounts. But it's still a trifle unsettling to see your business's net worth reported as zero. (Of course, until you distribute the firm's profits, Microsoft Money calculates and displays a figure for net worth on the Net Worth Report. This figure equals the profits the firm has earned since the last profit distribution—the amount that will be allocated to the partners' capital accounts or the shareholder accounts.)

Another problem with respect to corporations is that you typically use several additional pieces of information to account for owners' equity, such as the number of shares a shareholder owns, the par value per share, the additional capital paid in excess of the par value per share, retained earnings, and so forth. You don't need to keep track of this information using Microsoft Money, but you or your attorney must track it somewhere else. (Accounting for these factors is beyond the scope of this book. If you're interested because they apply in your case, you can learn what's involved from any introductory college textbook in accounting.)

Month-End and Year-End Bookkeeping Procedures

One final important business accounting topic is the procedures you'll want to perform at the end of each month and at the end of each year. Table 9-1 is a checklist of common month-end bookkeeping procedures, along with the reasons for performing them; Table 9-2 covers common year-end bookkeeping procedures.

Procedure	*Reason*
Print monthly Income and Expense Report	Evaluate firm profits on monthly basis and have a permanent record of profits
Print month-end Net Worth Report	Evaluate firm's financial condition—cash, inventory, receivables, credit-line balances, and so on—and have a permanent record of them
Print and review agings of receivables	Use as a credit and collections tool; e.g., to remind you to call every customer with invoices over 30 days past due
Reconcile bank accounts and credit lines	Catch and correct bank errors and your own record-keeping errors before they cause problems—e.g., an overdrawn account

Table 9-1.
Common month-end bookkeeping procedures.

Procedure	*Reason*
Print annual Income and Expense Report	Evaluate firm profits on annual basis and have a permanent record of profits
Print year-end Net Worth Report	Evaluate firm's year-end financial condition—cash, inventory, receivables, credit-line balances, and so on—and have a permanent record of them
Print a Summary Report by payee	Meet legal requirement to report payments made to unincorporated businesses and individuals, using a 1099 form; the Summary Report provides the necessary data

Table 9-2.　　　*(continued)*
Common year-end bookkeeping procedures.

Table 9-2. *continued*

Procedure	*Reason*
Print out complete Register Reports for year	Create a permanent hard-copy record of the year's transactions (print one copy of the Account Book in order of transaction date and another summarized by category or account for later reference about a previous year's transaction or income or expense total)
Print out a Tax Report showing transactions	Document the individual amounts that make up each of your tax deductions
Archive the year's financial records	Make a permanent copy of the Microsoft Money file, to restore lost transactions or in case of tax audit (the archive copy isn't the same as temporary backup copies you create on an ongoing basis)

Conclusion

This chapter describes a series of tricks and techniques that let you use Microsoft Money as a business accounting tool. If you're employing more than one or two of these techniques, you're pushing the boundaries of Microsoft Money's capabilities. However, if you're not ready to step up to a full-fledged business accounting program, Microsoft Money can be a solid alternative solution.

Chapter 10

MAKING FINANCIAL CALCULATIONS

There's no doubt about it: Microsoft Money lets you keep good financial records. But there is a financial management task that it can't perform—making financial calculations. Suppose, for example, you want to know how much money you'll have in a savings account if you put away $50 a month for 10 years and earn 10 percent interest. Or perhaps you want to figure your monthly payments on a new car loan. You might need to make such calculations before you can record or budget for certain income or expense items. This chapter describes how to make financial calculations using the Windows Calculator.

You don't have to be a mathematical wizard or financial genius. Even beginners can make these powerful calculations—and make them correctly. In the following paragraphs, I'll show you how to display the Windows Calculator and set it up for making financial calculations. Then I'll describe the four basic financial calculations.

Displaying the Windows Calculator

The first step in making financial calculations is getting to the Windows Calculator window and setting it up. Start Microsoft Money in the usual way, and then choose the Calculator command from the Options menu as shown in Figure 10-1.

 MICROSOFT MONEY TIP: *You can also get to the Windows Calculator directly from Windows without starting Money. Start Windows in the usual way, and then choose Accessories from the menu displayed on the Program Manager window or any program group window. When the Accessories program group window appears, start the Calculator by double-clicking on the Calculator icon.*

Options	
Balance Account...	
Pay Bills...	Ctrl+P
Calculator	**Ctrl+K**
Entire Transaction View	Ctrl+T
Settings...	
Password...	

Figure 10-1.
The Options menu.

Windows displays the standard version of the Calculator window. (See Figure 10-2.) However, you need the scientific version of the Calculator, which provides more powerful buttons. To display the scientific version, choose the Scientific command from the Calculator's View menu. When you do, Windows displays the scientific version of the Calculator window used to make financial calculations. (See Figure 10-3.) This version provides four buttons not available on the standard Calculator: the parentheses buttons [(and)], the

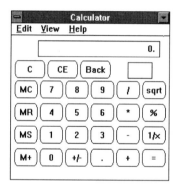

Figure 10-2.
The standard version of the Calculator window.

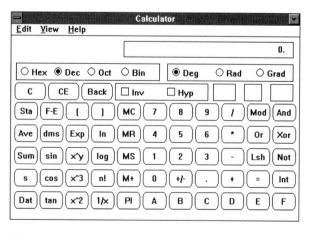

Figure 10-3.
The scientific version of the Calculator window.

exponent button (x^y), and the natural logarithm button (ln). Take a minute or two to locate these buttons before going further if you intend to try out the formulas as I discuss them.

Loan Payment and Balance Calculations

Two of the common financial calculations you'll want to make concern loans. You might want to calculate what a loan payment will be or how much you still owe on a loan. Using the scientific version of the Windows Calculator, you can do both types of calculations.

Calculating Payments on a Loan

Perhaps the single most common financial calculation you'll make is estimating payments on a loan. Suppose, for example, you're considering buying a car, for which you'll need to borrow $10,000 at 12 percent annual interest and make monthly payments over five years.

To calculate the payments on such a loan, you need only three pieces of information: loan amount, number of payments, and interest rate per payment period. In this case, the loan amount is, of course, $10,000. The number of payments is 60, calculated as five years of 12 monthly payments a year. And the interest rate per payment period is .01, or 1 percent per month—the 12 percent annual rate divided by the 12 monthly payments made during the year. Once you have this information, use the following formula to make the calculation.

Monthly payment = loan amount * interest rate per payment period /
[1 − (1 + interest rate per payment period) ^ (− number of loan payments)]

Before you complain that this formula is much too complicated to work with, let me relate it to the example above, using the correct calculation buttons.

If you plug the numbers from the car loan example into the formula, the sequence of buttons you select is as follows:

```
10000 * .01 / ( 1 − ( 1 + .01 ) x^y ( 60 +/− ) ) =
```

When you select the equals button (=) after clicking the last closing parenthesis, the Calculator window displays the monthly loan payment, which equals $222.44 rounded to the nearest cent.

To use for other loan payments, simply substitute the correct variables—the loan amount, the interest rate per payment period, and the number of payments—for those shown in the example.

For example, suppose you want to calculate the mortgage payment on a $100,000 mortgage bearing interest of 9 percent annually and requiring semi-monthly payments over the next 30 years. As noted earlier, you need three pieces of information to make the calculation: the loan amount, $100,000; the interest rate per payment period, which is 9 percent divided by 24 half-months, or .00375; and the number of payments, which is 24 half-months of payments over 30 years, or 720. To calculate this loan payment, you enter the following sequence of buttons.

```
100000 * .00375 / ( 1 - ( 1 + .00375 ) x^y ( 720 +/- ) ) =
```

When you select the equals button at the end of the sequence to complete the calculation, the Calculator displays the monthly mortgage payment, which is $402.16 rounded to the nearest cent.

Calculating the Outstanding Balance on a Loan

Another common financial calculation is computing the outstanding balance on a loan. Continuing the car loan example, suppose you had made a year's worth of payments on the $10,000 loan at 12 percent interest requiring 60 monthly payments of $222.44. To calculate the outstanding balance after making the twelfth payment, you use the following formula.

> Loan amount = [1 − (1 + interest rate per payment period) ^ (− number of payments remaining)] / interest rate per payment * period payment amount

Using the example above, you calculate the outstanding loan balance after the twelfth payment by using these buttons:

```
( 1 - ( 1 + .01 ) x^y (48 +/- ) ) / .01 * 222.44 =
```

When you select the equals button after entering in this set of numbers and operators, the Calculator displays the outstanding loan balance as a negative number. Rounded to the nearest penny, this figure is $8,446.93.

To calculate the principal paid, you simply calculate the change in the loan balance. In the case of the $10,000 car loan, which shows $8,446.93 outstanding after the twelfth payment, you obviously have paid $1,553.07 (calculated as $10,000 minus $8,446.93) in principal over the first 12 months, because that's the change in the loan balance.

To calculate the interest paid, you calculate the total payments made and then subtract the principal portions of those payments. So, in the case of the $10,000 car loan with payments of $222.44 a month, you paid $2,669.28 over the 12 months ($222.44 times 12). As calculated in the previous paragraph, $1,553.07 of this amount went toward reducing the principal balance. Therefore, the remainder, $1,116.21, ($2,669.28 minus $1,553.07) represents loan interest.

Investment Calculations

You can also make several investment calculations with the scientific Calculator. For example, you can calculate the future value of an initial investment or a series of investments, how long it takes for an investment to grow to a certain size, and the interest rate earned on some types of investments.

Calculating the Future Value of a Lump Sum

One of the easiest financial calculations you can make is determining the future value of a lump sum investment, given the annual interest rate and the number of years the investment will earn interest. To illustrate this type of calculation, suppose you want to invest $5,000 for your daughter's college expenses, which will begin in 18 years. Further suppose that you estimate you can earn an annual interest rate of 10 percent because that's roughly the historical interest rate produced by the stock market, which is where you will invest the $5,000.

PERSONAL FINANCIAL TIP: Because you can easily calculate the outstanding loan balance after a payment, you can also calculate the interest and principal paid as part of a payment or series of payments.

To calculate the future value of such an investment, you use the following formula.

> Future investment value = initial investment * (1 + annual interest rate)
> ^ number of years interest is earned

Therefore, to calculate the future value of the $5,000 stock investment, you use the following sequence of numbers and operators.

`5000 * ( 1 + .10 ) x^y 18 =`

When you select the equals button after entering the final number, the Calculator displays the estimated future value of your $5,000 investment. Rounded to the nearest penny, the value is $27,799.59.

Calculating the Future Value of an Annuity

Calculating the future value of an annuity, or equal stream of payments, is only slightly more involved than calculating the future value of a lump sum. This is another calculation that many people need to make. For example, suppose you contribute $2,000 a year to a retirement account that you expect will earn 8 percent annual interest. You'll find it helpful to estimate what the balance in such an account will be after you make contributions for, say, 30 years.

To calculate the future value of an annuity, you use the following formula.

> Future investment value = [(1 + period interest rate) ^ number of periods in which interest is earned and payments are made − 1] / period interest rate * payment amount

Therefore, you calculate the future value of the retirement account—assuming you make annual payments of $2,000 for 30 years and that you earn 8 percent annually—with the following sequence of numbers and operators.

`( ( 1 + .08 ) x^y 30 − 1 ) / .08 * 2000 =`

When you select the equals button after entering the last number, the Calculator displays the estimated future value of your retirement account. Rounded to the nearest penny, this value is $226,566.42.

Calculating the Term of a Lump Sum

Using the scientific Calculator's natural logarithm button, ln, you can calculate how long it takes an investment to grow to a given value at a certain interest rate. Suppose, for example, you want to become a millionaire and you currently have $10,000—money that is invested in speculative-grade corporate bonds you believe will produce average annual earnings of 14 percent.

To calculate the number of years it will take for $10,000 invested at 14 percent to grow into $1 million, you use the following formula.

Term or number of periods = ln (future investment value / present value or initial investment) / ln (1 + period interest rate)

The sequence of numbers and operators you enter is

```
(1000000 / 10000) ln / ( 1 + .14 ) ln =
```

When you select the equals button to display the calculation result, the Calculator displays the number *35.14638827847*, which means it will take slightly more than 35 years to become a millionaire based on an initial lump sum investment of $10,000 and a 14 percent annual interest rate.

Calculating the Term of an Annuity

You can also use the natural logarithm button to calculate the time it takes for an annuity, or series of equal payments, to grow to a future value. For example, imagine that you plan to save $5,000 a year using your employer's 401(k) plan. To calculate the number of years it will take for an annual $5,000 payment invested at 14 percent to grow to $1 million, use the following formula.

Term = ln [1 + (period interest rate * future investment value) / payment amount] / ln (1 + period interest rate)

Thus, the sequence of numbers and operators you enter is

```
( 1 + ( .14 * 1000000 ) / 5000 ) ln / ( 1 + .14 ) ln =
```

When you select the equals button, the Calculator displays the number *25.6990039259*, which means it will take a little less that 26 years to become a millionaire if you make $5,000 annual payments and earn interest at an annual rate of 14 percent.

PERSONAL FINANCIAL TIP: One variable that isn't explicitly included in future value calculations is inflation. But inflation can play a large part in both the period interest rates and the ultimate value of your savings.

When you start playing around with compounding interest, it seems too good to be true. For example, back when almost everybody qualified for an individual retirement account, some banks and stock brokerage houses ran advertisements showing that if you invested $2,000 a year for 35 years at 12 percent, you would end up with about $900,000. That was true as far as it went. But to get a realistic picture of such an investment, you need to consider inflation. You could earn 12 percent annually, but inflation might be 8 to 10 percent.

Although the future-value calculation was correct in showing that you, too, could be almost a millionaire by saving $2,000 a year, inflation would eat away at the value of your savings. If inflation averaged 8 percent over the 35 years you saved, in 35 years the minimum wage would be about $100,000 a year, a car that today costs $12,000 would cost about $180,000, and two movie tickets that cost $6 each today would cost close to $200. (You can estimate the future inflated price of an item by multiplying its current price by a factor of 1 plus the inflation rate for each year of inflation.)

Calculating an Interest Rate

You can't do most interest rate calculations with the scientific Calculator because they're too complex and require interactive calculations. However, you can calculate the interest rate required for an initial investment to grow to a given value over a specified number of periods. For example, suppose you want to invest a lump sum distribution of $100,000 from your former employer's pension fund so that when you retire in 20 years, you'll have $300,000. What you want to know is what annual interest rate you'll need to earn to make this dream come true. To make this calculation, you use the following formula.

Period interest rate = (future investment value / initial lump sum investment) ^ (1 / number of years investment will earn interest) − 1

The sequence of numbers and operators you would enter to calculate the annual interest rate necessary for $100,000 to grow to $300,000 over 20 years would be as follows:

```
( 300000 / 100000 ) x^y ( 1 / 20 ) − 1 =
```

When you select the equals button, the Calculator displays the number *.05646731,* which means your investment must earn roughly 5.65 percent annually to grow from $100,000 to $300,000 in 20 years.

Some Tips for Making Financial Calculations Easier

Here are some tips for making your calculations easier and more reliable.

Be sure to double-check your calculations. Particularly with long sequences of numbers and operators, it's all too easy to enter the wrong number or misplace an operator. Because you're unlikely to make the same error twice in a row, making a calculation twice increases the reliability of the result. If you have repeated problems making the calculations, attempt to duplicate the calculations in this chapter to make sure you're correctly interpreting the calculator buttons. Remember, too, to select the equals sign when you finish. And be especially careful about the parentheses buttons. (I find it particularly easy to foul up the double parentheses.)

 PERSONAL FINANCIAL TIP: Income tax is the final factor you need to think about when you work with future value calculations. This is particularly true when you project your savings over a long time, during which you might earn a good deal of interest income. Unless your interest income is either tax exempt or tax deferred, you will have to pay income tax on it. Tax-exempt interest income, as the name implies, is interest you don't have to pay taxes on (for example, interest from municipal bonds). Tax-deferred interest income is interest you're taxed on when you withdraw the money but not in the interim. An individual retirement account (IRA) and a 401(k) plan provided by your employer (or your spouse's employer) are examples of tax-deferred interest income sources.

To calculate your income taxes, you need to know your marginal income tax rate, or the percentage of the interest income you'll pay in federal and state taxes. Three marginal federal income tax rates were in effect for 1991: 15, 28, and 31 percent. To one of these federal tax rates you need to add any marginal state and local income tax rates. Most likely, your federal marginal income tax rate is 28 percent, so you can start with that.

Be especially careful about entering the interest rates. I see two mistakes over and over. The first is forgetting that the interest rate is actually a percentage. That is, the rate 12 percent is entered as *.12* and not 12. A second mistake is forgetting that the interest rate is the rate per period. If your periods are years, you use the annual interest rate. But if your periods aren't years—say you're calculating a monthly loan payment—then you need to convert the annual interest rate to an equivalent period rate. To convert an annual interest rate to a monthly rate, for example, you can divide the annual rate by 12.

One final issue about the formulas involving annuities is that they assume the payments occur at the end of the period—the end of month, the end of the year, and so forth. This is what's called an ordinary annuity, or a payments-in-arrears annuity. It is typically the way you'll want to make financial calculations. However, when a financial calculation involves a loan or investment for which payments occur at the beginning of the period, this is called an annuity due, or payment-in-advance annuity, and it requires an additional calculation.

For a loan payment and outstanding loan balance calculation, you need to divide the payment or balance amount by (1 + the period interest rate). If the loan payment formula calculates an ordinary annuity payment equal to $222.44, the annuity payment due equals $222.44 divided by (1 + interest rate). If the loan balance formula calculates the ordinary annuity outstanding balance as $8,446.93, the equivalent outstanding balance in an annuity-due situation equals $8,446.93 / (1 + interest rate).

For an investment formula that calculates a future value, such as the future value of a lump sum or an annuity formula, you need to multiply the future value amount produced by the formula by (1 + the period interest rate).

Finally, for the investment formula that calculates the term of an annuity, you need first to divide the future value input used in the formula by (1 + the period interest rate) before actually using it in the formula.

Conclusion

This chapter describes how to make seven standard financial calculations using the scientific view of the Windows Calculator. It discusses the steps for calculating loan payments and balances, for estimating the future values of investments, for forecasting the years it takes for investments to reach certain sizes, and for calculating the implicit interest earned by some investments. Of course, you won't need to make all these calculations, but you probably will want to make at least one or two.

This chapter concludes *Microsoft Money*. The book has covered a lot of material, and I hope it has been successful in teaching you how to use Microsoft Money to manage your personal or business finances. Best wishes in those endeavors.

Appendix

INSTALLING MICROSOFT MONEY

Although installing Microsoft Money on your computer isn't difficult, it involves a fair number of steps. If you're new to computers—and particularly if you're new to Microsoft Windows—it will help to have someone walk you through the steps of installing the software on your hard disk.

In these directions, I assume that you know next to nothing about your computer or how Microsoft Windows works. Of course, there's a good chance you know quite a lot, but this approach makes it less likely that I'll leave out some critical piece of information you need to install Microsoft Money.

To install Microsoft Money on your computer, follow these steps.

1. Start your computer, and turn on your monitor.

2. Insert the Microsoft Money disk into your floppy drive.

3. Start Microsoft Windows by typing *win* at the DOS prompt (C:>).

4. Activate the File menu by using the mouse to point to the word *File* and clicking the left mouse button. (The File menu is located at the top left of the Program Manager window; see Figure A-1.) When you do this, Windows displays the File menu. (See Figure A-2.) (In future steps, when I tell you to click on an object, I'm referring to the process of pointing to an object and then clicking the left mouse button.)

5. Choose the Run command from the File menu by clicking on the word *Run* or by typing the letter *R* and pressing enter. When you do, Windows displays the Run dialog box, shown in Figure A-3.

6. Be sure the cursor is in the text box labelled Command Line, and type *b:setup* in the box if you're using the B drive; otherwise, type *a:setup* in the box. If you make a mistake, use the Backspace key to erase the incorrect entry, and then retype the entry. After correctly typing the letters, press Enter. After a few moments, Windows displays the Microsoft Money Setup screen, shown in Figure A-4.

7. To start the setup or installation, press Enter or click on the button labelled Continue. When you do, the Setup program displays another dialog box that provides text boxes in which you enter your name and (if applicable) your company name.

8. Type your name in the appropriate text box. If you make a mistake, use the Backspace key to correct it.

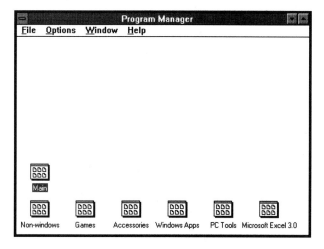

Figure A-1.
*The Program Manager window with the File menu name in the top left-hand corner.
You activate the File menu by pointing to and clicking on the word* File.

Figure A-2.
The File menu.

9. Press Tab to move the cursor to the Company text box.

10. Type the name of your company. If you make a mistake, use the Back-space key to correct it.

11. Press Enter to move to the next step in the installation process: identify-ing the directory in which the Microsoft Money program and data files will be stored. When you do, the Setup program displays the Destina-tion Path dialog box, shown in Figure A-5.

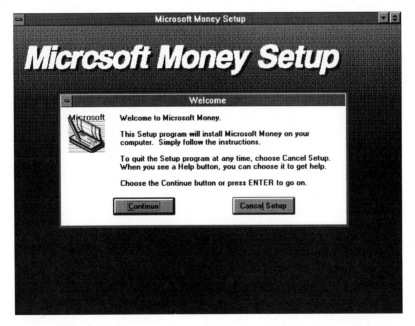

Figure A-3.
The Run dialog box.

Figure A-4.
The Microsoft Money Setup screen.

12. By default, the Setup program installs Microsoft Money's program and
    data files on your hard disk in a directory named MSMONEY. To accept
    the default directory, press Enter or click on the Continue button. If you
    want to store the files in a different directory or drive, press the Back-
    space key to erase the default drive and directory (C:\MSMONEY), type
    the drive and directory you want to use, and press Enter or click on the
    Continue button.

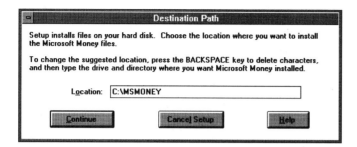

Figure A-5.
The Destination Path dialog box.

If you're new to computers, you'll probably want to use the default drive and directory. It's easy to do because you won't have to worry about the correct punctuation for specifying a drive and directory.

13. After you complete step 12, the Setup program begins copying the Microsoft Money program files to the drive and directory you specified. As the Setup program works, it displays a message box telling you what percentage of the copying it has completed.

14. When the Setup program is complete, it displays the Installation Complete message, shown in Figure A-6. To return to the Windows Program Manager window (refer to Figure A-1), click on the Exit To Windows button. However, for the installation of Microsoft Money to be truly complete, you must first set up an account. To do so, first start Microsoft Money by clicking on the Run Money button.

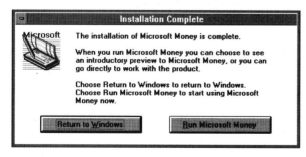

Figure A-6.
The Installation Complete message box.

15. When you start Microsoft Money, you'll see the hourglass icon appear briefly on your screen, followed by the Microsoft Money copyright notice screen.

    Microsoft Money also displays a dialog box that allows you to select several useful income and expense categories, depending on your needs. (These categories can be modified, deleted, or added to at any time later on.) Select one category from Home Categories, Business Categories, Both Home And Business, or None.

16. Money next displays a message box prompting you to create an account. When you choose OK to continue, Money displays the Create New Account dialog box shown in Figure A-7.

17. Type the name you want to use for the account, such as *Checking* or *Visa*. Microsoft Money assumes by default that you want to name the first account Checking. If you begin to type a different account name, it replaces the default account name.

18. Using the mouse, click on the option button describing the type of account you're setting up: Bank, Credit Card, Cash Or Other, Asset, or Liability. Then choose OK.

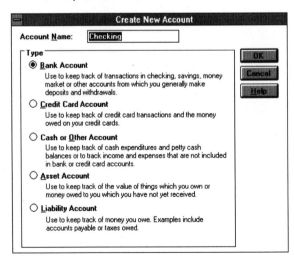

Figure A-7.
The Create New Account dialog box.

19. When Money asks for the account's starting balance, use the Opening Balance dialog box, shown in Figure A-8, to enter the starting balance. Then choose OK. Microsoft Money next displays the Account Book window. (See Figure A-9.)

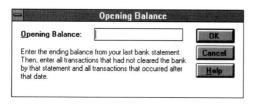

Figure A-8.
The Opening Balance dialog box.

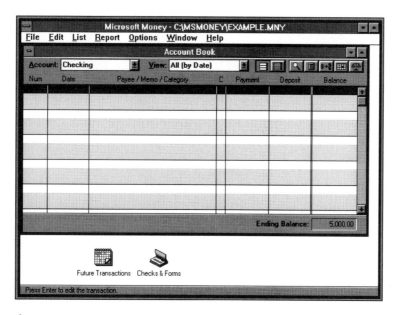

Figure A-9.
The Account Book window.

Microsoft Money is now ready for use, although you might need to create additional accounts. Chapter 2, "Preparing to Use Microsoft Money," describes the steps for creating new accounts in more detail; refer to it if you have questions about creating additional accounts.

After you open your first account, a Confirmation message box appears on the screen, asking if you would like to see a short demonstration of Microsoft Money. Click Yes if you do.

Index

A

MICROSOFT MONEY

Removing
items, 94
payees, 85
sub-items, 94
Rename command
in Account List dialog box, 81–82
in Category List dialog box, 41, 42
in List dialog box, 95
in Payee List dialog box, 86
Renaming
accounts, 79, 81–82
category and subcategory names, 41–42
classifications, 90–91
items, 95
payees, 85, 86
sub-items, 95
Report Column Width dialog box, 184
Report command, in Payee List dialog box, 86
Report menu, 150, 153
Report printing
basics of, 151–55
multiple copies, 154–55
print setup for, 152–53
quality of, 153–54
Reports. *See also* Budget Report; Customizing reports; Income and Expense
Report; Net Worth Report; Register
Report; Summary Report; Tax Report
customizing, 161–85
exporting, 159–61
importing into other applications, 160–61
producing, 150–85
titles for, 163
transaction data in, 163–64
type style and size in, 161, 184
viewing on screen, 153
width of, 161, 184
Report Transfers By options, for Income and
Expense Report, 175–76
Report type, specifying for Tax Report, 176
Residence
gathering account information on, 29
tracking adjusted cost basis of, 29
tracking fair market value of, 201–2
Resizing windows, with mouse, 16–17
Restore Backup dialog box, 122–23
Restore command, in Windows, 13, 17
Restoring files, to hard disk, 121–23

Retirement accounts, calculating future value
of, 239

S

Schedule In Future command, in Edit menu,
73–77
Schedule Future Transaction dialog box, 73–74
Scientific Calculator, 235–41
investment calculations on, 238–41
loan payment and balance calculations
on, 236–38
Scroll bars, 11, 17–18
Scroll boxes, 11, 18
Scrolling, list boxes, 10–11
Search icon, in Help window, 24
Select Account dialog box, 105
Select Checks option, in Print Checks dialog
box, 148
Select Checks To Reprint dialog box, 150
Select Font dialog box, 184–85
Select Import Account dialog box, 130–31
Select Transactions dialog box, 167–69, 171–
72, 174–75, 179, 182
Self-employment taxes, 37, 38
Seller-financed mortgages, 205
Service Charge text box, in Balance Checking
dialog box, 107
Service fees, recording, 52, 107
Settings command, Options menu, 96, 100–101
Settings dialog box, 100–101
elements of, 8–12
turning SmartFill on and off in, 61
Setup For Report Printing option, in Print
Setup dialog box, 152
Setup New File dialog box, 135
Setup program, for Microsoft Money, 246–49
Shareholders, liability accounts for, 230
Shortcut field, in Payee List dialog box, 84
Shortcut keys, choosing commands in
Windows with, 6
Shortcut text box, 36
in Account List dialog box, 80, 81
in Sub-Property List dialog box, 93
Show Message Bar check box, in Settings
dialog box, 100
Size buttons, sizing windows with, 17
Size command, in Windows, 14
SmartFill, 60–61, 83–84, 86

Stephen L. Nelson

A CPA and former senior consultant with the systems consulting group of Arthur Andersen & Co., Stephen L. Nelson provides financial and personal computer applications consulting to businesses in a variety of industries.

Nelson has written more than 80 articles on personal computer applications for national publications such as *LOTUS Magazine, PC Computing, PC Magazine, Macworld,* and *Home Office Computing.* He is the author and architect of the *Microsoft Excel Small Business Consultant, Microsoft Excel Money Manager,* and *Lotus 1-2-3 Money Manager,* collections of worksheet templates published by Microsoft Press. In addition, he is the author of *Inside PC Tools Deluxe,* second edition, and coauthor of *Quattro Pro 3 Companion,* also published by Microsoft Press. Nelson's bestselling computer tutorials include *Using 1-2-3 Release 3* and *Using Quicken,* published by Que.

Nelson holds a bachelor of science degree in accounting from Central Washington University and a master's degree in business administration from the University of Washington.

The manuscript for this book was prepared and submitted to Microsoft Press in electronic form. Text files were processed and formatted using Microsoft Word.

Principal word processor: Janet Lemnah
Principal proofreader: Sarah St. Onge
Principal typographers: Joan Beardslee and Hagop Hagopian
Interior text designer: Kim Eggleston
Cover designer: Becky Geisler
Cover color separator: Color Control

Text composition by Editorial Inc. in Garamond Light with display type in Futura Extra Bold Condensed, using Xerox Ventura Publisher and the Linotronic 300 laser imagesetter.

Printed on recycled paper stock.

Great Resources for the Microsoft® Windows™ User!

RUNNING WINDOWS™
Craig Stinson and Nancy Andrews

"RUNNING WINDOWS does not skirt a subject, but instead dives right in....The text is clear and concise....Its detailed explanations will save you much more time than it takes to read it." **PC Magazine**
Build your confidence and enhance your productivity with the Microsoft Windows—quickly and easily—using this hands-on introduction. This Microsoft-authorized, best-selling volume provides detailed coverage of every aspect of installing and using Windows 3, and it incorporates real-world examples to help you optimize Windows' performance.

522 pages, softcover $24.95 ($32.95 Canada)   Order Code RUWI2

WINDOWS™ 3 COMPANION
The Cobb Group: Lori Lorenz and Michael O'Mara

"An excellent reference featuring dozens of live examples of how different functions work." **PC Magazine**
This resource covers everything from installing and starting Windows to using all its built-in applications and desktop accessories. Novices will value the book for its step-by-step tutorials and great examples; more experienced users will turn to it again and again for its expert advice, tips, and information. The authors detail the features and use of Windows' Program Manager, File Manager, and Printer Manager so that you'll be able to expertly maneuver through Windows, control the environment, and easily manage files, disks, and printers.

536 pages, softcover $27.95 ($36.95 Canada)   Order Code WI3CO

MICROSOFT® WORKS FOR WINDOWS™
JoAnne Woodcock

An information-filled tutorial and reference for beginning to intermediate users. Ideal for small businesses computerizing their offices. This combination tutorial and reference offers clear instruction on each element in the Works package—the word processor, the spreadsheet, the database, the drawing package, the charting tool, the communications module, and the report generator. In addition, Woodcock demonstrates how to share data within Works and with Microsoft Money and Microsoft Publisher, and how to integrate Works into any small business.

400 pages, softcover $22.95 ($27.95 Canada)   Order Code WOWI

RUNNING MICROSOFT® EXCEL, 2nd ed.
The Cobb Group

No matter what your level of expertise—longtime Lotus® 1-2-3® user, veteran Microsoft Excel user, beginning or occasional Microsoft Excel user—this will be your primary source of information and advice. RUNNING MICROSOFT EXCEL is packed with step-by-step instruction, superb examples, and dozens of screen illustrations to help you understand and use every function and command of the program. In addition, special "Excel Tips" throughout the book spotlight effective shortcuts. New information covers version 3.

848 pages, softcover $27.95 ($36.95 Canada)   Order Code RUEX2

Microsoft Press books are available wherever quality computer books are sold. Prices subject to change.
Or call **1-800-MSPRESS** for ordering information or placing credit card orders.
Please refer to **BBK** when placing your order.

In Canada, contact Macmillan Canada, Attn: Microsoft Press Dept., 164 Commander Blvd., Agincourt, Ontario, Canada M1S 3C7. 416-293-8141
In the U.K., contact Microsoft Press, 27 Wrights Lane, London W8 5TZ.

More Titles From Microsoft Press